Arabic Hijazi Reader

Arabic Dialect Series
(Saudi Arabia)

Habaka J. Feghali

Edited by
John D. Murphy

Dunwoody Press
1991

All questions and inquiries should be directed to:

Dunwoody Press, P.O. Box 1825, Wheaton, MD, 20915

First Edition: 1991
Printed and bound in the United States of America
Library of Congress Catalog Number: 91-70-530
ISBN: 0-931-745-72-1

Table of Contents

The Forty Selections

Translations of the Selections

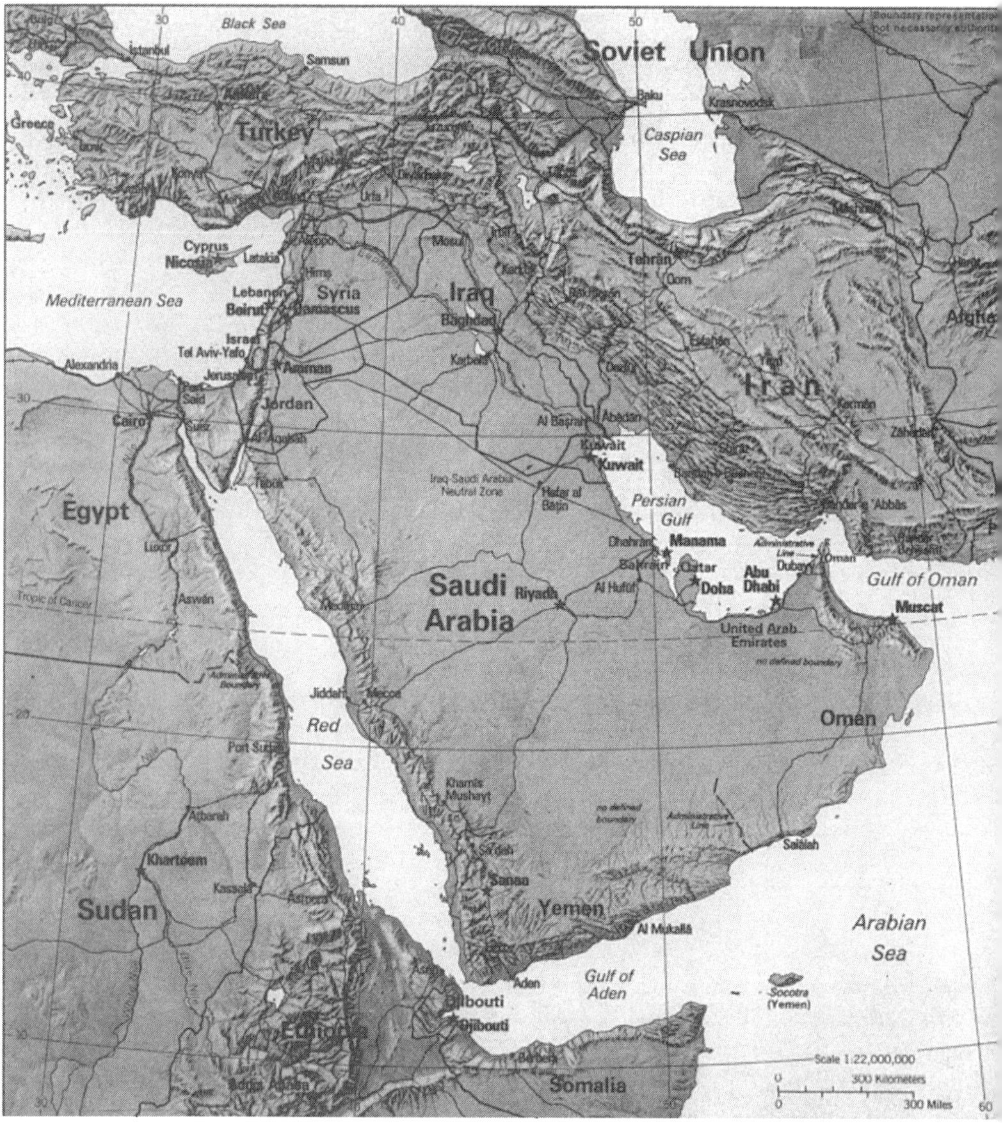
Black Sea
Soviet Union
Istanbul
Samsun
Baku
Krasnovodsk
Turkey
Greece
Caspian Sea
Cyprus
Nicosia
Latakia
Mosul
Tehran
Qom
Syria
Iraq
Lebanon
Beirut
Damascus
Mediterranean Sea
Baghdad
Israel
Tel Aviv-Yafo
Amman
Alexandria
Karbala
Iran
Jordan
Cairo
Kerman
Al Basrah
Abadan
Kuwait
Iraq-Saudi Arabia Neutral Zone
Hafar al Batin
Persian Gulf
Egypt
Luxor
Dhahran
Manama
Bahrain
Qatar
Doha
Abu Dhabi
Dubayy
Oman
Gulf of Oman
Saudi Arabia
Riyadh
Al Hufuf
Aswan
Tropic of Cancer
Muscat
United Arab Emirates
no defined boundary
Jiddah
Mecca
Red Sea
Oman
Port Sudan
Khamis Mushayt
Administrative Line
Salalah
Khartoum
Sanaa
Sudan
Yemen
Al Mukalla
Arabian Sea
Aden
Gulf of Aden
Socotra (Yemen)
Djibouti
Djibouti
Ethiopia
Berbera
Addis Ababa
Somalia
Scale 1:22,000,000
300 Kilometers
300 Miles

Preface

For the past two decades or so there has been an ever-increasing interest in the West in Arabic and Arabic dialects. This fact is reflected in the number of studies devoted to the Arabic language and in the numerous intermediate and advanced courses in Arabic dialects. As a result of this demand, many universities, colleges, institutes, and companies offer courses in Modern Standard Arabic and Arabic dialects. Furthermore, the study of Arabic at all levels in our universities has increased significantly in the last two decades.

Many major studies on Saudi Arabian dialects have been made, and even some oil companies have published basic language material to meet the needs of their personnel. However, I am not aware of any advanced Hijazi Arabic reader similar to this book. This reader is designed for students who have some background in Modern Standard Arabic, and who are interested in Hijazi Arabic beyond the basic level. Presumable the student has already completed an introductory Hijazi Arabic course such as Margaret K. Omar's Saudi Arabic, Urban Hijazi Dialect, Basic Course (see the bibliography). The reader may also be of interest to Arabists and Arabic dialectologists.

The language of this reader is used in informal situations by educated native speakers of the Hijaz area. There are some variations within Hijazi Arabic which correlate with the level of education, occupation, age, social class, travel, etc. of native speakers. Highly educated natives speak with some admixture of pan-Arabic koine, depending on circumstances and situations. This fact is apparent in some selections of the reader.

The reader consists of forty selections, some of which are based on recordings of spontaneous, unrehearsed conversations of unsophisticated native speakers from Mecca, Medina, and Ta'if. The remaining selections are based on accounts of current events which appeared in Saudi newspapers such as *Al-Jazzira, Al-Medina* and *Al-Sharq Al-Awsat*. These survey the progress made by Saudi Arabia in the areas of education, industry, agriculture, medicine, infrastructure and improving the standard of living as a whole. The selections also describe life in Saudi Arabia and treat various social, political and religious problems.

The introductory section on the transcription and the sound system is designed to acquaint the user with the transcription employed throughout the reader. The symbols used for the transliteration are those most commonly employed for Arabic dialects. In daily speech, short vowels are often omitted because of elision and assimilation, and because of the difference in pronunciation among native speakers.

Each selection is followed by a vocabulary list. The words are listed in the order they appear in the text. Verbs are listed in the third person singular masculine in both the perfect and imperfect aspects. Grammatical and cultural notes are also provided for each selection in order to facilitate a better understanding of the dialect as well as the society in which it is spoken. Quite often the notes make comparisons of the Hijazi dialect to some features of Modern Standard Arabic.

The second part of the reader provides the English translations of the Hijazi selections, from which the user will benefit whether he is studying independently or with a teacher. The translations were kept as close as possible to the Hijazi text in order to enable the user to see the relationship between the two. As a result, he may occasionally find the English somewhat stiff or unidiomatic. The words and phrases enclosed in brackets do not have equivalents in the Hijazi text. They were added for a better and smoother English translation. Words and phrases which appear in the Hijazi text but which are not necessary for the English translation are enclosed in parentheses preceded by "literally".

The last part of the reader provides an alphabetized general glossary containing all the entries in the individual vocabulary lists and the words used in the notes as well.

My deepest gratitude goes to my Saudi friends who spent many hours sharing with me their fascinating culture and traditions, and who assisted me in bringing this work to completion. Special thanks are due Mrs. Sandra Walden who was responsible for keyboarding and formatting the reader from beginning to end. Stephen A. Bladey managed the production throughout.

H.F.
Washington DC
January 1991

Introduction

Saudi Arabia is a Middle Eastern Arab country about which almost everyone in the West has heard. Because of the Saudi influence on OPEC, Saudi Arabian Arabic, in particular the dialect of the Hijaz or western part of the country (containing the two holiest cities in Islam, Mecca and Medina, in addition to the large metropolitan thriving port city of Jiddah), has become one of the principal colloquial vehicles in the entire Persian Gulf area. Considering the vast number of foreigners in Saudi Arabia, one need not spend much time explaining that a knowledge of Saudi Arabian Arabic will facilitate life for anyone going to this Kingdom of nine million people. The forty selections which follow will not only introduce the reader to the history and culture of the Kingdom, but will also greatly facilitate the acquisition of colloquial Hijazi (Saudi) Arabic.

The linguistic situation in Saudi Arabia today is quite complicated because the Kingdom has been, especially over the past 25 years, a melting pot of different Arabic dialects. Muhammad Bakalla, a Saudi linguist trained in the United Kingdom, estimated that there are more than 200 dialects scattered over the country. This situation has led to the creation of a rather large stylistic variation between Modern Standard Arabic (MSA) and the colloquials. One will soon see that, in many respects, the Hijazi dialect is closer to MSA than, e.g., the Najdi (the Najd, which contains the capital city of Riyadh, is in the central part of the country). Thus the word **kēf** *'how'* is pronounced with a /**k**/ sound in the Hijaz just as it is in the MSA **kayfa**. In the Najd, however, the velar stop /**k**/ is replaced by the affricate /**ch**/. These phonological adjustments may take some getting used to.

In one way or another, then, every Saudi Arab will understand the dialect represented in this book throughout the Kingdom's 870,000 square miles because there is quite a bit of pan-Arabic used. It should be firmly kept in mind though, that Arabs throughout the Arab world speak their local dialects, but the more educated the person, the greater the tendency to interject MSA expressions and vocabulary. On formal occasions, the educated Saudi will use MSA, or at least upgrade his colloquial or code switch between MSA and his/her dialect.

This is the first advanced reader in Hijazi Arabic. As is stated in the Preface, it is assumed that the user has already studied a basic textbook of Hijazi Arabic such as the one by Margaret K. Omar; however, that is not an absolute prerequisite to the enjoyment of the following texts. He/she will be greatly helped by idiomatic, i.e., non-literal translations, grammatical notes pertaining to linguistic areas of comparative or descriptive interest, as well as cultural notes pertaining to life in this Islamic society.

Assuming that many users of this book have studied MSA but have little familiarity with colloquial Arabic, it is important to keep in mind that there are fundamental differences between them. Although there are vocabulary and phonological differences, a more pronounced contrast can be seen in the elimination of such grammatical features as the case endings, the dual markers for verbs and adjectives, and mood markers such as the **-u** for the indicative. The grammatical notes for the selections will often greatly facilitate your switching your colloquial "hat" for your MSA one. Thus, in the first selection one can compare the verbal form **tiḥtal** *it occupies* with MSA **taḥtallu** (p.2, note 2). One can, in my opinion, acquire a knowledge of the language faster via these grammatical and cultural notes.

A word now about the transcription of the texts. Arabic is not normally written in English (Latin) script, but colloquial Arabic dialects often are, because the transcription is much more accurate than if the Arabic script were used. Thus these texts are transliterated according to the phonological principles and conventions used by Arabists and Orientalists.

The student may "teach himself/herself" Arabic with these splendid readings because the difficult, new vocabulary items are listed in each selection. Many of these words, sometimes with proper adjustments, are also used in MSA.

These narratives all come from native Saudis. I have many favorites among the forty, such as "Some Cities of Saudi Arabia." All of them are remarkably interesting, authentically transcribed for a native-like pronunciation, and accurately translated. You will soon have many favorites, too. This method of learning a foreign language is reminiscent of the sound, philological approach to foreign language teaching common in the more traditional, academic environments. You will soon come to appreciate the culturally relevant "emic" (i.e. significant) aspects of Saudi culture and civilization as a whole. The interrelatedness of language and culture, thought and society, will make the student glad indeed that she/he has decided to closely scrutinize the texts.

For anyone interested in Saudi Arabia in general or the Hijaz in particular, this book is a must. Take your time and study these texts slowly and carefully. If you have the services of a teacher or assistant, so much the better. If you do not, do not despair as this material can be studied and mastered heuristically. "Go for it!," and remember the old Arabic saying about learning Arabic:

samع fataqlīd fatakrār faṣabr
listening, and imitation, and repetition and patience.

Please keep in mind that Arabic is not hard, just different. Good luck!

Alan S. Kaye

Professor of Linguistics and Arabic
Director, Laboratory of Phonetic Research
California State University
Fullerton, CA 92634 USA

Abbreviations

act.	active
adj.	adjective
adv.	adverb
coll.	collective
comp.	comparative
cf.	compare; refer to
conj.	conjunction
CV	consonant followed by a vowel
def.art.	definite article
du.	dual
e.g.	for example
f.	feminine
fig.	figurative
i.e.	that is (to say)
impf.	imperfect
imp.	imperative
intr.	intransitive
lit.	literally
m.	masculine
MSA	Modern Standard Arabic
ng.	negative
n.	noun
pl.	plural
part.	participle
pass.	passive
prep.	preposition
pron.	pronoun
pro.n.	proper noun
rel.pron.	relative pronoun
s.	singular
s.o.	someone
s.th.	something
tr.	transitive
v.	verb
v.n.	verbal noun
– āt	suffix for regular feminine plural
– īn	suffix for regular masculine plural

The Transcription System

Urban Hijazi Arabic has many sounds that do not have exact equivalents in English. On the following page is a list of the symbols used in the transcription of the sounds of Hijazi Arabic with their approximate English equivalents. This list is intended to help the user acquire a reasonably accurate Hijazi Arabic pronunciation and to introduce the system of transliteration used through-out the reader. The list also provides the movements and positions of the lips, tongue, throat, and nasal passages which produce the sounds. The user should master this part before any attempt at reading the selections.

The Arabic letter **θ**, as in *thin,* is pronounced **t** as in *tom* in Hijazi, but since the pronunciation model presented below is that of an educated speaker, the student should also expect to hear the Modern Standard Arabic pronunciation, e.g., **talāta**, *three* pronounced **θalāθa**. It is also worth noting that the same letter is sometimes pronounced **s** as in *Sam,* e.g., **maθalan**, *for example* is pronounced **masalan**.

The letter **ð**, as in *this,* is often pronounced **d** as in *dad,* e.g. **ðahab**, *gold* becomes **dahab**. This same letter is also pronounced **z** as in *zoo,* e.g., **iða**, *if,* becomes **iza**. The Modern Standard Arabic pronunciation is often heard in the Hijaz area.

Hijazi Symbol	*English Equivalent*
ʔ	a glottal stop; the glottal catch in the throat (glottis closed) between the two vowels as in *oh-oh.*
a; ā	short **a** as in *bat;* long **ā** as in *father* depending on the surrounding consonants.
b	**b** as in *bed* (a voiced bilabial stop).
d	**d** as in *dad* (a voiced dental non-emphatic stop).
ḍ	no English equivalent; raise the back of the tongue while producing this sound (a voiced dental emphatic stop).
ē	**ai** as in *bait.*
f	**f** as in *foot* (a voiceless labio-dental fricative).
g	**g** as in *got* (a velar stop).
gh	no English equivalent; similar to the French **r** in *Paris* (a voiced uvular fricative).
h	**h** as in *hat* (a voiceless glottal fricative).
ḥ	no English equivalent; tighten the muscles of the tongue and whisper without voicing (a voiceless pharyngeal fricative).
i; ī	short **i** as in *hit,* long **ī** as ee in *feet.*
k	**k** as in *kit* (a voiceless velar stop).
kh	no English equivalent; similar to the Scottish **ch** in *loch* (a voiceless uvular fricative).
l	**l** as in *light* (a voiced alveolar lateral).
m	**m** as in *mad* (a voiced bilabial nasal).
n	**n** as in *net* (a voiced alveolar nasal).
ō	**oa** as in *boat,* but without diphthongization.
q	no English equivalent; say *chalk* and hold the **k** longer in the back of the throat (a voiceless uvular stop).
r	like the Spanish **r** in *pero* (a voiced alveolar trill).
s	**s** as in *sofa* (a voiceless alveolar non-emphatic fricative).
ṣ	no English equivalent; raise the back of the tongue when producing this sound (a voiceless alveolar emphatic fricative).
sh	**sh** as in *shut* (a voiceless palatal fricative).
t	**t** as in *tent* (a voiceless dental non-emphatic stop).
ṭ	no English equivalent; produce it with the back of the tongue raised (a voiceless dental emphatic stop).
u; ū	short **u** like the **oo** in *foot;* long **ū** like the **oo** in *fool.*
w	**w** as in *wind* (a voiced labiovelar semivowel).
y	**y** as in *yellow* (a voiced palatal semivowel).
z	**z** as in *zinc* (a voiced alveolar non-emphatic fricative).
ẓ	no English equivalent; produce it with the back of the tongue raised (a voiced alveolar emphatic fricative).
ع	no English equivalent; produce it while tightening the very back of the throat (a voiced pharyngeal fricative).

Pronunciation

Consonants

Most of the Arabic consonants have identical or slightly different English equivalents which a student of Hijazi Arabic will have no difficulty in pronouncing. However, there is a group of consonants that does not have equivalent sounds in English. Usually the student needs more time to acquire an acceptable pronunciation of these consonants. Such consonants are **q, ṭ, ṣ, ḍ, ḥ. kh, gh**, and **ع**.

q

The **q** sound usually becomes **g** in Hijazi Arabic, but it sometimes occurs in the speech of educated speakers, rarely in the speech of uneducated speakers, except in certain words, e.g., **qur?ān**. To pronounce this voiceless uvular stop say *chalk*, hold the final **k** a little longer, then let the back of the tongue touch the soft palate. The consonant **q** requires a back pronunciation of a following vowel, e.g., **ā** is like the **a** in *father*.

ṭ

The pronunciation of the consonant **ṭ** requires a great deal of tightening of the muscles of the mouth and the throat while raising the back of the tongue towards the roof of the mouth. The consonant ṭ requires a back pronunciation of a following vowel. It is a voiceless dental emphatic stop.

ṣ

The consonant ṣ is pronounced differently than the English s. In pronouncing this sound try to curve the tongue upward slightly at the edge almost touching the upper gum, and tighten the muscles of the mouth as well as the back of the throat. This voiceless alveolar emphatic fricative requires a back pronunciation of a following vowel.

ḍ

The consonant ḍ is a voiced dental emphatic stop. When pronouncing the sound ḍ, allow the whole middle of the tongue to cover the roof of the mouth. Feel the muscular tension in the mouth and in the back of the throat as well. The consonant **d** requires a front pronunciation of the following vowel, e.g. **Dan**, whereas the consonant ḍ requires a back pronunciation of a following vowel, e.g., **ā** is like **a** in *father*.

ḥ

Most Westerners find the consonants **ḥ** and ع the most difficult to pronounce. The consonant **ḥ** is produced by tightening the muscles of the throat and then forcing the air through the throat while keeping the very back of the tongue as low as possible. Try to whisper **ah** very forcefully while keeping the throat muscles very tense.

kh

The consonant **kh** is a voiceless uvular fricative. It has no English equivalent. To produce the sound **kh** raise the back of the tongue close to the uvula, then force the air through this very tense passage. The sound **kh** is similar to the **ch** in Scottish *loch* or German *ach.*

gh

The consonant **gh** is the voiced counterpart of **kh**. It is also produced by raising the back of the tongue close to the soft palate without blocking the air passage. An excellent practice for producing the **gh** sound is to gargle without water. The consonant **gh** is similar to the French **r** in *Paris.*

ع

This voiced faucalized pharyngeal fricative has no English equivalent. It is the voiced counterpart of **ḥ**. In producing the sound ع, tighten the muscles of the throat used in gagging and make the sound of being strangled.

Vowels

Hijazi Arabic has five vowels; **a**, **i**, **u**, **ō**, **ē**. The vowels **a**, **i** and **u** can be either short or long. Their long forms are represented by **ā**, **ī**, and **ū**. The pronunciation of a vowel depends to a large extent on the consonants adjacent to it. Furthermore, there is variation in pronunciation within the Hijazi dialect area. The difference between short vowels and long vowels is, of course, one of length. A carefully stressed long vowel is twice as long as a stressed short vowel. Since English speakers are not used to distinguishing the differences in vowel length, it is very important that the user recognize that this factor has a great affect on meaning, e.g., **dam**, *blood*; **dām**, *lasted.*

a

The vowel **a** is pronounced like the u in *fun*; its long form **ā** is like the a in *cab*, but sometimes like the a in *car*, depending on the surrounding consonants.

u

The vowel **u** is pronounced like the **u** in *put;* its long form **ū** is pronounced like the **u** in *rude* or the **oo** in *fool.*

i

The vowel **i** is pronounced like the **i** in *sit;* its long form **ī** is pronounced like the **ee** in *need* or the **i** in *machine.*

e

The vowel **ē** corresponds to the MSA diphthong **ay**, e.g., **bayt**, becomes **bēt**, **bintayn** becomes **bintēn**. The vowel **ē** does not have a short form. It is pronounced like the **ai** in *bait.*

o

The vowel **ō** corresponds to the MSA diphthong **aw**, e.g., **yawm** becomes **yōm**, and **nawm** becomes **nōm**. The **ō** also does not have a short form in Hjazi Arabic. It is pronounced like the **oa** in *boat,* but without diphthongization.

The Definite Article **al-**

The definite article **al-** (**adāt attaɛrīf**, the sign of making known) is prefixed to nouns and adjectives, e.g., **bēt**, **albēt**; **gaṣīr**, **algaṣīr**. The definite article is pronounced **al-** when prefixed to a word beginning with one of the "moon letters", **alḥurūf alqamariyya a**, **b**, **g**, **h**, **ḥ** **kh**, **ɛ**, **gh**, f, q, k, **m**, w, and **y**. Note the following:

akhḍar	green	al?akhḍar
bint	girl	albint
garya	village	algarya
hadiyya	gift	alhadiyya
ḥarb	war	alḥarb
ɛamal	work	alɛamal
ghalṭa	mistake	alghalṭa
finǰān	cup	alfinǰān
khabar	news	alkhabar
qānūn	law	alqānūn
kātib	writer	alkātib
madrasa	school	almadrasa
waṭan	country	alwaṭan
yad	hand	alyad

The rest of the consonants **d**, **ḍ**, **n**, **r**, **s**, **ṣ**, **sh**, **t**, **ṭ**, **z**, **ẓ** are referred to as "sun letters," **alḫurrūf ashshamsiyya**. The **-l-** of the definite article is assimilated to a following sun letter to form a double consonant. Note the following:

dars	lesson	addars
ḍarb	hitting	aḍḍarb
ruz	rice	arruz
sāɛa	watch, hour, clock	assāɛa
shēkh	sheik	ashshēkh
ṣabāḥ	morning	aṣṣabāḥ
ṭarīg	road	aṭṭarīg
namla	ant	annamla
ẓābiṭ	officer	aẓẓābiṭ
tarbiya	teaching	attarbiya

The Forty Selections

Selection One

maʕlūmāt ʕan almamlaka lʕarabiyya ssuʕūdiyya[1]

assuʕūdiyya tiḥtal[2] akbar gism min shibh alǰazīra lʕarabiyya. masāḥat almamlaka taman miyya[3] wu sabʕīn alf mīl murabbaʕ tagrīban. tarwatha lmaʕdaniyya tishmil addahab, alfiḍḍa, annaḥās, arraṣāṣ, alḥadīd, wu baʕḍ almaʕādin attānya. ʕadad sukkān assuʕūdiyya tisʕa malyōn nasma tagrīban.

dīn almamlaka alʔislām. fīha wulid annabi muḥammad ṣalla llāh ʕalēh wu sallam[4]. wu fīha alḥaramēn[5], makka lmukarrama wa lmadīna lmunawwara. humma yiʕtagdu bi[6] mūsa wa bi abūna[7] ibrāhīm wa bi sayyidna ʕīsa ʕalēh assalām. alḥukūma mā tismaḥ[8] li ghēr almuslimīm yiṣallu fi kanāʔis aw fi maʕābid. mū masmūḥ[9] buna lkanāʔis fi kull assuʕūdiyya.

alʔislām ʕindahum attagwīm alhiǰri[10], wu huwwa yiʕtamid ʕala shshahr algmari illi huwwa tisʕa wu ʕishrīn yōm wu nuṣ. abtada hāda ttagwīm lamma hāǰar annabi min makka ila lmadīna fi lqarn assābiʕ mīlādi. kull almuslinīn lāzim yiṣūmu shahr ramaḍān, yaʕni lāzim yitwaggafu ʕan alʔakl wu shshurb wu ttadkhīn ṭūl annahār. algānūn assuʕūdi yiǰbur kull annās muslimīn wu ghēr muslimīn innu mā yāklu wala yishrabu wala yidakhkhinu fi amākin ʕāmma fi wagt ṣōm[11] ramaḍān. alʔashhur alʔislāmiyya hiyya: muḥarram, ṣafar, rabīʕ alʔawwal, rabīʕ attāni, ǰumād alʔawwal, ǰumād attāni, raǰab, shaʕbān, ramaḍān, shawwāl, zu lgiʕda, wu zu lḥiǰǰa. fi khams arkān fi ddīn alʔislami humma: ashshihāda bi anna lā ilāha illa llāh wu anna muḥammad rasūlu allāh, wu ṣṣalā khams marrāt fi lyōm, wu zzakā itnēn wu nuṣ fi lmiyya, wu ṣōm shahr ramaḍān, wu ḥaǰǰ albēt.

Vocabulary

maʕlūmāt *n.*	information
aḥtal/yiḥtal *v.tr.*	to occupy
shibh alǰazzīra lʕarabiyya	the Arabian Peninsula
masāḥa *n.pl.* -āt	area
murabbaʕ *pass.part.*	square
maʕdaniyya *adj.*	mineral
dahab *n.coll.*	gold
fiḍḍa *n.coll.*	silver

naḥās *n.coll.*	brass
raṣāṣ *n.coll.*	lead
ḥadīd *n.coll.*	iron
nasma *n.*	inhabitant; breeze; breath
alḥaramēn *n.du.*	the two holy places of Mecca and Medina
aʕtagad/yiʕtagid + bi *v.intr.*	to believe
kanīsa *n.pl.* kanāyis, kanāʔis	church
tagwīm hiǰri	the Islamic calendar
aʕtamad/yiʕtāmid + ʕala *v.intr.*	to depend on
hāǰar/yihāǰir *v.intr.*	to immigrate; to emigrate
qarn *n.pl.* qurūn	century
mīlādi *adj.*	A.D.
aǰbar/yiǰbur *v.tr.*	to obligate, force s.o.
atwaggaf/yitwaggaf + ʕan *v.intr.*	to abstain from
ṣōm *n.*	fasting
rukn *n.pl.* arkān	pillar
s̲hihāda *n.*	declaration; certificate; witness
rasūl, *n.pl.* rusul	messenger; prophet
zakā *n.*	almsgiving
fi lmiyya	percent
ḥaǰǰ *n.*	pilgrimage

Notes

1. **almamlaka lʕarabiyya ssuʕūdiyya:** *the Kingdom of Saudi Arabia.* Saudi Arabians as well as other Arabs do not use the full name of the country. Usually they refer to it either as **almamlaka**, *the Kingdom,* or **assuʕūdiyya.**

2. **tiḫtal:** *It occupies.* Cf. MSA **taḫtallu.** Note the change of the preformative vowel **a** ---> i as well as the deletion of the final vowel, which is a common phenomenon in Hijazi Arabic.

3. **taman miyya:** *eight hundred.* Cf. MSA **θamān miʔah** (pausal form). Note the change of MSA **θ** ---> **t** and the shortening of the vowel a. Note also the double **yy** to compensate for the deletion of the glottal stop.

4. **ṣalla llāh ʕalēh wu sallam:** *God bless him and grant him salvation.* This expression is borrowed from MSA and is used as a eulogy after the name of the Prophet Muhammad.

5. **alḫaramēn:** *the two holy places, Mecca and Medina.* Hijazi dual nouns are marked with the suffix **-ēn** for masculine nouns and **-tēn** for feminine nouns which end in a. Hijazi Arabic borrows the genitive-accusative form only. Cf. MSA **ḫaramayni** with the Hijazi change of **-ay** ---> **ē** which is very common. However, there is another dual pattern in this dialect which is **itnēn** m.; **tintēn** f. followed by the plural form of the noun, e.g., **itnēn riǰāl**, *two men;* **tintēn banāt**, *two girls.*

6. **yiʿtagdu bi**: *they believe in.* Cf. MSA **yaʿtaqidūna**. Note the change of the preformative marker **a** ---> i with the loss of the third vowel as well as the deletion of the suffix -na and the shortening of the vowel preceeding it.

7. **abūna**: *our father.* Cf. MSA **abīna** (nominative **abūna** and accusative **abāna**). Hijazi Arabic uses only the nominative form of **ab** and **akh**.

8. **mā tismaḥ**: *does not allow.* The negative particle **mā** is used in Hijazi Arabic to negate verbs.

9. **mū masmūḥ**: *It is not allowed.* The negative particle **mū** precedes an adjective, an adverb, a noun or a prepositional phrase, e.g., **huwwa mū kabīr**, *he is not big*, **huwwa mū hina**, *he is not here;* **hiyya mū muʿallima**, *she is not a teacher;* **humma mū fi lmaktab**, *they are not in the office.*

10. **attagwīm alhiǰri**: *the Hegira calendar.* This calendar in use in Muslim countries, reckons time from July 16, A.D. 622, the day after Muhammad's flight from Mecca to Medina. It is based on a cycle of 30 years, nineteen of which have 359 days, and eleven of which are leap years having 355 days each.

11. **ṣōm**: *fasting.* Cf. MSA **ṣawm** (pausal form). It is characteristic of Hijazi Arabic to change MSA **-aw** ---> **ō**, as is the case here.

Selection Two

tārīkh assuɛūdiyya wa ḥukūmatha

assuɛūdiyya liɛbat[1] dōr muhim fi ttārīkh min gadīm azzamān fi majālāt attijāra wu ddīn wu ttagāfa. timtad almamlaka min albaḥr alʔaḥmar fi lgharb ila lkhalīj alɛarabi fi shsharg. alʔarāḍi ssuɛūdiyya munawwɛa wu lākin hiyya arḍ gāḥla[2] ijmālan, wu muɛẓamha[3] ṣaḥra[4]. arrubɛ alkhāli huwwa akbar[5] manṭiga ramliyya fi lɛālam. bas mā lāzim ninsa annu fi ssuɛūdiyya fī wudyān, wu suhūl, wu arāḍi ḥajariyya, wu jibāl khāṣṣa fi manṭigat ɛasīr. fī kamān[6] masāḥāt ẓaghīra[7] nisbiyyan min alʔarāḍi lmukayyafa zirāɛiyyan. yigūlu innu hādi lʔarāḍi min akhṣab wu min aktar alʔarāḍi lmuntija fi shsharg alʔawṣaṭ, zay wāḥāt alqaṭīf masalan[8].

shaɛb assuɛūdiyya shaɛb sāmi, kulluhum min aṣl ɛarabi wu tagrīban ɛashara bi lmiyya minhum baduw. assuɛūdiyyīn mā tjānasu maɛ shuɛūb tānya. bi lwāgiɛ innu assuɛūdiyya mā kānat wala marra taḥt ay istiɛmār. hāda shshi sāɛad ɛala wiḥdat albilād wa istigrārha lʔijtimāɛi. assuɛūdi huwwa insān fakhūr bi giyamu ddīniyya wu lʔakhlāgiyya wu bi turāθu.

alɛarabiyya ɛindaha tārīkh ghani jiddan. ibtidāʔan min alqarn[9] assābiɛ mīlādi alɛarb nasharu risālat alʔislām min makka wu min almadīna wu nasharu lughathum alɛarabiyya wu turāθhum. hāda ddīn antashar bi surɛa ila shimāl afrīqya wu ila āsya lwusṭa. amma tārīkh assuɛūdiyya lḥāḍir yibtadi min sanat 1902, lamma ɛabdu lɛazīz astarjaɛ bēt gabīlatu fi rriyāḍ. baɛd ḥarb talatīn sana ɛabdu lɛazīz waḥḥad kull alɛanāṣir almuḥārba (almutnāzɛa) wu aɛlan nafsu malik assuɛūdiyya.

muɛḍam khazzānāt annafṭ infataḥat baɛd alḥarb alɛālamiyya ttānya. ɛabdu lɛazīz abtada yistaɛmil kull fulūs annafṭ minshān yiɛajjil marḥalat alḥaḍāra wu ttagaddum fi bilādu. wu hādi lmarḥala kānat titgaddam taḥt giyādat khulafāʔu almalik fēṣal wu lmalik khālid wu lmalik fahd. assuɛūdiyya fīha malakiyya muṭlaqa. tiḥkimha ɛēlat[10] suɛūd, sulālat ɛabdu lɛazīz. guwwād alɛēla yiɛayyinu lmalik. qānūn assuɛūdiyya lḥāḍir huwwa ashsharīɛa lʔislāmiyya, yaɛni alqurʔān alkarīm.

Vocabulary

dōr *n.pl.* adwār	role, part (played by s.o. or s.th.); turn; floor
gadīm azzamān	ancient times, former times

amtad/yimtad + min...ila *v.intr.*	to stretch, extend from...to
gāḥla *adj.*	dry, arid, barren
iǰmālan *adv.*	on the whole, in general, generally speaking
arrubɛ alkhāli	the Empty Quarter
wādi *n.pl.* wudyān	valley
sahl *n.pl.* suhūl	level, soft ground, plain
ḥaǰariyya *adj.*	rocky, stony
nisbiyyan *adv.*	relatively
mukayyafa *adj.*	cultivated; conditioned; molded
khaṣīb *adj.comp.* akhṣab	fertile, productive
wāḥa *n.pl.* -āt	oasis
a/tǰānas/yitǰānas *v.intr.*	to intermarry
bi lwāgiɛ	indeed, as a matter of fact
istigrār *n.*	stability
fakhūr *adj.*	proud
gīma *n.pl.* giyam	value
giyam akhlāgiyya	moral values
turāθ/t *n.*	culture; heritage; inheritance, traditions
a/istarǰaɛ/yistarǰiɛ *v.tr.*	to get back, recover, regain; recapture
ɛunṣur *n.pl.* ɛanāṣir mutnāzɛa	hostile factions
ɛaǰǰal/yiɛaǰǰil *v.tr.*	to expedite
marḥala *n.pl.* marāḥil alḥaḍāra	stages of modernization
khalīfa *n.pl.* khulafa	successor; caliph
malakiyya muṭlaqa	absolute monarchy
ɛayyan/yiɛayyin *v.tr.*	to appoint; specify
ashsharīɛa alʔislāmiyya	Islamic law

Notes

1. **liɛbat** impf. **tilɛab:** *It plays.* Cf. MSA **laɛibat** with the Hijazi change of the first vowel **a** ---> i and the deletion of the second vowel.

2. **gāḥla:** *arid.* Cf. MSA **qāḥilah** (pausal form). Note the change of **q** ---> g which is a common phenomenon in Hijazi Arabic; however, in some words the **q** sound never changes, e.g., **qurʔān.**

3. **muɛḍ/ẓamha:** *most of it, the majority.* This word may be followed by a noun or a pronominal suffix, e.g., **muɛẓam alʔarāḍi**, or **muɛẓamha.** Cf. MSA **muɛðamuha**, with the change of **ð** ---> **ẓ** and the deletion of the final vowel before the pronominal suffix.

4. **ṣaḥra:** *desert.* Cf. MSA **ṣaḥrāʔ**. Hijazi Arabic and most other Arabic dialects delete the glottal stop and shorten the final vowel of words ending in **-āʔ**, as is the case here.

5. **akbar:** *the biggest.* Hijazi Arabic uses the pattern aCCaC to form the comparative and superlative of adjectives.

6. **kamān:** *also, as well.* This word is not used in MSA. However, it is possible that it is based on the two MSA fused elements **kama anna,** *as well as, as, as also.* Most Arabic dialects use this word.

7. **ẓi/agh̲īra:** *small.* Cf. MSA **ṣagh̲īratun** (nominative). The **gh̲** sound may have caused the assimilation of **ṣ** ---> **ẓ**. This shift occurs in many Arabic dialects.

8. **masalan:** *for example.* Cf. MSA **maθalan** with the change of **θ** ---> **s**. The student should expect the MSA pronunciation as well.

9. **i/abtada:** *began, started.* Cf. MSA **ibtada?a.** Note the deletion of the glottal stop and the final vowel. The form **bada?** is very common in Hijazi Arabic. The phrase **ibtidā?an min** means *starting from, beginning with...*

10. **ɛēla:** *family.* Cf. MSA **ɛā?ilah** (pausal form). The glottal stop drops causing the change of the vowel **ā** ---> **ē**.

Selection Three

baɛḍ almudun assuɛūdiyya

1. makka almukarrama hiyya ɛāṣimat kull almuslimīn. ta?assasat makka min lamma allāh khalag bīr[1] zamzam ɛashān yikhalliṣ hājar wu ibnha ismāɛīl min almōt ɛaṭash. kull wāḥad yiɛrif innu alɛarab aǰu[2] min nasl ismāɛīl. ibrāhīm wu ibnu ashtaghalu katīr ɛashān yibnu lkaɛba illi kānat makān li lɛibāda ḥatta min gabl al?islām. addīn al?islāmi biygūl[3] innu kull muslim fi lɛālām lāzim yiǰi yizūr makka fi wagt alḥaǰǰ, ɛala lgalīla marra wāḥda fi lḥayā. daḥḥīn[4] makka taghayyarat marra[5] ɛan almāḍi. fīha ɛamāyir kabīra wu shawāriɛ wāsɛa wu ?utīlāt katīra khāṣṣa li lḥuǰǰāǰ.

2. almadīna almunawwara hiyya madīna muhimma ɛind almuslimīn li ann fīha ǰāmiɛ arrasūl almashhūr wu gabru wu lmaktaba ḥaggatu[6] kamān, wu fīha lǰāmɛa al?islāmiyya. kull ḥaǰǰ lāzim yizūr gabr annabi fi lmadīna. ayyām zamān kānat almadīna ẓaghīra wa lākin daḥḥīn kibrat albalad w kitrat[7] annās fīha. fa bitshūf innu ɛādu buna[8] lmadīna min hadāk alwagt ḥatta inn alwāḥad mā yiɛrifha. ṣār fīha aswāg ḥadīsa w ɛamāyir katīra.

3. arriyāḍ madīna ḥadīsa wu btinma[9] bi surɛa. almalik ɛabdul ɛazīz illi maɛrūf ɛādatan bi ibn suɛūd ɛimilha ɛāṣimat assuɛūdiyya. arriyāḍ ɛindaha tārīkh gadīm, tuɛtabar awwal ɛāṣima li manṭgat alyamāma. li ghāyat awwal alkhamsīnāt mā kān fī wala ṭarīg mzaffata tiwṣal[10] ila rriyāḍ. kānat ṣaḥra fīha guṣūr min turāb wu ṭīn. ǰō nnās ila rriyāḍ li?annu fīha wāḥāt wāsɛa min shaǰar annakhl wu lkhuḍār, wu kān fīha mōya kāfya. kilmat 'arriyāḍ' tiɛni basātīn aw ǰannāt. manākhha ǰāf marra, wu yinzal fīha maṭar galīl. arriyāḍ kānat ɛāṣimat gabīlat āl auɛūd wa lākin ṭaradūhum minha. fi sanat 1902 ḥāṣarha almalik ɛabdul ɛazīz w akhadha (istarǰaɛha) min ibn rashīd.

4. ǰidda yisammūha ɛarūsat albaḥr al?aḥmar. astaslamat ǰidda li ɛabdul ɛazīz wu riǰālu sanat 1925, wa lākin tārīkhha mā btada illa li sanat 1933, lamma wazīr al?igtiṣād waggaɛ ittifāgiyya maɛ sharikat stāndard ōyl ḥaggat kalifōrnya. dafaɛu khamsa wu talatīn alf ǰunēh inglīzi dahab. wu min hadāk alwagt taghayyarat ǰidda w irtafaɛ ɛadad sukkānha min 25 alf nasma li malyōn tagrīban fi sanat 1980. fīha aḥdas maṭār ismu maṭār almalik ɛabdul ɛazīz addawli, illi masāḥatu aktar min 40.5

mīl murabbaع. hāda lmaṭār yiʔammin kull sana safar malyōn wu nuṣ min alḥuǰǰāǰ almuslimīn. wu sittat malāyīn musāfir tānyyīn.

5. ǰubēl wu yunbuع byitḥassanu bi shakl hāyil[11]. humma mudun ṣināعiyya wu fīhum mashārīع ḍakhma marra.

Vocabulary

almukarrama *adj.*	the honored, the revered; (with def.art.) epithet of Mecca
taʔassasat/titʔassas *v.intr.*	to be established, founded
khalag/yikhlag *v.tr.*	to create, make; to shape, form
bīr *n.pl.* ābār	well
عaṭash *n.*	thirst
nasl *n.*	progeny, descendant
عibāda *n.*	worship
عala lgalīla	at least
munawwar *adj.*	lighted; shining; radiant; (with def.art. plus f. ending) epithet of Medina
mashhūr *act.part.*	famous
عādu/yiعīdu *v.tr.*	to repeat an action
buna *v.n.*	building
ḥadīsa *adj.*	modern, up-to-date
nama/yinma *v.intr.*	to grow
tuعtabar *v.pass.*	to be considered
li ghāyat	until
mzaffata *pass.part.*	paved
turāb *n.coll*	dirt, soil; mud
ṭīn *n.coll.*	clay
wāḥa *n.pl.* -āt	oasis
shaǰar nakhl	palm trees
bustān *n.pl.* basātīn	garden
ǰanna *n.pl.* -āt	paradise, garden
manākh *n.pl.* -āt	weather, climate
ǰāf *adj.*	dry
ṭarad/yiṭrud *v.tr.*	to expel, drive out, chase away
ḥāṣar/yiḥāṣir *v.tr.*	to surround, besiege
a/istarǰaع/yistarǰiع *v.tr.*	to regain, recapture
astaslam/yistaslim + li *v.intr.*	to surrender

waggaع/yiwaggiع *v.tr.*	to sign (one's name); to drop s.th.
irtafaع/yirtafiع *v.intr.*	to go up
amman/yiʔammin *v.tr.*	to provide; to trust s.o.; to insure
hāyil *adj.*	huge, vast, gigantic
mashrūع *n.pl.* masharīع	project
ḍakhma *adj.*	huge, gigantic

Notes

1. **bīr:** *well.* MSA uses **biʔr.** Note the deletion of the glottal stop and the compensatory lengthening of the vowel.

2. **aJu:** *they came.* Cf. MSA **Jāʔu.** Hijazi Arabic as well as many other Arabic dialect metathesize this MSA verb. Hijazi Arabic uses **Jō** also.

3. **biygūl:** *he says.* Cf. MSA **yaqūlu.** The prefix **bi-** is used in Hijazi Arabic to mark a habitual, progressive or future action. This marker does not occur in MSA. Note the deletion of preformative vowels, the change of **q** ---> **g** and the deletion of the final vowel.

4. **daḥḥīn:** *now.* MSA does not use this word, it uses **alʔān.** The cognates for this Hijazi lexeme are **ða** the demonstrative pronoun without **hāʔ attanbīh** and the word **ḥīn** (pausal form) *time.*

5. **marra:** *very much.* Hijazi Arabic uses this word as an intensifier. It may modify adjectives or verbs, and it either precedes or follows the word it modifies, e.g., **taghayyarat marra,** *it changed a lot,* or **marrra taghayyarat.**

6. **ḥaggatu:** *his.* This word agrees with the noun it modifies in gender and number, e.g., **almaktaba ḥaggatu,** *his library;* and **alkutub ḥaggōni,** *my books.* This usage does not occur in MSA.

7. **kitrat:** *increase, multiply.* Cf. MSA **kaθurat** with the change of **a** ---> **i** and the **θ** ---> **t** (a common phenomenon in Hijazi Arabic) and the deletion of the second vowel.

8. **buna:** *building.* Cf. MSA **bināʔ** (pausal form). Note the change of the first vowel **i** ---> **u** and the deletion of the glottal stop with the shortening of the final vowel. MSA uses **aعādu bināʔa lmadīnati,** *they have rebuilt the city,* instead of **عādu buna lmadīna.**

9. **btinma:** *is growing.* Cf. MSA **namā** impf. **t/yanmu.** Hijazi Arabic does not adhere to the MSA rule that the final **alif ṭawīla** of a defective verb is changed to **wāw** in the imperfect, e.g., MSA **daعā** impf. **yadعu** is equivalent to Hijazi Arabic **daعa** impf. **yidعi,** *to call; to pray.*

10. **tiwṣal:** *taking to/linking to/leading to.* Most MSA verbs having the initial vowel **wāw,** drop the **wāw** in the impf. and imp., e.g., **waṣal/yaṣilu, waJada/yaJidu.** Unlike MSA Hijazi Arabic maintains the diphthong **iw** in the impf.

11. **hāyil:** *huge, gigantic.* Cf. MSA **hāʔilin** (genitive case). Note the deletion of the glottal stop and the substitution of the **y,** a common phenomenon in many Arabic dialects.

Selection Four

alfarg bēn alḥayāt fi lmamlaka wa lḥayāt fi amrīka

amrīka tikhtalif ikhtilāf kulli ɛan almamlaka. awwal ḥāǰa[1] alḥaḍāra. hina fī ɛindahum ḥaḍāra aktar mima ɛindana. bas mush[2] bi maɛna innu iḥna mā ɛindana ḥaḍāra. fī[3] ɛindana ɛamāyir w shawāriɛ. kull ḥāǰa yitkhayyalha lʔinsān, mawǰūda fi ssuɛūdiyya, bas innu mush bi nnissba lli bi amrīka, aw fi dduwal lʔōrōbbiyya.

min nāḥiyat alǰaw, alǰaw mukhtalif tamāman, bard, w talǰ. iḥna mā ɛindana talǰ illa fi lmanāṭig shshamāliyya. baɛḍ awgāt byiǰīna talǰ mū dāʔim. zay alɛām[4], bi ḥāyil nizil ɛindana talǰ fi lmurtafaɛāt hināka. kān alǰaw ǰiddan bārid, liʔannu ḥāyil fi shshamāl garība min lʔurdun. aḥyānan byiǰīna hawa zay ma ngūl iḥna shamāli, w biykūn alǰaw bārid. almamlaka lɛarabiyya ssuɛudiyya ṣaḥra, fa bardaha ǰāf wa ḥarraha ǰāf, mā ɛada lmanāṭig albaḥriyya, ṭabɛan bīkūn fīha ruṭūba bi sabab albaḥr.

min nāḥyat alɛādāt fī farg kabīr ǰiddan. aṣlan ɛindana alḥarīm mā tiṭlaɛ tigaḍḍi[5] bi nafsaha, yaɛni trūḥ assūg w tishtari aghrāḍaha lkhāṣṣa fīha. ɛindana arriǰǰāl huwwa masʔūl ɛan kull ḥāǰa. huwwa lli yǰīb aghrāḍ albēt wa lmagāḍi. alḥurma law ṭilɛat min albēt, lāzim[6] tkūn lābsa llibs alkāmil, alli huwwa lmiṣfaɛ, alḥāǰa ssōda lli ɛa[7] lwaǰh, wa lɛaba, w lāzim tkūn sōda. fī anwāɛ katīra min alɛuby. lḥurma law ṭalaɛat min albēt lāzim tkūn lābsa ṭawīl. maɛnātu[8] lāzim tkūn musattara min arrās wu rragaba ila rruǰūl. wa lmiṣfaɛ yitlibis[9] ṭabagatēn[10] ɛashān ykūn mā yiwarri lwaǰh.

Vocabulary

farg *n.pl.* furūg	difference
ikhtalaf/yikhtalif + ɛan *v.intr.*	to be different from
ḥaḍāra *n.pl.* -āt	modernization; development; civilization
ɛimāra *n.pl.* -āt, ɛamāyir	building
atkhayyal/yitkhayyal *v.tr.*	to imagine
mush bi nnisba illi	not to the extent that
min nāḥiyat	concerning, with respect to
ǰaw *n.*	weather
talǰ *n.coll.pl.* tulūǰ	snow

ɛām *n.*	(with def.art.) last year
hawa s̲h̲amāli	northern wind
ǰāf *adj.*	dry
mā ɛada	except
ruṭūba *n.*	humidity
gaḍḍa/yigaḍḍi *v.intr.*	to go shopping
g̲h̲araḍ *n.pl.* ag̲h̲rāḍ	household items
magāḍi *n.pl.*	groceries
miṣfaɛ *n.pl.* maṣāfiɛ	veil
ɛaba *n.pl.* ɛuby	cloak, aba
musattara *adj.*	covered, hidden
ragaba *n.pl.* -āt	neck
ṭabaga *n.pl.* -āt	layer

Notes

1. **awwal ḥāǰa:** *the first thing, first of all.* Arabic dialects often borrow MSA words and assign them different meanings, as is the case here. MSA **ḥāǰatun** means *need, necessity.*

2. **mus̲h̲:** *not.* This word is borrowed from Egyptian Arabic. Another variation of this word is **mis̲h̲**. Hijazi Arabic uses **mū**.

3. **fī:** This word may mean *there is/there are.* It is often used at the beginning of a sentence followed by an indefinite noun. It is also used by Saudis in interrogative sentences with the meaning *is...there?* e.g., **abu aḥmad fī**? *Is Abu Ahmad there?*

4. **zay lɛām:** *last year, for example.* The word **zay** may mean *as, like, for example.* The word **ɛām** when used as a definite noun means *last year* in Hijazi Arabic as well as in many other Arabic dialects.

5. **tigaḍḍi:** *to shop (for household things).* This word does not occur in MSA. It is a good isogloss for Hijazi Arabic. Note also the derived noun **magāḍi**.

6. **lāzim:** *must.* This is an active participle of the verb **lazima**; however, it has lost its function as an active participle and serves as an auxiliary verb. MSA uses the verb **yaǰibu** + **an**.

7. **ɛa:** *on.* This is the short form of **ɛala**. Another variation is **ɛal**. When pronominal suffixes are added to **ɛala**, the **a** changes to **ē**, except for the first person singular.

8. **maɛnātu:** *this means (lit., its meaning).* Many Arabic dialects use the verb **yaɛni** in this situation. Cf. MSA **maɛnāhu**, *its meaning.*

9. **yitlaba/is:** *is worn.* pf. **atlabas**. In Hijazi Arabic the passive verb is formed by adding the prefixes **an-** or **at-** to the perfect. However, this prefix becomes an infix in the impf. verb, e.g., **ankatab**, *was written,* impf. **yinkatib**. There is no rule stating which is to be used in a given case.

10. **ṭabagatēn:** *two layers.* Cf. MSA **ṭabaqatayni**. The dual in Hijazi Arabic is formed by adding the suffix **-ēn** (**-tēn** to nouns with the feminine ending **a**) to the noun. In some cases the equivalent of the dual is formed by placing **itnēn**, **tintēn** before or after a plural noun, e.g., **ɛindu banāt tintēn**, *he has two girls.*

Selection Five

maǰālis alḥarīm

alḥurma tiǰlis fi maǰālis alḥarīm bas. mū mumkin tiǰlis maɛ arriǰāl. fī maḥallāt la lɛazāyim maɛmūla khiṣṣīṣan gism li lḥarīm wu gism li rriǰal. ḥatta madkhal alḥarīm yikūn la ḥālu[1]. mā fī[2] madkhal mushtarak li lḥarīm wa li rriǰāl sawa[3]. lāzim almadkhal matalan shamāli wu lmadkhal attāni ǰanūbi aw shargi wu gharbi. mustaḥīl yikūn alʔitnēn ǰamb[4] baɛḍ. fī biyūt maɛmūla bi madkhal wāḥad. w ḥatta wa law fī bēt wāḥad fī riǰāl w ḥarīm, dāyman[5] yiḥāwil rāɛi lwalīma/ lɛazūma nafsu innu yikhalli lḥarīm madkhalhum ɛala ǰanb wu rriǰāl madkhalham ɛala ǰǰanb attāni. la ḥad baɛḍ awgāt byiḍṭar alwāḥad iza mā ɛindu illa madkhal wāḥad aw shugga wāḥda byākhud[6] bēt ǰāru ɛashān yifṣul bēn alḥarīm wa bēn arriǰāl. hādi lɛādāt ṭabɛan wu ttagālīd, mush mumkin yikūn mushtarak.

ɛindana fi ssuɛūdiyya alḥarīm bitṣāfiḥ baɛḍhum albaɛḍ mush arriǰāl. alḥurma mā tgāblak ḥatta law kunt garīb laha. fī ɛindana baɛḍ awgāt, fī ɛādāt innu ibn alɛam mā yishūf bint ɛammu, lēsh?[7] liʔannaha tiḥil lu fi zzawāǰ. w ibn alkhāl mā yishūf bint ɛammatu kamān. alli yiḥggillhum yishūfu lḥurma humma, akhūha, khālaha, ɛammaha, walad ukhtaha, ashshakhṣ illi mā tiḥiggillu yitzawwaǰha, hāda illi mumkin yikshif ɛalēha. innama shakhṣ mumkin yitzawwaǰha ngūl iḥna mush maḥram laha. maḥram maɛnāta innu mā yiḥiggillu yitzawwaǰha, mush maḥram maɛnāta mumkin yitgaddam w yitzawwaǰha. lākin iḥna fi lbalad ḥaggatna mā nimshi ḥasab hādi lɛādāt. lamma arūḥ ɛind ahli baɛḍ awgāt bi lʔiǰāza nigɛud nitɛashsh kullana sawa. mā fī ḥad bīghīb ɛan assufra illa ida kān fī wāḥad ṭāliɛ mīɛād[8] aw mashghūl wu mā yigdar yiǰi ɛala lghada aw ɛala lɛasha. kullana nigɛud ɛala sufra wāḥda w nākul[9] sawa ḥarīm ɛala riǰāl. lēsh? liʔannu ana mutzawwiǰ w akhūy mutzawwiǰ yanɛni mumkin yikshif ɛalā zōǰati, lākin dīniyyan hāda ḥarām.

Vocabulary

maǰlis *n.pl.* maǰālis	get together, social gathering; chamber; board; council; conference room
khiṣṣīṣan *adv.*	especially
li/a ḥālu	by itself, alone
mushtarak *act.part.*	common, joint, combined
sawa	together

mustaḥīl *adj.*	impossible
rāɛi lwalīma	the host of the feast
shugga *n.pl.* -āt, shugag	apartment
gābal/yigābil *v.tr.*	to meet, to face; to compare
ḥal/yiḥil + li *v.intr.*	to be lawful, permitted, allowed
kashaf/yikshif ɛalēha *v.intr.*	to look at her unveiled; to examine her medically
maḥram	unlawful; unmarriageable, being in a degree of consanguinity precluding marriage; taboo, forbidden
ijāza *n.pl.* -āt	vacation, leave; license, authorization
ghāb/yighīb + ɛan *v.intr.*	to be absent; to hide
sufra *n.*	dining table
ṭāliɛ mīɛād	has an appointment
ḥarīm ɛala rijāl	women and men
ḥarām *adj.*	unlawful, forbidden; sin; sacred; offense

Notes

1. **li/a ḥālu:** *by itself, off by itself, separate (lit., for its condition).* The usage of this phrase is typical of Hijazi Arabic.

2. **mā fī:** *there is not.* The preposition **fī** with the long vowel ī functions as a pseudo-verb. Therefore it is negated by the negative particle **mā**. It is used to introduce a sentence and is usually followed by an indefinite noun, e.g., **fī madkhal mushtarak**, *there is a common entrance.* However, in interrogative sentences such nouns are often plural, e.g., fī **madākhil mushtaraka li rrijāl wu li ḥarīm?** *Are there common entrances for men and women?*

3. **sawa:** *together, jointly.* Cf. MSA **sawiyyan** or **sawiyyatan.**

4. **jamb:** *beside, next to.* Cf. MSA **janb** (pausal form) with the dissimilation of **n** ---> **m.** The MSA pronunciation is also used.

5. **dāyman:** *always.* Cf. MSA **dāʔiman.** Hijazi Arabic as well as many Arabic dialects change the **hamza** to **y** in the active participle of form-one hollow verbs, as is the case here. It is worth noting that the accusative nunation serves to indicate that this active participle functions as an adverb.

6. **byākhud:** *he takes.* Cf. MSA **yaʔkhuðu**, with the deletion of the glottal stop, the compensatory lengthening of the vowel **ā**, and the loss of the final vowel.

7. **lēsh:** *why.* This word functions as an interrogative adverb in Hijazi Arabic. MSA does not use **lēsh**, but uses **limāða** instead.

8. **ṭāliɛ mīɛād:** *has an appointment (lit., going appointment).* MSA does not use this construction but uses **kāna ɛala mīɛādin maɛa** instead.

9. **nākul:** *we eat.* Cf. MSA **naʔkulu.** See #6 above for further details.

Selection Six

ḥādis sayyāra

marra kunna nāzlīn ana w zōǰti ɛashān nigaḍḍi[1] iǰāza ʔusbūɛiyya ɛind abūy w ʔummi. lli ḥaṣal, innu taɛaṭṭalna fi ṭṭarīg, wu ssabab, kān fī ḥādis. waggafna wagt. nizilt min assayyāra ɛashān ashūf nōɛ alḥādis ēsh. fa ḥaṣṣalt innu kān fī wāḥad min assawwāgīn musriɛ, wu fi nafs alwagt kān fī wāḥad biḥāwil yigṭaɛ alkhaṭ, fa mā kān ɛindu furṣa, ṭiliɛ guddāmu w atṣādamat assayyārāt. tgaffal alkhaṭ ɛalēna liʔannu fī sayyāratēn, w fī sayyāra tālta ǰāyya[2] mwāǰha. fa iḍṭarrēna nūgaf lēn[3] albulīs yiǰi. ɛindana ddawriyyāt ḥaggat alkhaṭ hāda shaghghāla arbaɛa w ɛishrīn sāɛa.

kān fī wāḥad min sawwāgīn assayyārāt lli ḥaṣal bēnhum alḥādis mughma ɛalē. ṭabɛan fi lḥāla hādi lāzim ykūn fī isɛāf. nizil wāḥad min annās alwāgfīn w ḥāwal yisāɛdu. waggaf annazīf, ṭabɛan awwal ḥāǰa, ɛabāl ma[4] ǰāt almustashfa. iḥna ɛindana kull baɛd khamsīn kīlu fī mustashfa. maḥaṭṭa kāmla, mōgif kāmil. istirāḥa fīha maṭɛam w fīha masǰid w fīha maḥaṭṭat banzīn, w ṣiyāna ḥag assayyārāt, w fīha maǰālis ḥag alḥarīm, buyūt kida ghuraf bi lʔaǰār, bi ssāɛa. almsāfrīn yiǰu yirtāḥu fīha. almaḥaṭṭa hādi kānat tibɛid ɛan makān alḥādis mū agal min talātīn kīlu. fa min aṣṣaɛb innak tishīl insān mughma ɛalē wu twaddī kull hādi lmasāfa.

intaḍarna ila ann albulīs ǰā w ḥaggag bi lḥādis. bēn ma hu yiḥaggig ǰa lʔisɛāf w akhad ashshakhṣ almughma ɛalē. baɛdēn ittaḍaḥ innu rāɛi ssayyāra alli gāṭiɛ alkhaṭ huwwa lmukhṭi[5], lli huwwa mughma ɛalē. akhadu rukhṣatu awwal shay ɛashān yiktubu ɛalē lmukhālafa lli sawwāha. katabu ɛalē lmukhālafa[6] w ǰābu lwinsh w saḥabu ssayyārāt w waḍḍaḥu lkhaṭ w ṣārat ḥāǰa ɛādiyya.

ṭabɛan assawwāg almukhṭi mulzam yidfaɛ attaɛwīḍ ɛan addāmiǰ li rāɛi ssayyāra lli tahashshamat minshān yiṣalliḥha. bi nnisba li ttaʔmīn ḥag assayyārāt mawǰūd, bas mush kull wāḥad bisawwīha. ɛindana mush farḍ innak tisawwi taʔmīn, yaɛni ḥāǰa ikhtiyāriyya. mumkin tiʔammin ɛala ḥayātak aw ɛala ay ḥāǰa, bas attʔamīn ɛala lḥayāt dīniyyan ɛindana ḥarām, w ḍud addīn. ida kān[7] alwāḥad muʔammin ɛala ssayyāra, ṭabɛan sharikat attaʔmīn hi lli tidfaɛ kull shay.

law[8] ḥad māt fi lḥādis, w kān lkhaṭa? mush mutaɛammad, assawwāg muǰbūr fi lḥādis, assawwāg maǰbūr yidfaɛ gharāma, alli ngullaha ddiyya[9]. w ida kān mutaɛammad yūgaɛ ɛalē lḥukm addīni, lli huwwa lgatl. addīn ygūl assin bi ssin wu lɛēn bi lɛēn, ay ḥāǰa yisawwīha l?insān lāzim yitlagga ǰazāha. ɛindana ssārig ida sarag byigṭaɛu yaddu.

Vocabulary

ḥādis *n.pl.* ḥawadis	accident
gaḍḍa/yigaḍḍi *v.tr.*	to spend (time)
iǰāza ?usbūɛiyya	weekend
khaṭ *n.pl.* khuṭūṭ	(here) lane, line
furṣa *n.pl.* furaṣ	(here) chance, opportunity
atṣādam/yitṣādam *v.intr.*	to collide, hit
tgaffal alkhaṭ ɛalēna	the road was blocked
mwāǰha *adj.*	opposite (direction)
iḍṭarr/yiḍṭarr *v.intr.*	to find it necessary, have to
dawriyya ḥaggat alkhaṭ	highway patrol
shaghghāla *adj.*	(here) on duty, working
mughma ɛalē	unconscious
isɛāf *n.*	first aid; ambulance
nazīf *n.*	bleeding
ɛabāl ma + *v.*	until, while
istirāḥa *n.*	(here) rest area
maḥaṭṭat banzīn	gas station
ṣiyāna *n.*	maintenance (of a machine, a car)
aǰār bi ssāɛa	rent on an hourly basis
irtāḥ/yirtāḥ *v.intr.*	to rest
ḥaggag/yiḥaggig + bi *v.intr.*	to investigate
a/ittaḍaḥ/yittaḍiḥ *v.pass.*	to be clear, obvious, evident
mukhālafa *n.*	violation, traffic ticket
winsh *n.*	tow truck
waḍḍaḥ/yiwaḍḍiḥ alkhaṭ	to clear the road
mukhṭi *act.part.*	at fault

mulzam *pass.part.*	obligated
taẓwīḍ *n.*	compensation, restitution
dāmiǰ *n.*	damages
taha<u>shsh</u>am/yitha<u>shsh</u>am *v.pass.*	to be broken, destroyed, wrecked
farḍ *n.*	order, command
i<u>kh</u>tiyāri *adj.*	optional, voluntary
mutaẓammad *pass.part.*	intentional, deliberate, premeditated
maǰbūr *pass.part.*	obligated
<u>gh</u>arāma *n.*	fine, penalty
diyya *n.*	blood money, indemnity for bodily injury
assin bi ssin wa lẓēn bi lẓēn	a tooth for a tooth and an eye for an eye
gaṭaẓ/yigṭaẓ yaddu	cut off his hand, amputate his hand

Notes

1. **nigaḍḍi:** *we spend (time).* MSA does not use this verb with this meaning. It uses **qaḍa**, impf. **yaqḍi**, or it may use the verbal noun **qaḍāʔ** in this case. Cf. MSA **linaqḍi iǰāzatan ʔusbūẓiyyatan**, or **liqaḍāʔi iǰāzatin ʔusbūẓiyyatin** (fully vocalized), *to spend a weekend.*

2. **ǰāyya:** *coming.* The usage of this act. part. is characteristic of Hijazi Arabic. MSA never uses the act. part. or the imp. form of the verb **ǰāʔa**, rather it uses **ātiyah** and **taẓāl** respectively.

3. **lēn:** *until.* When **lēn** is used with **ma** it is normally followed by a verb, e.g., **lēn ma yiǰi lbūlīs**, *until the police come.* Usually **ma** is dropped before a noun, e.g., **lēn assāẓa arbaẓa**, *until four o'clock.*

4. **ẓabāl ma:** *until, by the time.* This conjunction can only be followed by a verbal clause, e.g., **ẓabāl ma ǰāt almusta<u>sh</u>fa**, *until the ambulance came* (the student might expect the use of the word **musta<u>sh</u>fa**, *hospital* instead of **sayyārat isẓāf**, *an ambulance).*

5. **mu<u>kh</u>ṭi:** *at fault.* Cf. MSA **mu<u>kh</u>ṭiʔun** (nominative) with the loss of the glottal stop and the case ending. Hijazi Arabic does not have case endings for either nouns or adjectives. The final vowel is simply replaced by a sukūn no matter what function the noun or adjective plays in the sentence.

6. **katabu ẓalē mu<u>kh</u>ālafa:** *They gave him a ticket (lit., they wrote on him the violation).* This expression does not occur in MSA.

7. **ida kān:** *if.* The word **ida** introduces a conditional sentence whether the verb is in the pf., impf. or future tense (**iza** is another variation).

8. **law:** *if.* The particle **law** introduces a conditional sentence which is contrary to fact.

9. **ngullaha diyya:** *We call it (lit., say to it) blood money.* Hijazi Arabic as well as some Levantine dialects use the verb **gāl** to mean *name* or *call s.th.* as is the case in this text. It is also used as the equivalent of the English passive, e.g., **gāl annu ssawwāg kān musriẓ**, *It was said (lit., he said) that the driver was speeding.*

Selection Seven

ǰaza[1] ssukr fi lmamlaka

assukr fi lmamlaka mush mawǰūd bi nisba kabīra. ṭabɛan ɛindana lḥukūma gawiyya, law ay insān sakrān wu tmasak, lā bud[2] ma yilga ǰazā. mustaḥīl innu yiṭlaɛ barī?. gabl kull shay hādi ḥikāya[3] dīniyya. wu ssuɛudiyya balad islāmi. ṭabɛan tinfi kull alḥāǰāt hādi. ida shshakhṣ sikir, miɛnātu innu kharaǰ ɛan addīn. anniḍām ḥaggana wu lganwānīn timishi bi ddīn[4]. masalan assārig tigṭaɛ yaddu, shay maktūb fi lqur?ān. fi ddīn ḥaggana maktūb algātil yugtal wa zzāni yurǰam. iḥna nimshi bi ddīn. mā nǰīb hādi l?umūr min nafsana. hādi qawānīn maḥṭūṭa bi lqur?ān wu bi shsharīɛa bi ihdā? rrasūl ṣalla llāh ɛalē. ɛindana hu kalām allāh subḥānahu wa taɛāla[5]. ṭabɛan iḥna nimshi ɛala kalām allāh. fa ssakrān bigāḍū mugāḍāt assukr alli hiyya sitta shuhūr ḥabs w ǰald kull yōm ǰumɛa baɛd aṣṣalā. yinḍarib bi khēzarān, allāh aɛlam, yimkin sittīn ǰalda. alǰald barḍu[6] ɛala ṭṭarīga l?islāmiyya. mū mafrūḍ alǰallād yirfaɛ yaddu la fōg w yiḍrub bi guwwa. lāzim yḥuṭ ḥāǰa taḥt yaddu ɛashān timsiku. alɛaskar byilbasu gubbaɛa dā?iriyya kida. yshīlha wu yḥuṭṭaha taḥt yaddu w yiḍrub bi sharṭ innu mā yirrfaɛ yaddu ɛashān lā ṭṭīr[7]. law rafaɛ yaddu w ṭāḥat miɛnātu huwwa lmukhālif li lqānūn. aṭṭarīga di[8] mush mu?lima mitl law wāḥad ḍarab bi guwwa. fa yḥuṭṭu shay taḥt alyadd ra?fa bi lmudnib minshan yitūb w yirǰaɛ li rabbu

Vocabulary

ǰaza *n.*	punishment, penalty
sukr *n.*	drinking, drunkenness
tmasak/yitmasak *v.pass.*	to be held, caught, arrested
mustaḥīl *adj.*	impossible
barī? *adj.*	innocent
ḥikāya *n.pl.* -āt	(here) matter, story
nafa/yinfi *v.tr.*	to refute, repudiate; to exile; to banish
sikir/yiskar *v.intr.*	to be drunk
kharaǰ/yikhruǰ + ɛan addīn	to deviate, drift away from the religion
masha/yimshi + bi *v.intr.*	(here) to live according to
masalan	for example
gātil *act.part.pl.* -īn, qatala	killer
zāni *act.part.pl.* zunāt	adulterer

ruǰim/yurǰam *v.pass.*	to be stoned
ashsharīɛa lʔislāmiyya	Islamic law
bi ihdāʔ	by the guidance of
rasūl *with def.art.*	the Prophet Muhammad
kalām allāh	God's word
subḥānahu wa taɛāla	(God) to whom be ascribed all perfection and majesty
gāḍa/ yigāḍi *v.tr.*	to judge, punish, sentence
mugāḍāt *n.*	punishment; sentence, (judicial, court) ruling
ǰald *n.*	lashing
allāh aɛlam	God knows
khēzarān *n.*	reed, bamboo, cane, rattan
ǰalda *n.pl.* -āt	a lash, a lashing
barḍu	still
mafrūḍ *pass.part.*	supposed; ordered, requested
ǰallād *act.part.pl.* -īn	person who performs the lashing
gubbaɛa *n.pl.* -āt	hat
dāʔiriyya *adj.*	circular
gubbaɛa dāʔiriyya	beret
bi sharṭ	on the condition that
ṭār/yiṭīr *v.intr.*	to fly
ṭāḥ/yiṭīḥ *v.intr.*	to fall
muʔlim *adj.*	painful
raʔfa + bi	being merciful, having pity
mudnib *act.part.*	offender

Notes

1. **Jaza:** *punishment, penalty.* Cf. MSA **Jazāʔu** with the shortening of the second vowel to **a**, and the deletion of the glottal stop along with the final vowel.

2. **lā bud ma:** *it is unavoidable; must.* Usually when **ma** follows **lā bud**, it is in turn followed by a verbal sentence as is illustrated in the text. It is worth noting that **lā bud** often expresses possibility and probability rather than necessity and certainty, e.g., **hu la bud marīḍ**, *he is probably sick.*

3. **ḥikāya:** *matter, story.* The word **ḥikāya** has several meanings in Hijazi Arabic. It may mean *matter* or *issue*, e.g., **hādi ḥikāya dīniyya**, *this is a religious matter.* It also may mean *story*, e.g., **ibni azzaghīr yiḥub alḥikāyāt**, *my little son likes stories.* Note also its use in the expression **ēsh alḥikāya?** *What is wrong* or *what is the problem?*

4. **timshi bi ddīn:** *is in accordance with the religion (lit., walks in the religion).* MSA does not use this contruction. It is typical of Hijazi Arabic.

5. **subḥānahu wa taʕāla:** *(God) to whom be ascribed all perfection and majesty.* This expression is borrowed from MSA. It is a term of praise and honor to God and His creations.

6. **barḍu:** *also.* This word does not occur in MSA. It is a good Hijazi Arabic isogloss.

7. **ṭṭīr:** *it flies.* Cf. MSA **taṭīru.** Note the deletion of the preformative vowel causing the regressive assimilation of **t** ---> **ṭ.**

8. **di:** *this.* This is a contraction of **hādi**. It is borrowed from Egyptian Arabic.

Selection Eight

ṣandūg attabarruɛāt wu dafɛ addiyya

zay ma gulna iza l?insān gatal gatīl bi gaṣd, ashsharīɛa tiḥkum innu lāzim yingatal. lākin iza lgatl kān mū mutaɛammid, alḥukūma tifriḍ ɛala lgātil innu yidfaɛ diyyat algatīl w lāzim yidfaɛ gharāma li lḥukūma. iza ahl almagtūl sāmaḥūh w gālu khalaṣ mā nibgha[1] diyya, alḥukūma tgūl hāda shay[2] min ḥaggahum. bas alḥukūma tākhud ḥaggaha. masalan tisǰin algātil wu tdaffiɛu algharāma ḥaggatha.

ɛindana fi ssuɛūdiyya fī gabāyil[3] katīr. kull gabīla tsawwi laha ṣandūg tabarruɛāt. masalan inta wāḥad min afrād algabīla tidfaɛ kamasīn riyāl fi shshahr. algabīla fīha lā yigil ɛan ɛishrīn, talatīn alf shakhṣ. fa tḥuṭ inta khamsīn w hāda yḥuṭ khamsīn, fa titkawwam alfulūs kull sana. ay[4] wāḥad yṣīr ɛalē mushkil, aṣṣandūg hu illi yidfaɛ ɛannu[5]. hāda shay mumkin yisāɛid alfard katīr iza wagaɛ fi mushkil.

mush aghlab alḥālāt ahl algatīl byiṭlubu diyya, li?annu in kān fagadt yā imma abūk, yā imma akhūk, yā imma ?ummak, yā imma waladak. alfulūs mā ḥatɛawwiḍ[6]. hada shay tagrīb ɛindana asāsi, bas fī baɛḍ alɛawāyil tgūl, nistafīd bi lfulūs[7]. naɛṭīha li l?awlād iza kān abūhum illi twaffa. w illi ɛindu kullhum aṭfāl akbar wāḥad ḥawāli arbaɛtaɛsh khamstaɛshar sana wu byidrus, ṭabɛan byistafīd. imma yaɛṭu ddiyya li l?awlād ɛashān masalan agal ḥāǰa yibnūlhum bēt yiskunu fīh, aw yishtaru bēt yiskunū fīh. algaṣd min innak tākhud addiyya mush innak tistaɛmilha istiɛmāl tarfīhi aw trūḥ titmashsha, tistaɛmilha istiɛmāl fi maḥallu.

Vocabulary

tabarruɛ *n.pl.* -āt	donation; contribution
diyya *n.pl.* -āt	blood money, indemnity for bodily injury
bi gaṣd	intentionally, deliberately
mutɛammid *adj.*	intentional, deliberate
faraḍ/yifriḍ + ɛala *v.intr.*	to impose; to order; to make incumbent
gharāma *n.pl.* -āt	fine; compensation; penalty
bagha/yibgha *v.tr.*	want
fard *n.pl.* afrād	individual

lā yigil ɛan	no less than
atkawwam/yitkawwam *v.intr.*	to be piled up
wagaɛ fi mushkil	got into trouble
aghlab alḥālāt	in most cases
fagad/yifgid *v.tr.*	to lose; to miss; to be bereaved
yā imma	either
ɛawwaḍ/yiɛawwiḍ *v.tr.*	to make up to s.o. for a loss; replace
twaffa/yitwaffa *v.intr.*	to pass away, die
istafād/yistafīd + min *v.intr.*	to benefit from s.o. or s.th.
tarfīhi *adj.*	luxurious, comfortable and pleasant; leisure
atmashsha/yitmashsha *v.intr.*	to have a good time; take a walk, stroll; to go on a trip
fi maḥallu	appropriately

Notes

1. **nibgha:** *we want.* This is a pure Saudi Arabic verbal form. It may be used alone or as an auxiliary verb. It is always imperfect in form even when the verbal complex of which it is a part is perfective in meaning, e.g., **kān yibgha yirūḥ aṭṭā?if**, *he wanted to go to Ta'if.* When speaking with non-natives, Saudis tend to use **biddi**, borrowed from Palestinian Arabic, or **ɛāwiz**, borrowed from Egyptian Arabic.

2. **shay:** *thing, something.* Cf. MSA **shay?** (pausal form) with the deletion of the glottal stop.

3. **gabāyil**, pl. of **gabīla:** *tribes.* Cf. MSA **qabā?il.** Note the common Hijazi Arabic change of **q** ---> **g**, and the substitution of the glottal stop by **y**. These changes are very common in other Arabic dialects as well.

4. **ay:** This particle is borrowed from MSA. It is used before a noun; in a statement it means *any* and in a question it means *which,* e.g., **ay suɛūdi mumkin yirūḥ almadrasa**, *any Saudi can go to school,* and **ay dars mā fahimtu?** *Which lesson did you not understand?*

5. **ɛannu:** Cf. MSA **ɛanhu.** Note the gemination of the **n** to compensate for the deletion of the **h**.

6. **ḥatɛawwiḍ:** *will compensate.* Hijazi Arabic uses the prefix **ḥa-** as a marker for the future tense. Sometimes the invariable auxiliary verb **raḥ** followed by the imperfect form of the verb expresses the future, e.g., **raḥ tɛawwiḍ**.

7. **nistafīd bi lfulūs:** *We benefit from the money.* Cf. MSA **nastafīdu min alfulūsi.** The major distinction here, other then the change of the preformative vowel **a** ---> **i** and the deletion of the final vowel, is that the Hijazi Arabic verb collocates with the preposition **bi**, while the MSA verb collocates with the preposition **min**.

Selection Nine

tārīkh sharikat arāmkō fi ssuɛūdiyya

giṣṣat assuɛūdiyya mū kāmla iza mā nitkallam ɛan giṣṣat annafṭ. tārīkh arāmkō badaʔ sanat 1933 lamman[1] waggaɛat alḥukūma ssuɛūdiyya ittifāgiyyat alʔimtiyāz alʔasāsiyya maɛ sharikat stāndard ōyl (sōkāl) ḥaggat kalifōrnya. baɛdēn[2] hādi shsharika ḥawwalat alʔimtiyāz li sharikat kalifōrnya arēbyān stāndard ōyl (kasōk). wu fi sanat 1936 ṣārat sharikat teksās timluk nuṣ[3] sharikat (kasōk) illi baɛdēn ghayyarat ismaha sanat 1944 li arāmkō, wu ɛaddalat ittifāgiyyat alʔimtiyāz alʔasāsiyya ɛiddat marrāt. fi sanat 1948 sharikatēn min ashsharikāt alʔamrīkiyya lkabīra ashtarat ashum (ḥuṣaṣ) fi arāmkō, fa ṣārat ḥuṣṣat (sōkāl) talatīn bi lmiyya, wu iksōn wu teksākō talatīn bi lmiyya kull wāḥda wu ḥuṣṣat mōbil ɛashara bi lmiyya. fi sanat 1980 ṣārat almamlaka ssuɛūdiyya timlik kull ḥugūg imtiyāz arāmko fi zzēt alkhām wu lmarāfig wu lʔintāǰ.

lamman lagu zzēt sanat 1932 badaʔt amrīka tibɛat rīǰāl mutkhaṣṣiṣīn wu mawād wu maɛaddāt alḥafr ila ḍḍahrān, albalad illi banatha shsharika fōg ḥagl addammām. fi lʔawwal ḥafaru ɛiddat ābār wu lākin mā lagu zēt bi nnisba illi atṣawwarūha. fi māris sanat 1938 ḥafaru bīr ghamīg marra[4], wu lagu zēt bi kammiyyāt kabīra.

almamlaka waggafat kull ɛamaliyyāt intāǰ albatrōl lamman gāmat alḥarb[5] fi ōrōbba. wu fi sanat 1943 ashsharika aɛlanat innaha ḥatibni maɛmal li ttakrīr fi rās tannūra[6]. fa zād ṭalab albatrōl baɛd alḥarb wu ṣārat ashsharika tizīd intāǰha ziyāda kabīra ɛashān tiʔammin li nafsha naṣīb fi ssūg alɛālamiyya.

tuɛtabar arāmkō akbar[7] sharika muntiǰa li zzēt alkhām wu sawāʔil alghāz aṭṭabīɛi fi lɛālam. li hāda ssabab almamlaka akhadat almartaba lʔūla bēn albuldān illi tintiǰ annafṭ fi shsharg alʔawṣaṭ wu ttālta fi lɛālam baɛd alwilāyāt almuttaḥida wu lʔittiḥad assōfyāti. lāzim nizkur inn assuɛūdiyya hiyya akbar balad muṣaddir li zzēt wu sawāʔil alghāz aṭṭabīɛi fi lɛālam.

arāmkō ɛindaha mashārīɛ tānya muhimma ǰiddan fi taṭwīr almanṭiga shshargiyya. wu minha mashrūɛ shabakat alkahraba. alḥukūma ṭalabat min arāmkō ɛashān tʔassis wu tdīr sharikat alkahraba fi lmanṭiga shshargiyya. w hādi shsharika lilḥīn btiṭlub musāɛadāt idāriyya min arāmkō. hādi shsharika hiyya illi tiʔammin alkahraba li kull mudun almanṭiga shshargiyya wu lgura wu li mashrūɛ alghāz wu li kull aṣṣināɛāt attānya fi lmanṭiga.

Vocabulary

kāmla *adj.*	complete
naft *n.*	petroleum
waggaɛ/yiwaggiɛ *v.tr.*	to sign; to drop; to cause to fall
ittifāgiyyat alʔimtiyāz	concession agreement
asāsiyya *adj.*	basic
ḥawwal/yiḥawwil *v.tr.*	to assign s.th. to s.o.; to transform; to transfer
malak/yimli/uk *v.tr.*	to own
ɛaddal/yiɛaddil *v.tr.*	to revise; to adjust; to amend, modify
sahm *n.pl.* ashum	share (of stock); arrow
ḥuṣṣa *n.pl.* ḥuṣaṣ	share, portion
zēt khām	crude oil
marfag *n.pl.* marāfig	facilities
intāj *n.*	production
laga/yilāgi *v.tr.*	to find
mukhaṣṣaṣ *adj.pl.* -īn	specialized
mādda *n.pl.* mawād	material
maɛaddāt *n.pl.*	equipment
ḥafr *v.n.*	drilling, digging
atṣawwar/yitṣawwar *v.tr.*	to imagine; to expect; to photograph; to draw
ghamīg *adj.*	deep
kammiyya *n.pl.* -āt	quantity
maɛmal takrīr	(here) refinery
zād/yizīd *v.tr.*	to increase
amman/yiʔammin *v.tr.*	to insure; to provide; to guarantee
naṣīb *n.*	share; portion; luck, chance; fate
sūg ɛālamiyya	international market
sāʔil *n.pl.* sawāʔil	liquid
ghāz ṭabīɛi	natural gas
martaba *n.pl.* -āt	rank
muṣaddir *act.part.pl.* -īn	exporter
taṭwīr *n.*	development

s̲habakat alkahraba	electric power network
lilḥīn	until now
garya *n.pl.* gura	village

Notes

1. **lamman:** *when.* Cf. MSA **lamma.** This is a subordinating conjunction which introduces a verbal sentence.

2. **baɛdēn:** *afterward, later.* MSA uses **baɛdaʔiðin.**

3. **nuṣ:** *half.* Cf. MSA **ni/uṣf** (pausal form). Hijazi Arabic as well as many other Arabic dialects delete the **f.** This word may also mean *middle,* e.g., fi nuṣ **allēl,** *in the middle of the night.* Note also imtiḥān nuṣ assana, *the semiannual examination.*

4. **g̲hamīg marra:** *very deep.* Cf. MSA **ɛamīq ǰiddan.** Hijazi Arabic changes the ɛ ---> g̲h and **q** ---> **g.** The word **marra** as an intensifier does not occur in MSA. It is used in Hijazi Arabic to modify adjectives or verbs. It can either precede or follow the word it modifies.

5. **gāmat alḥarb:** *the war started, broke out.* This expression is pure Hijazi Arabic. Note that Hijazi Arabic treats the word **ḥarb** as a feminine noun. MSA does not use this expression; it uses many other expressions, one of which is indalaɛati lḥarbu.

6. **rās tannūra:** Cf. MSA **raʔs tannūrah** with the common Hijazi Arabic deletion of the glottal stop and the lengthening of the vowel **ā** to compensate for its loss.

7. **akbar:** *bigger, biggest.* Both the comparative and the superlative adjectives have the same pattern aCCaC.

Selection Ten

dirāsat mushkilat ghala lmuhūr

gism[1] addirāsāt alʔiǰtimāɛiyya bi kulliyyat alʔādāb bi ǰāmiɛat almalik suɛūd, bi tawǰīh min wizārat alɛadl, gām bi dirāsa li ẓāhirat ghala lmuhūr fi lmuǰtamaɛ assuɛūdi[2]. waṣal ila lgurayyāt yōm arrubūɛ[3] almāḍi farīg min gism ɛilm alʔiǰtimāɛ illi huwwa mukallaf bi dirāsat hādi lmushkila. alfarīg mitkawwin min alʔustāz almusāɛid bi gism addirāsāt alʔiǰtimāɛiyya bi lkulliyya, adduktōr mḥammad hāni ɛīsa, almuɛīd fi lgism ṣāliḥ ibrahīm alkhuḍēri wu khamsa ṭalaba.

istagbal alfarīg maɛāli mufattish alḥudūd algharbiyya wu amīn manṭagat algurayyāt, sulṭān bin ɛabdul ɛazīz aṣṣudēri, w raḥḥab bīhum[4] w ḥaṭ taḥt taṣarrufhum ǰamīɛ attashīlāt.

gām alfarīg bi ǰawlāt mīdāniyya fi gura lmanṭaga, w kamān[5] sawwu ǰawlāt fi dākhil aḥyāʔ lmadīna lmikhtalfa, minshān yiǰmaɛu lmaɛlūmāt min almuwāṭinīn min mukhtalaf almustawayāt alʔiǰtimāɛiyya. shakar adduktōr hāni maɛāli amīr almanṭaga ɛala taǰawubu maɛ alfarīg. kamān shakar adduktōr almuwāṭinīn fi lgurayyāt ɛala taɛāwinhum likwayyis[6]. huwwa gāl innu lhadaf min hādi ddirāsa huwwa tawḍīḥ ḥagīgat ghala lmuhūr fi kull anḥāʔ lmamlaka, w tagdīm dirāsa mitkāmla[7] li wizārat alɛadl. kamān innu shughl aṭṭalaba bi ǰamɛ almaɛlūmāt w mugābalat almuwāṭinīn ḥatsahhil lahum ɛamalhum baɛd takharruǰhum bi izni llāh, ɛashān yikhdimu muǰtamaɛhum almuslim.

Vocabulary

ghala *n.*	inflation, high cost, rising cost
mihr *n.pl.* muhūr	dowry
gām/yigūm *v.intr.*	to undertake; to get up
gism *n.pl.* agsām	department; part, portion
dirāsāt iǰtimāɛiyya	social studies
ẓāhira *n.*	phenomenon
farīg *n.*	team, group
mukallaf *pass.part.pl.* -īn	authorized; commissioned, delegated
ustāz musāɛid	assistant professor
muɛīd *n.pl.* -īn	intern

istagbal/yistagbil *v.tr.*	to receive (people), to welcome
maʕāli	his excellency
mufattis͟h *act.part.pl.* -īn	inspector
ḥudūd *n.*	borders, boundaries
raḥḥab/yiraḥḥib *v.intr.*	to welcome
taḥt taṣarrufhum	at their disposal
tashīl *n.pl.* -āt	facilitation; facility
ǰawla mīdāniyya	field trip
garya *n.pl.* gura	village
ḥay *n.pl.* aḥyāʔ	neighborhood
maʕlūmāt *n.*	information
muwāṭin *n.pl.* -īn	native, citizen
mustawa iǰtimāʕi	social class
taǰāwub *n.*	response, reaction; cooperation
taʕāwun *n.*	cooperation
kwayyis *adj.*	good, fine
anḥāʔ almamlaka	every part of the kingdom
dirāsa mi/utkāmla	comprehensive study
mugābala *n.pl.* -āt	interview, meeting s.o.
sahhal/yisahhil *v.tr.*	to make something easier, simplify
tak͟harruǰ *n.*	graduation
bi izni llāh	if God is willing; if God permits

Notes

1. **gism:** *department.* Cf. MSA **qism** (pausal form) with the change of **q** ---> **g**, which is a common phenomenon in Hijazi Arabic. This word may also mean *part or portion.*

2. **assuʕūdi:** *Saudi.* The final **-y** of a masculine adjectival **nisba**, unlike in MSA, is not doubled in Hijazi Arabic, e.g., **suʕūdi, suʕūdiyy.**

3. **yōm arrubūʕ:** *on Wednesday.* Cf. MSA **alʔarbaʕāʔ.** This word is a good isogloss for Hijazi Arabic. **arrubūʕ** is an MSA word which means *region, area, territory, land.* It is not uncommon for Hijazi Arabic to borrow words from MSA and assign them different meanings.

4. **raḥḥab bīhum:** *He welcomed them.* MSA uses **raḥḥabba bihim.** The major distinction other than the deletion of the final vowel is that, in accordance with the operation of vowel harmony, MSA uses **bihim** rather than **bihum.**

5. **kamān:** *also, besides, moreover.* As was previously mentioned, this word does not occur in MSA. It is a typical colloquial Arabic word, used as an affirmative particle to emphasize an action.

6. **kwayyis:** *well, good, fine.* This is another colloquial word used either as an adverb or as an adjective, e.g., **huwwa yitkallam inglīzi kwayyis**, *he speaks English well,* and **aḥmad riʤāl kwayyis**, *Ahmad is a good man.* The word **zēn** is also used with the same meaning.

7. **mi/utkāmla**, m. **mitkāmil:** *complete.* The active participle of some verbs is formed in Hijazi Arabic by adding the prefix **m-**, **mi-**, or **mu-** to the imperfect of the verb after deleting the personal prefix, and changing the short vowel before the final consonant to i, e.g., **yitkāmal mitkāmil.** Note that the final i is dropped from the feminine form.

Selection Eleven

khaṭar almurabbiyāt alʔaǰnabiyyāt yishghil ihtimām wuzara[1] lɛamal bi lkhalīǰ

wuzara shshuʔūn alʔiǰtimāɛiyya ḥaggōn adduwal assitta illi humma aɛḍāʔ fi maǰlis attaɛāwun alkhalīǰi ṭalabu[2] dirāsa shāmla[3] ɛala mawḍūɛ ziyādat istikhdām alɛāyilāt alɛarabiyya fi lkhalīǰ ḥarīm min alhind wu min ǰanūb shargi āsya, ɛashān yirabbu lbuzūra[4] ḥaggōnhum. hāda lmawḍūɛ yiglig alwuzara. iǰtamaɛu wuzara maǰlis attaɛāwun fi masqaṭ ɛashān yibḥasu khaṭar almurabbiyāt alʔaǰnabbiyyāt. gālu lwuzara annu lʔawlād illi yirabbūhum[5] aǰnabiyyāt mā yiɛrifu yitkallamu ɛarabi kwayyis, w kamān humma yitɛallamu ɛādāt mā tittafig maɛ attagālīd alqawmiyya.

mā fī iḥṣāʔiyyāt shāmla fi lkhalīǰ, wu lākin fi lbaḥrēn kān fī 13 alf murabbiya aǰnabiyya fi sanat '82. hādi nisba bi muɛaddal wāḥda li kull ʔusratēn[6] aw talāt ʔusar. maɛ alɛilm innu[7] lbaḥrēn hiyya agall duwal alkhalīǰ fi lghina w illi yiblugh ɛadad sukkānha 360 alf nasma maɛ almuhāǰirīn w ghēr almutzawǰīn.

aṣṣaḥīfa lbaḥrēniyya 'akhbār alkhalīǰ', ams naddadat bi hādi ttagllīɛa illi tafashshat min ɛashr sinīn. kān hadaf annās innu yigtanu murabbiya ɛashān tiṭbukh, wu tinaḍḍif albēt, wu tirabbi lbuzūra. w baɛdēn ṣārat hādi lɛāda ɛunṣur asāsi fi haykal almuǰtamaɛ.

kull ṣuḥuf alkhalīǰ tizkur bi istimrār ɛan ḥawādis illi bitṣīr maɛ hadōla lʔaṭfāl bi sabab ɛadam khibrat hadōla lʔānisāt wu ssayyidāt illi byirǰaɛ aṣlhum li manāṭig rīfiyya fi āsya, w bi nōɛ khāṣ li sirilānka. fi muɛḍam alḥālāt, alḥukūma ḥakamat ɛala hadōl almurabbiyāt bi ssiǰn aw bi ṭardhum min albilād min aǰl sulūkhum almuɛīb maɛ muhāǰrīn min nafs alǰinsiyya. w hāda matal mū kwayyis bi nnisba li lɛāyilāt.

fi ɛām '81 nādat ǰarīda khalīǰiyya bi tawgīf manḥ rukhaṣ alɛamal li hadōla lʔaǰnabiyyāt illi yitruku asar salbi ɛala lʔawlād. yōm alʔitnēn aɛlanat sulṭāt albaḥrēn tawgīf taṣārīḥ alɛamal. w dalḥīn fī ḥamla ḍud alʔigāma ghēr almashrūɛa fi lbilād li lɛummāl alhārbīn min kafīlhum ṣāḥib alɛamal.

wizārat attakhṭīṭ fi dawlat alʔimārāt alɛarabiyya sawwat dirāsa w lāgat innu mawǰūd mā bēn malyūnēn wu nuṣ li talāt malāyīn min almaṭrūdīn min bilādhum yishtaghlu fi manṭagat alkhalīǰ. w hāda yisāwi tisɛīn bi lmiyya min alyad alɛāmla fi lʔimārāt w arbɛīn bi lmiyya fi ssuɛūdiyya wu lbaḥrēn.

shaddadu wuzara lɛamal wa shshuʔūn alʔiǰtimāɛiyya bi duwal alkhalīǰ alɛarabiyya fi nihāyat iǰtmāɛhum fi masqaṭ ams ɛala ahamiyyat dirāsat taʔsīr almurabbiyāt alʔaǰnabiyyāt ɛal ɛāyila lɛarabiyya fi manṭagat alkhalīǰ.

kallafu lwuzara maktab almutābaɛa bi dirāsa shāmla ḥawalēn[8] hāda lmawḍūɛ bināʔan ɛala ddirāsāt illi ḥatsawwīha kull dawla. w lāzim yiɛruḍu kull natāyiǰ hādi ddirāsāt ɛala dawrat maǰlis wuzara lɛamal wa shshuʔūn alʔiǰtimāɛiyya lgādma.

Vocabulary

khaṭar *n.pl.* akhṭār	danger, threat
murabbiya *n.pl.* -āt	governess, educator; nanny
aǰnabiyya *adj.,n.*	foreign; foreigner
ashghal/yishghil *v.tr.*	to occupy
ihtimām *n.pl.* -āt	concern, care
khalīǰ *n.*	gulf
maǰlis attaɛāwun alkhalīǰi	the Gulf Cooperation Council
ṭalab/yiṭlub *v.tr.*	to request, order, ask
mawḍūɛ *n.pl.* mawāḍīɛ	subject, issue, matter; title
ziyāda *n.*	increase
istikhdām *n.*	using
alhind *pro.n.*	India
ǰanūb sharg āsya	South East Asia
buzūra *coll.n.*	children
ḥaggōn *poss.pron.*	their
aglag/yiglig *v.tr.*	to worry, concern, upset, disturb, trouble
baḥas/yibḥas *v.tr.*	to discuss; (with **ɛan**) to look for something, to search
ɛāda *n.pl.* -āt	habit, customs, traditions
attafag/yittafig + maɛ *v.intr.*	to agree with; to suit; (with the preposition **ɛala**) agree on
taglīd *n.pl.* -āt, tagālīd	traditions, rituals
qawmiyya *adj.,n.pl.* -āt	national; nationalism
iḥṣāʔiyyāt *n.*	statistics, census
nisba *n.*	percentage, proportion

muɛaddal *n.pl.* -āt	average; (if used as adj.) amended, modified, adjusted
ʔusra *n.pl.* ʔusar	family
ghina *n.*	riches, wealth
nasma *n.*	inhabitant; breeze; breath
muhāǰir *act.par.pl.* -īn	immigrant
ṣaḥīfa *n.pl.* ṣuḥuf	newspaper
naddad/yinaddid + bi *v.intr.*	to denounce, degrade, expose (someone's faults)
taglīɛa *n.pl.* -āt	fad, trend
tafashsha/yitfashsha *v.intr.*	to spread (often of an epidemic)
agtana/yigtani *v.tr.*	to own, possess
ṭabakh/yiṭbikh *v.tr.*	to cook
naḍḍaf/yinaḍḍif *v.tr.*	to clean
ɛunṣr *n.pl.* ɛanāṣir	element
asāsi *adj.*	basic
haykal *n.pl.* hayākil	temple; skeleton, framework (of a structure), frame
bi istimrār	continuously, always
ḥādis *n.pl.* ḥawādis	event, happening; accident
ṭifl *n.pl.* aṭfāl	children
ɛadam khibra	lack of experience
ānisa *n.pl.* -āt	unwed girl
sayyida *n.pl.* -āt	lady, married woman
raǰaɛ/yirǰaɛ *v.intr.*	to go back, return
aṣl *n.pl.* ʔuṣūl	roots, background
rīfiyya *adj.*	rural
bi nōɛ khāṣ	especially
muɛḍam	most (of)
ṭard *n.*	expelling; firing (someone)
sulūk *n.*	behavior
muɛīb *adj.*	shameful
ǰinsiyya *n.pl.* -āt	nationality
matal *n.pl.* amtāl	example; proverb; lesson
nāda/yinādi *v.tr.*	to call
tawgīf *n.*	stopping
manḥ *n.*	granting
rukhṣat ɛamal	work permit
asar *n.pl.* asār	trace; effect, influence

salbi *adj.*	negative
taṣrīḥ *n.pl.* -āt, taṣārīḥ	permit
ḥamla *n.pl.* -āt	campaign, expedition
igāma *n.*	residence, stay
mas̲h̲rūɛa *adj.*	legal, lawful
hārib *act.part.pl.* -īn	escapee
kafīl *n.pl.* kufala	sponsor, legal guardian; responsible
yad ɛāmla	labor force
s̲h̲addad/yis̲h̲addid *v.tr.*	to emphasize, reinforce, stress
kallaf/yikallif *v.tr.*	to commission, authorize
mutābaɛa *n.*	follow up, continuing
binā?an ɛala	based on, on the basis of
ɛaraḍ/yiɛruḍ *v.tr.*	to present, exhibit
natīǰa *n.pl.* natāyiǰ	result

Notes

1. **wuzara:** *ministers.* Cf. MSA **wuzarā?u** with the deletion of the glottal stop and the final vowel, and the shortening of the final vowel **ā** ---> **a**. This form of plural is very common in Hijazi Arabic.

2. **ṭalabu:** *they requested.* This verb has many meanings in Hijazi Arabic as well as in MSA, e.g., **ṭalab min rabbu almag̲h̲fira**, *he asked his God for forgiveness;* **almalik ṭalab waqf iṭlāg annār**, *the king demanded a cease-fire;* **ṭalabna lɛas̲h̲a**, *we ordered dinner.*

3. **s̲h̲āmla:** *complete.* This is the feminine active participle of **s̲h̲āmil**. Note the deletion of the vowel **i** in the feminine form. See Selection 10 #7.

4. **buzūra:** *children.* This word does not occur in MSA. It is possible that the plural form **buzūr**, *seeds,* is the cognate for this Hijazi Arabic word. MSA uses **awlād** or **aṭfāl.**

5. **yirabbūhum:** *They raise them.* Cf. MSA **yurabbīnahum.** In Hijazi Arabic the third person feminine plural of the verb is identical in form with the third person masculine plural, as is the case here.

6. **?usratēn**, pl. **?uar**, s. **?usra:** *family.* This word is borrowed from MSA with the change of the dual suffix **-ayn** (genitive and accusative) to **-ēn.** The word **ɛāyila** is more common.

7. **maɛ alɛilm innu:** *knowing that, keeping in mind, (lit., with the understanding that).* This expression is borrowed from MSA. **maɛa lɛilmi anna...** MSA also uses **ɛilman bi anna.**

8. **ḥawalēn:** *around; about, concering.* This is a Hijazi Arabic word. Cf. MSA **ḥawla.**

Selection Twelve

mushkilat ɛadam attawǰīh almihani

yā[1] ǰamāɛa, aɛtagid innu taɛlīm almuǰtamaɛ li abnāʔu yuɛtabar[2] sarwa igtiṣādiyya hāyla, byiǰni tamarha baɛd attawǰīh wu ttadrīb wu ttaɛlīm albannāʔ. bi lḥagīga innu lḥāǰa li ttaɛlīm lʔakadīmi wu lmihani ḍarūriyya ǰiddan. almuǰtamaɛ yiḥtāǰ li sawāɛid abnāʔu ɛashān yinbana buna salīm[3]. lāzim nirabbi aǰyāl wāɛya illi ɛindahum alʔistiɛdād yitɛallamu ḥiraf w mihan ṣināɛiyya, mitl mīkānīkiyya, w kahraba ssayyārāt, wu nniǰāra wu lḥdāda, wu lbuna, wu lgiṣāra[4], wu ttamdīdāt aṣṣiḥḥiyya, w mihan tānya illi mū mumkin[5] nistaghni ɛanha fi lḥayāt alɛādiyya.

min almunāsib nibdaʔ fi ɛumr mubakkir ɛashān nizraɛ mafāhīm taɛlīm almihan alḥurra w iḥtirāmha fi nufūs attalāmīz fi lmadāris. min lmufaḍḍal ḍarrūrat idkhāl wurash mihaniyya fi lmadāris li taɛlīm almabādiʔ lʔasāsiyya ɛan baɛḍalmihan aṣṣināɛiyya. lāzim tiballish[6] hādi lfikra fi ṣṣufūf lʔibtidāʔiyya lɛālya, w tistamir lēn nihāyat attānawiyya lɛāmma. w lāzim yikūn fī ɛalāmat ɛala hādi lmawād mitl almawād attānya, ɛashān yikhallu[7] ṭṭullāb yihtammu bi hādi lmihan.

barnāmaǰ almihan alḥirafiyya fi lmadāris yisāɛid lʔidāra wu ṭṭalaba ɛala farz almuyūl wu rraghbāt wu lmagdira. baɛdēn yiwaǰǰihu ttalāmīz ḥasab gudrāthum, fi nihāyat albarnāmaǰ ḥaykūn fī ɛadad min attalmāmīz illi yikhtāru lmihan wu yḥubbu yishtaghlu fīha. hadōla attalāmīz lāzim yiltaḥgu bi marākiz mihaniyya, w daḥḥīn ḥaykūn ɛindahum attawǰīh almihani ssalīm. hāda lbarnāmaǰ fi ɛumr mubakkir ḥayiɛti natāyiǰ ɛaẓīma fi lmustagbal.

katīr min annās yinẓuru li lmihan aṣṣināɛiyya wu lḥiraf naẓra tigallil min gīmatha. humma yiḍunnu annu illi yitwaǰǰah li hādi lmihan huwwa fāshil fi ttaɛlīm alʔakadīmi. hāda mū ṣaḥ. liʔann dars alḥiraf amr muhim fi tagaddum almuǰtamaɛ w izdihāru, w lāzim nisud alḥāǰa li hādi lmihan illi iḥna niḥtāǰha fi kull lʔawgāt, w hadōla ttalāmīz humma shabāb almustagbal w ḥaygūdu lmuǰtamaɛ li lʔafḍal.

min wāǰbāt almadrasa ziyāda ɛala ttarbiya wu ttaɛlīm, huwwa taḥḍīr talāmīz wāsgīn min nufūshum wu yistaɛmlu khibrāthum w shaṭārathum. w lāzim tiktashif muyūlhum w mawāhibhum wu twaǰǰihhum attawǰīh assalīm. wu khuṣūṣan attalāmīz illi ɛindahum algudra li lʔaɛmāl alfanniyya mitl arrasm wu lḥiraf. hāda raḥyikhalli lmuwāṭin yiḥiss innu lmadrasa laha dōr ɛaẓīm fi buna lmuǰtamaɛ lʔigtiṣādi wu ṣṣināɛi.

fa iḥna bi ḥāǰa li lmihan aṣṣināɛiyya wu lḥiraf, wu lgaṣd min hāda lbarnāmaǰ huwwa lfāyda li kull afrād almuǰtamaɛ wu lkhēr li lǰamīɛ.

Vocabulary

mihani *adj.*	vocational
yā ǰamāɛa	people! (vocative)
sarwa *n.pl.* -āt	wealth, treasure
ǰana/yiǰni *v.tr.*	to reap
tamar *col.n.pl.* atmār	fruits; results
tawǰīh *n.*	guidance
tadrīb *n.*	training
bannāʔ *adj.*	productive, constructive
bi lḥagīga	frankly, in fact, indeed
ḍarūri *adj.*	necessary
sāɛid *n.pl.* sawāɛid	wrist, hand, arm
rabba/yirabbi *v.tr.*	to raise (a child, a beard)
ǰīl *n.pl.* aǰyāl	generation
wāɛi *adj.*	alert, aware, vigilant
istiɛdād *n.pl.* -āt	readiness; willingness; ambition
ḥirfa *n.pl.* ḥiraf	vocation, career, trade
kahraba ssayyāra	automotive electricity
niǰāra *n.*	carpentry
ḥidāda *n.*	smithery, the trade of a smith
buna *n.*	building, construction
giṣāra *n.*	brick laying
tamdīdāt ṣiḥḥiyya	plumbing, installing pipes for water and sewers
astaghna/yistaghni + ɛan *v.intr.*	to be able to do without
mafhūm *n.pl.* mafāhīm	understanding, concept, idea
iḥtirām *n.*	respect
warsha *n.pl.* wurash	workshop
mabdaʔ *n.pl.* mabādiʔ	principle, ideology
ballash/yiballish *v.tr.*	to start, begin
ɛalāma *n.pl.* -āt	grade, mark, sign

ahtamm/yihtamm *v.intr.*	to be concerned, take care
farz *n.*	sorting out, classifying
mēl *n.pl.* muyūl	desire, inclination
raghba *n.pl.* -āt	desire, inclination
magdira *n.pl.* -āt	ability
akhtār/yikhtār *v.tr.*	to choose, select
naẓar/yinẓur *v.intr.*	to look at
naẓra *n.*	glance, look,
gīma *n.*	value, price
fāshil *act.part.*	failure
tagaddum *v.n.*	advancing, improvement
izdihār *n.*	progress
wāsig min nafsu	confident of oneself
khibra *n.*	expertise
shaṭāra *n.*	skill, cleverness
aktashaf/yiktashif *v.tr.*	to discover
mawhiba *n.pl.* mawāhib	talent, gift
rasm *n.*	drawing
gaṣd *n.*	purpose, goal
fāyda *n.pl.* fawāyid	benefit, interest (on money); gain, profit
fard *n.pl.* afrād	individual

Notes

1. **yā:** The vocative particle **yā** is used in direct address. It is placed before an indefinite form of the noun, e.g., **yā Jamāʿa**, *people!* It is also used before proper names or titles in addressing persons, e.g., **yā muḥammad**, *Oh Muhammad.*

2. **yuʿtabar:** *is considered.* This passive verb is strictly MSA; however, it is often used in Hijazi Arabic as well as in some other dialects.

3. **yinbana buna slīm:** *to be built well (lit., to be built well building).* In MSA, as well as in Hijazi Arabic, all verbs whether transitive or intransitive, active or passive, may take their own abstract nouns as cognate accusatives **almafʿūlu lmuṭlaqu** to emphasize or magnify the action or state expressed by the verb. Cf. MSA li **kay yubna binā?an salīman**.

4. **giṣāra:** *brick laying.* This word occurs in MSA but with a different meaning. The MSA meaning of this word is *shrinking and bleaching cloth, fulling.*

5. **mū mumkin:** *impossible.* The word **mumkin** used before the imperfect form of the verb means *you may...,* e.g. **mumkin tākhud hada lgalam**, *you may take this pen.* It also introduces a question, e.g., **mumkin tiʿallimni hādi lḥirfa?** *Could you teach me this trade?*

6. **tiballish:** *starts.* This is strictly colloquial. It is often used as an auxiliary verb, e.g., **lāzim tiballish titʿallam mihna**, *you have to start learning a trade.*

7. **yikhallu:** *they let.* This is a pan-colloquial verb. It may be used as an auxiliary verb as is the case here, **yikhallu ṭṭullāb yihtammu**, *they let the students be concerned.* It also functions as a primary verb, e.g., **khalli l?awlād fi lbēt**, *leave the children at home.*

Selection Thirteen

izāɛat arriyāḍ tiḥaḍḍir barnāmiǰ li taɛlīm allugha lɛarabiyya

almamlaka ṭāl ɛumrak[1], btihtam bi maṣlaḥat[2] kull muwāṭin suɛūdi. fa binshūf attagaddum alʔiǰtimāɛi wu ttagāfi fi kull manṭaga fi ssuɛūdiyya. zay ma garētu fi ddurūs assābga, almamlaka ḥassanat maɛīshat almuwāṭin assuɛūdi bi ṣūra khayāliyya. hāda ttagaddum mū bas li ssuɛūdiyyīn wu lākin li kull alʔaǰānib alli ɛāyshīn ɛindana[3].

zay ma tiɛrufu annu aktariyyat[4] alyad alɛāmla fi ssuɛūdiyya hum aǰānib wu mā yiɛrifu yitkallamu ɛarabi. fa binshūf annu lmamlaka btihtam bi taɛlīm allugha lɛarabiyya li hadōla lɛummāl.

daḥḥīn izāɛat arriyāḍ bi lmushāraka maɛ maɛhad allugha lɛarabiyya bi ǰāmɛat muḥammad bin suɛūd alʔislāmiyya biyḥaḍḍiru durūs izāɛiyya[5] li taɛlīm allugha lɛarabiyya. hādi ddurūs maktūba khuṣūṣan[6] li taɛlīm alɛarabi li ghēr alɛarab. maɛhad allugha lɛarabiyya ḥaḍḍar hāda lbarnāmiǰ bi ṣifatu ǰuzʔ min mashrūɛu lkabīr illi huwwa nashr allugha lɛarabiyya, lughat dīnana lḥanīf fi lɛālam kullu. byishmil hāda lbarnāmiǰ kutub asāsiyya wu kutub tānya li llugha lɛarabiyya maktūba kullaha fi iṭār attagāfa lʔislāmiyya, wu kutub tānya maktūba bi lughat alḥayāt alyōmiyya.

min ǰihha tānya minshān yisahhilu taɛallum allugha li kull ghēr annāṭgīn fīha alli yirghabu yitɛallamūha, almaɛhad aṣdar ɛadad min almaɛāǰim/algawāmīs. fa maslan gāmūs alif bāʔi ɛarabi muzawwad bi rrusūm almulawwana alli tidil ɛala lmaɛāni lwārda fi ssilsila alli ḥayiṣdirha lmaɛhad li taɛlīm allugha lɛarabiyya li ghēr abnāʔha. wu iṣdār gāmūs tāni li nafs almufradāt assābga murattaba ḥasab almawḍūɛāt, masalan kull shay ɛan alʔakl biykūn taḥt mawḍūɛ wāḥad. hadi lgawāmīs muṣammama ɛala asās dirāsa taḥlīliyya li ttaǰārib almutwaffra fi hāda lmaǰāl bi llugha lɛarabiyya aw bi llughāt attānya.

Vocabulary

izāɛa *n.pl.* -āt	broadcasting; network
ḥaḍḍar/yiḥaḍḍir *v.tr.*	to prepare, make ready
maṣlaḥa *n.pl.* maṣāliḥ	well-being; benefit; business

sābig *act.part.*	previous; former
ḥassan/yiḥassin *v.tr.*	to improve
maɛīsha *n.*	way of life/living; livelihood
aktariyya *n.*	majority, most of
yad ɛāmla	labor, labor force
mushāraka *n.*	cooperation, collaboration; participation
bi ṣifatu	in its capacity as
nashr *v.n.*	spreading; publication; announcement
ḥanīf *adj.*	true (in reference to the Islamic religion)
asāsi *adj.*	basic, important
iṭār *n.pl.* -āt	framework; frame
sahhal/yisahhil *v.tr.*	to make s.th. easy
nāṭig *act.part.*	speaker
alif bāʔi	in alphabetical order
muzawwad *adj.*	provided, supplied; equipped
rasm *n.pl.* rusūm	drawing, picture
mulawwana *adj.*	colored, colorful
wārda *adj.*	mentioned; found
silsila *n.pl.* -āt, salāsil	episode; chain; range
muṣammama *adj.*	designed
ɛala asās	based on, on the basis of, according to
taḥlīli *adj.*	analytic
taǰruba *n.pl.* taǰārib	experiment
mutwaffra *adj.*	available, provided

Notes

1. **ṭāl ɛumrak:** *May [God] extend your life.* This is a polite expression used when addressing a person. It indicates respect as well as a wish for a long life. The expression **yā ṭawīl alɛumr** is as common.

2. **maṣlaḥa:** *welfare of s.o.* Hijazi Arabic uses this word with many different meanings, e.g., **almaṣlaḥa lɛāmma**, *public welfare;* **maṣlaḥa ḥukūmiyya**, *a government agency;* li **maṣlaḥat aḥmad**, *Ahmad's well-being;* **mā ɛindu maṣlaḥa**, *he does not have a career.*

3. **ɛindana:** *we have, in our (country).* Cf. *French chez nous.* Note its usage as the equivalent of the prepositions *to* and *for* respectively, e.g., **hu rāḥ ɛind almudīr**, *he went to the director;* hu **yishtaghil ɛindana**, *he works for us.*

4. **aktariyyat alyad alɛāmla:** *most/the majority of the labor force.*

5. **izāɛiyya:** *via radio/TV.* This **nisba** adjective (that is, a relative adjective) indicates something characteristic of, or having to do with the noun from which it is derived. This type of adjective ends in **-i** in the masculine and **-yya** in the feminine.

6. **khuṣūṣan:** *especially.* Nouns are not ordinarily inflected for case in Hijazi Arabic. However, there are a few nouns which take the accusative nunation **-an**, e.g., **yōm**, *day,* **yōmiyyan**, *daily.*

Selection Fourteen

taḥḍīr dawra fi maǰāl taɛlīm alkubār[1] ɛashān yimḥu l?ummiyya[2] fi manṭagat addarɛiyya

wāfag maɛāli wazīr almaɛārif ɛala taǰhīz dawra tadrībiyya fi maǰāl taɛlīm alkubār wu maḥw al?ummiyya, bi markaz attadrīb wu lbuḥūs alɛilmiyya ttaṭbīgiyya fi ddarɛiyya. ɛammāl[3] tinaẓẓim hādi ddawra al?idāra lɛāmma bi manṭagat arriyāḍ, fi gism taɛlīm alkubār. ashshurūṭ almuḥaddada minshān l?iltiḥāg bi hādi ddawra hiyya:

1. lāzim yikūn[4] almultlaḥig mudarris fi lmarḥala l?ibtidā?iyya.
2. lāzim yikūn gaḍa muddat talāt sinīn fi ttadrīs.
3. lāzim tikūn tagdīrātu lfanniyya fi ākhir sanatēn lā tgill ɛan ǰayyid.
4. mā lāzim yikūn ḥaḍar dawrāt zay hādi.

wu min ǰihha tānya ballagh mudīr ɛām attaɛlīm ǰamīɛ almadāris ɛashān[5] yiɛaǰǰilu w yirsilu asāmi kull arrāghbīn fi l?shtirāk bi hādi ddawra. w lāzim ykhalliṣu tiɛbāyat kull almaɛlūmāt allāzma[6] bi hāda lkhuṣūṣ li?an ākhir mawɛid li gubūl ṭalabāt attarshīḥ huwwa yōm 11-6-1404 hiǰriyya[7].

Vocabulary

dawra *n.pl.* -āt	(here) workshop
maǰāl *n.pl.* -āt	area, field, subject
ummiyya *n.*	illiteracy
wāfag/yiwāfig + ɛala *v.intr.*	to agree, approve
taɛlīm alkubār	adult education
maḥw *n.*	erasing, wiping out
buḥūs ɛilmiyya	scientific research
taṭbīgi *adj.*	applied
naẓẓam/yinaẓẓim *v.tr.*	to arrange
idāra ɛāmma	general administration
sharṭ *n.pl.* shurūṭ	condition, stipulation
gaḍa/yigḍi *v.tr.*	to spend (time)
tagdīrāt *n.*	evaluation
ǰayyid *adj.*	good
ballagh/yiballigh *v.tr.*	to notify

ɛaĵĵal/yiɛaĵĵil *v.intr.*	to speed, hasten, expidite
rāg̲h̲ib *act.part.pl.* -īn	the person who is interested
is̲h̲tirāk *n.pl.* -āt	participating, subscribing (to a magazine)
tiɛbāyat *n.*	filling out
bi hāda lk̲h̲uṣūṣ	concerning this matter
mawɛid *n.pl.* mawāɛīd	appointment, date
gubūl *n.*	acceptance
ṭalab *n.pl.* ṭalabāt	application; order (for making a purchase); request
tars̲h̲īḥ *n.pl.* -āt	nomination

Notes

1. **taɛlīm alkubār:** *adult education.* Cf. MSA **taɛlīmi alkibāri** (iɖāfa construction). Hijazi Arabic does not have case endings to indicate the genitive, accusative and nominative cases. A **sukūn** simply replaces the final vowel no matter what function the word has in the sentence.

   The Saudi government provides free education from grade school through college. It is said that Saudi Arabia spends a larger percentage of its GNP on education than any other country in the world. Increasing numbers of men and women are getting college degrees. The literacy rate is between 15% and 25%.

2. **ummiyya:** *illiteracy.* Many abstract nouns are formed by adding the suffix -iyya to a root or stem, e.g., **malakiyya,** *monarchy;* **dimuqrāṭiyya,** *democracy.*

3. **ɛammāl:** Hijazi Arabic uses this particle before the imperfect form of the verb to indicate an ongoing action or the progressive tense.

4. **lāzim yikūn:** *It is necessary that he be, he must be.* **lāzim,** an active participle in MSA, has assumed in Hijazi dialect the function of an auxiliary verb.

5. **ɛas̲h̲ān:** *in order to, so that.* This is a pan colloquial word. Hijazi Arabic uses **mins̲h̲ān** as well. This conjunction is usually followed by a verbal sentence, as is the case here. MSA uses **likay** or **li-** before the imperfect verb.

6. **almaɛlūmāt allāzma:** *the necessary information.* Inanimate plurals govern singular adjectives in Hijazi Arabic as well as in MSA. Cf. MSA **almaɛlūmāti allāzimati** (fully vocalized).

7. **11-6-1404 hiJriyya:** Saudi Arabia officially uses the Hegira calendar which started in 622 A.D. when Muhammad emigrated from Mecca to Medina. When writing a date in Arabic the day is written before the month. The Hegira calendar is based on a cycle of 30 years, 19 of which have 354 days each, and 11 of which are leap years having 355 days each.

Selection Fifteen

ǰaddati raḥamaha llāh[1]

marra kunt aḥib aǰāri rrabʕ[2] illi yizūghu ʕan ashghālhum, khāṣṣatan yōm illi yirūḥu w yitriku ʕibād allāh mintaẓrīn lēn[3] yirǰaʕu, fa ruḥt ʕind raʔīsi w ṭalabt minnu ʕashān yiʕṭīni iǰāza li muddat khams ayyām. ḥuǰǰati kānat annu ǰaddati ntagalat ila man bi yaddu malakūt assamawāt wu lʔarḍ[4]. huwwa gaddar ḍurūfi[5] ǰāzāh allāh ʕanni bi lkhēr[6], w manaḥni ʕishrīn yōm ʕashān adabbir ʔumūr alʕaǰūza. galli, "ʕaḍḍam allāh aǰrak[7] yā wlēdi[8], hād aṭṭarīg kullana māshyīnu[9]. lā tinsa ṣṣadaga w inta inshālla walad bār." lākin maʕ murūr azzaman nasēt ḥikāyat wafāt almarḥūma. fa bi kull barāʔat lʔaṭfāl, marra tānya ruḥt ʕind raʔīsi aṭlub minnu iǰāza li muddat khams ayyām. alʕuzr kān annu lǰadda ntagalat li bārīha subḥānahu wu taʕāla. faǰʔa, rafaʕ rāsu ʕan alʔawrāg lli guddāmu, w gāl bi taʕaǰǰub, "subḥān man yiḥyi lʕiḍām w hiyya ramīm, bas alli azkuru yā wlēdi annu ǰaddatak mātat min ʕashr ashhur, ēsh, hiyya gāmat min algabr? almuhim khudlak khams ayyām stirāḥa wa lā ʕād tʕīdaha."

Vocabulary

raḥamaha llāh	May God rest her soul. May God have mercy on her
ǰāra/yiǰāri *v.tr.*	to be in conformity with/in accordance with, to keep up with
zāgh/yizūgh + ʕan *v.intr.*	to depart from, leave; to deviate from
ʕibād allāh	God's servants, human beings, mankind
ḥuǰǰa *n.pl.* ḥuǰaǰ	reasoning; excuse
malakūt *n.*	kingdom (of God)
sama *n.pl.* samawāt	heaven (when with the definite article); sky
ntagalat/tintagil *v.intr.*	to be moved
gaddar/yigaddir + ẓ/ḍurūfi *v.tr.*	to be understanding of one's situation
ǰāzā/yiǰāzi *v.tr.*	to reward, punish
khēr *n.*	good, goodness; blessing; wealth
manaḥ/yimnaḥ *v.tr.*	to grant, give and receive nothing in return
ʕaḍḍam/yiʕaḍḍim *v.tr.*	to make great, make big; to exaggerate
aǰr *n.*	reward; wage, pay; fee, rate

māshi *act.part.pl.* māshyīn	walking, going; one who walks/goes
ṭarīg *n.pl.* ṭurgāt	road, way
ṣadaga *n.pl.* -āt	alms, giving for charity (normally in memory of the deceased)
bār *adj.*	righteous; good
maɛ murūr azzaman	as time goes by, with the passage of time
wafāt *n.*	death
marḥūma *pass.part.*	deceased, the late, May God rest her soul
barāʔa *n.*	innocence
ṭifl *n.pl.* aṭfāl	baby; child
bāri *act.part.*	creator (referring to God)
faǰʔa	suddenly
bi taɛaǰǰub	surprised, astonished
aḥya/yiḥyi *v.tr.*	to bring back to life, revive; to commemorate
ɛaḍma *n.pl.* ɛiḍām	bones
ramīm *adj.*	decayed, rotten (of bones)
gabr *n.pl.* gubūr	grave, tomb
lā ɛād tɛīdaha	Don't you ever do it again

Notes

1. **raḥamaha llāh:** *May God have mercy on her.* This expression, borrowed from MSA, maintains its MSA pronunciation even with illiterate speakers. It is noteworthy that most religious expressions are treated in this manner in Hijazi Arabic.

2. **arrabɛ:** *colleagues, associates; folks.* This word occurs in MSA meaning *home* and *its surroundings,* while in Hijazi Arabic, it refers only to *a group of people.*

3. **lēn:** This conjunction is characteristic Hijazi Arabic and is used to render *until, when, whenever, as soon as.* It is possible that MSA **ʔila an** is the cognate of this word.

4. **ntagalat ila man bi yaddu malakūt assamawāt wu lʔarḍ:** *She was moved to Him who has in His hand the heavens and the earth.* This expression, also borrowed from MSA, is a euphemism for dying.

5. **gaddar ḍ/ẓurūfi:** *He was understanding of my situation.* This is a common expression in Hijazi Arabic. Although both words occur in MSA, this expression is rarely used.

6. **ǰazāh allāh bi lkhēr:** *May God reward him with goodness, God bless him.* This expression is borrowed from MSA. It is very common in Hijazi Arabic as well as in other Arabic dialects.

7. **ɛaḍḍam allāh aǰrak:** *May (God) make your reward greater.* This expression is borrowed from MSA to express condolence. Note that the optative is expressed in Hijazi Arabic by the perfect form of the verb. See for example in this text **raḥamaha llāh**, and **ǰazāh allāh**.

8. **wlēdi:** *my boy.* Cf. MSA **wulaydi** with the deletion of short vowel **u** in rapid speech, and the common Hijazi Arabic change of **-ay** ---> **ē**. This form is the diminutive of **walad**.

9. **hāda ṭṭarīg kullana māshyīnu:** *All of us are going to walk this road, (lit., this road all of us will be walking it).* This expression is used to express condolence, to remind the bereaved that all human beings are going to die. Note that the pronominal suffix **u** added to **māshyīn** refers back to **ṭarīg**. This construction, known as interference modification, presents some difficulty for Arabs when they speak English.

Selection Sixteen

al<u>kh</u>ādim alban<u>gh</u>āli illi <u>kh</u>aṭaf ibn alɛēla illi akramūh

Part One

lamman alʔinsān yitǰarrad min insāniyyatu, ḥatta lḥayawānāt tiṣīr[1] ti<u>kh</u>ǰal bi aɛmālu. yōm alǰumɛa lmāḍya, <u>sh</u>urṭat alɛēn bi dōlt[2] alʔimārāt alɛarabiyya lmuttaḥida, miskat almuǰrim alban<u>gh</u>āli illi <u>kh</u>aṭaf ṭifl ɛumāni[3], ismu saɛīd ǰumɛa <u>sh</u>shāmi, w ɛumru agal min sanatēn. lāgu ǰuttat aṭṭifl madfūna ǰanb manṭagat alḥaǰar alǰadīda. bi hādi ṭṭarīga anfaḍaḥat alǰarīma illi hazzat ma<u>sh</u>āɛir alunuwāṭinīn fi manṭagat al<u>kh</u>alīǰ kullu, wu nntaha ɛazāb ahl aṭṭifl alma<u>kh</u>ṭūf[4].

hādi tafāṣīl alǰarīma. abtadat algiṣṣa fi <u>kh</u>amsa w ɛi<u>sh</u>rīn abrīl[5] sanat itnēn w tamanīn. aǰa wāḥad min aṣḥāb alɛēla w maɛu wāḥad ban<u>gh</u>āli, ɛa<u>sh</u>ān yi<u>sh</u>ta<u>gh</u>il ṭabbā<u>kh</u> fi bēt assayyid ǰumɛa <u>sh</u>shāmi. hādi lɛēla giblatu, w awatu, w kasatu, w dafaɛatlu maɛā<u>sh</u> zēn marra. astawat sigat alɛēla tizīd lamma <u>sh</u>āfu annu biyṣalli fi alʔawgāt almuɛayyana li ṣṣalā.

aṭṭabbā<u>kh</u> ṭālab bi ziyādat rātibu w asta<u>gh</u>all ṭībat alɛēla. baɛd ḥulūl <u>sh</u>ahr ramaḍān alkarīm <u>sh</u>āfat alɛēla taɛabbudu w ṣiyāmu, w zādūlu[6] uǰratu mitēn dirham. lākin ṭamaɛ hāda ṭṭabbā<u>kh</u> aɛmāh w nassāh kull algiyam alʔinsāniyya, w aṣarr ɛala ziyāda ǰadīda, w haddad alɛēla bi tark a<u>sh</u>shu<u>gh</u>l iz mā naffazu ṭalabu.

lamman assayyid ǰumɛa mā astaǰāb li ṭalabu, ǰammaɛ a<u>gh</u>rāḍu w ṭalab arraḥīl. lākin wālid aṭṭifl <u>sh</u>afag ɛalē[7] w aɛṭāh kull mustaḥggātu w zād ɛalēha. baɛd talāt arbaɛ asābīɛ raǰaɛ aṭṭabbā<u>kh</u> li bēt alɛēla w ṭalab minhum yaɛṭūh <u>sh</u>u<u>gh</u>l ka muzāriɛ fi mazraɛathum. ḥann galb alwālid ɛalē w ṣammam yiraǰǰiɛu li waḍīfatu alʔawwalāniyya ka ṭabbā<u>kh</u>. astamar yimattil ɛala[8] lɛēla wu yiwarrīhum[9] gaddē<u>sh</u>[10] a<u>kh</u>lāgu zēna. ṣammamat alɛēla mā yirfuḍu ay ṭalab min ṭalabātu liʔann ṭiflhum mitɛallig bīh li daraǰa[11].

Vocabulary

ban<u>gh</u>āli *adj.n.pl.* -yyīn	Bengali, native of West Bengal (India) or Bangladesh
<u>kh</u>aṭaf/yi<u>kh</u>ṭi/uf *v.tr.*	to kidnap, highjack, abduct, snatch; to elope

atǰarrad/yitǰarrad + min *v.intr.*	to be stripped, deprived; to be disarmed; to be detached, be free of
insāniyya *n.*	humanity, humanness, politeness, civility
ḥayawān *n.pl.* -āt	animal, beast
ǰutta *n.pl.* ǰutat	body, corpse, cadaver, carcass
madfūn *pass.part.*	buried, hidden
anfaḍaḥ/yinfaḍiḥ *v.pass.*	to be disclosed, be revealed, become public; to be dishonored
ma<u>sh</u>āʿir *n.*	senses, feelings
hazz/yihizz ma<u>sh</u>āʿir *v.tr.*	to shock
ʿazāb *n.*	suffering, pain, torment, agony, torture; punishment, chastisement
tafāṣīl *n.pl.*	details
awa/yiʔwi *v.tr.*	to shelter, lodge, accomodate, house, give refuge
kasa/yiksi *v.tr.*	to clothe, dress, garb
maʿā<u>sh</u> *n.pl.* -āt	livelihood, living, income
siga *n.*	confidence, trust, faith
ṭamaʿ *n.*	greed, avidity, covetousness
aʿma/yiʿmi *v.tr.*	to blind, cause to lose one's sight
giyam *n.*	values, norms; worth
aṣarr/yiṣirr + ʿala *v.intr.*	to insist, persist, be determined
raḥīl *n.*	departure, emigration, exodus; traveling
<u>sh</u>afag/yi<u>sh</u>fag + ʿala *v.intr.*	to feel pity, sympathize, have compassion, commiserate, have a tender heart
mustaḥaggāt *n.* in the *pl.* form	one's rightful due
muzāriʿ *n.pl.* -īn	farmer
ḥann galbu ʿalē	He had sympathy for him. His heart was full of compassion for him. He had pity on him.
a<u>kh</u>lāg *n.* in the *pl.* form	manners
mitʿallig bi	attached to; depending on, related to, connected with, linked to

Notes

1. **tiṣīr:** *becomes.* This verb loses its function as a copulative verb (it is one of **kāna's** sisters). **ṣār** may function as an auxiliary verb in Hijazi Arabic.

2. **dōla:** *country, nation.* Cf. MSA **dawla** with the common Hijazi shift of **aw** ---> **ō**. The MSA pronunciation is used by some Hijazi speakers also.

3. **ɛumāni:** *Omani.* In Hijazi Arabic the final sound in an adjectival **nisba** is not doubled, **mushaddad** as in MSA, e.g., **ɛumāniyy.**

4. **makhṭūf:** *kidnapped.* Hijazi Arabic uses the MSA passive participle pattern $maC_1C_2\bar{u}C_3$ for some triliteral verbs.

5. **khamsa w ɛishrīn abrīl:** *April 25.* The student should remember how dates are expressed in Arabic (as day, month, year).

6. **zādūluh ʔuǰratu:** *They increased his wages.* If a verb ends in a vowel, that vowel is lengthened when an indirect object pronoun with -l- is suffixed to it, as is the case here.

7. **shafag ɛalē:** *He felt pity for him.* Cf. MSA **shafiqa ɛalayhi** with the common Hijazi Arabic phonological changes. Both MSA and Hijazi Arabic verbs collocate with the preposition **ɛala.** Note that when a pronominal suffix is added to **ɛala**, the final vowel **a** changes to **ē.**

8. **yimattil ɛala:** *he deceives, misleads (lit., he acts on [s.o.]).* Although this is an MSA verb, it does not collocate with the preposition **ɛala** in MSA to render the above meaning.

9. **yiwarrīhum:** *he shows them.* MSA verb **yurīhim** (**him** instead of **hum** in conformity with vowel harmony) could be the cognate of this Hijazi Arabic verb.

10. **gaddēsh:** *how much.* This word does not occur in MSA. Hijazi Arabic uses it to refer to *time, amount, weight,* and *length.* Note the following: **gaddēsh assāɛ?** *What time is it?* **gaddēsh ɛumrak?** *How old are you?* **gaddēsh ashtarēt?** *How many did you buy?* and **gaddēsh ṭūl hada annahr?** *How long is this river?*

11. **li daraǰa:** *very much, to the extent that.....* This expression is used in MSA, but normally it has a modifier after **daraǰah**, e.g., **aḥabbaha lidaraǰatin ǰunūniyyatin**, *he loved her to the extent of madness.*

alkhādim albanghāli illi khaṭaf ibn alɛēla illi akramūh

Part Two

gabl ɛīd lʔaḍha bi talāt ayyām ǰā ṭṭabbākh w ṭalab min assayyid ǰumɛa ɛashān yismaḥlu yigaḍḍi furṣat alɛīd maɛ aṣḥābu fi ḍubay, w gallu, "iza mā ḥaʔarǰaɛ iɛtabirni tarakt ashshughl." w ṭalab uǰratu. aɛṭah assayyid ǰumɛa uǰratu w zawwadlu[1] miyyat dirham ɛīdiyya. tāni yōm baɛd aḍḍuhr rāḥ aṭṭabbākh maɛ aṭṭifl mitl alɛāda w akhtafa.

mā raǰaɛ li lbēt wagt ghurūb ashshams w astawat alɛēla mashghūl bālhum/galgānīn, bi nōɛ khāṣ umm aṭṭifl illi ṣārat tifattish ɛalēhum fi kull makān muḥtamal yiruḥlu ṭṭabbākh. w lamma mā lāgūhum, rāḥ wālid aṭṭifl li markaz ashshurṭa w khabbarhum ɛan alḥādis. min hina abtadat ɛamaliyyāt attaftīsh ɛan almukhtaṭif.

maḍat arbaɛ shuhūr. alʔumm aḍrabat ɛan lʔakl lēn yiɛūd ibinha. ṣār ɛindaha inhiyār ɛaṣabi min hādi ṣṣadma. astawa lwālid bi muṣībatēn, zōǰatu min nāḥiya w ṭiflu lmafgūd min nāḥiya tānya. azzōǰ mā khalla wala ṭabīb ikhtiṣāṣi illa w akhad[2] zōǰatu ɛindu ɛashān alɛilāǰ. lākin kānat tirfuḍ w tiṣrukh lēl wu nhār "ibni saɛīd! yā waladi! abghi waladi!"

baɛd kull hāda alwagt ǰann ǰunūn alwālid w gaddam ǰāʔiza māliyya kabīra li ay wāḥid yidullu ɛala ibnu. marrat shuhūr bidūn khabar w ṭār annōm min ɛuynūnu[3]. lākin mā gaṭaɛ alʔamal w astamarr yifattish ɛala ibnu fi kull makān. bas bidūn fāyda. ashshurṭa astaǰwabat katīr min aṣḥāb almuttaham w min illi shāfūh baɛd ma[4] khtafa. w arsalu firag almabāḥis fi kull anḥāʔ lʔimārāt, w rāgabu ṣanādīg albarīd wu lʔamākin illi maɛgūl yitraddad laha lmukhtaṭif.

yōm alǰumɛa fi sabɛa yanāyir miskat ashshurṭa almukhtaṭif w ibtadu ttaḥgīg. ḥāwal almuǰrim yimattil ɛalēhum dōr ǰadīd, lākinnu mā naǰaḥ hādi lmarra. lamman wāǰah kull lʔisbātāt anhār w aɛtaraf, w akhad ashshurṭa li lmakān illi dafan fīh aṭṭifl. waǰadu ǰuttat aṭṭifl madfūna fi ḥufra ghumgaha[5] tamanīn santi wu mghaṭṭāya[6] bi rraml.

ashshi lmukhīf alli yiǰannin min hādi lmuṣība huwwa annu lmuǰrim yiɛtarif bi maḥabbatu lgawiyya li ṭṭifl. li hāda ssabab khṭafu w khallāh maɛu ɛashān yirabbī. bigī ṭṭifl maɛu khamsa w ɛishrīn yōm. baɛdēn miriḍ w ṣār yiguḥ. almuǰrim khāf yākhdu li lmustashfa aw li ay ɛiyāda w tinkashaf ǰarīmatu. baɛd sitta wu ɛishrīn yōm min almaraḍ māt aṭṭifl. akhadu lmuǰrim w dafanu fi makān yibɛid khamsa kīlu min sakanu. baɛdēn harab li manṭaga tānya. ǰalas[7] hināk fatra maɛ wāḥad min rifāgu lēn algu lgabḍ ɛalē.

Vocabulary

ɛīdiyya *n.*	a present given on the occasion of a feast
akhtafa/yikhtafi *v.intr.*	to disappear, become invisible, be missing, vanish
galgān *act.part.pl.* -īn	worried, anxious, sleepless, agitated
aḍrab/yiḍrib + ɛan *v.intr.*	to abstain from; to go on strike
inhiyār ɛaṣabi	nervous breakdown
ṣadma *n.pl.* -āt	shock, jolt, blow, difficulty
muṣība *n.pl.* maṣāyib	misfortune, calamity, disaster
mā khalla wala ṭabīb	he did not leave out a single doctor
ṣarakh/yiṣrukh *v.intr.*	to scream, cry with a loud voice
ǰann ǰunūn + *poss.pro.*	to become frantic, become angry, become furious
ǰāʔiza māliyya	monetary award
gaṭaɛ/yigtaɛ lʔamal *v.tr.*	to give up hope
astaǰwab/yistaǰwib *v.tr.*	to interrogate, question, hear (a defendant or witness), examine
muttaham *pass.part.*	accused, charged; suspect
mabāḥis *n.*	intelligence agency, secret police
atraddad/yitraddad + ɛala or li *v.intr.*	to frequent a place
isbāt *n.pl.* -āt	proof, evidence; confirmation, documentation, verification
anhār/yinhār *v.intr.*	to collapse, break down
ḥufra *n.pl.* ḥufar	hole, pit
ghumg *n.*	depth
gaḥ/yiguḥḥ *v.intr.*	to cough
alga/yilgi lgabḍ + ɛala *v.intr.*	to arrest

Notes

1. **zawwadlu:** *increased; gave him more.* MSA uses this verb to mean *to supply, to provide.* It always takes a direct object. MSA **zāda** impf. **yazīdu** corresponds with this verb.

2. **mā khalla wala ṭabīb illa w akhad zōjatu ɛindu:** *He did not leave out a single doctor but that he took his wife to him.* Note that **illa** is an exceptive particle meaning *unless, except, but,* when preceded by a negative clause.

3. **ṭār annōm min ɛuyūnu:** *He could not sleep, (lit., the sleep flew away from his eyes).* This expression is very common in Hijazi Arabic and in many other Arabic dialects as well. Note that in Hijazi Arabic, the plural form of **ɛēn** is usually more frequent than the dual when one refers to one's eyes.

4. **baɛd ma:** *after.* These words function as a temporal conjunction.

5. **ghumgaha:** *its depth.* Cf. MSA **ɛumqaha** with the dissimilation of ɛ ---> gh and the normal change of **q** ---> **g**.

6. **mghaṭṭāya:** *covered.* Cf. MSA **mughaṭṭāt.** The vowel **u** following **m** often is deleted in Hijazi Arabic. The feminine form of the passive participle often ends in **ya**, especially when the participle is derived from a verb ending in the vowel **a.**

7. **jalas:** *he stayed.* This verb means *to sit* in MSA. MSA **makaθa**, *stay,* corresponds with the Hijazi meaning.

Selection Seventeen

wizārat attiǰara tākhud[1] iǰrā?āt shadīda bi nnisba li sharikat tawzīɛ wahmiyya

akhadat wizārat attiǰāra iǰrā?āt shadīda ḍud sharikat attawzīɛ assuɛūdiyya lwahmiyya alli hi sharika musāhima lissaɛ[2] taḥt atta?sīs. hādi shsharika baɛatat daɛwāt li baɛḍ almuwāṭinīn bi wāṣiṭat ṣanādīg albarīd. w bayyanat ashsharika lwahmiyya annu markazha fi ǰidda wu annu rasmālha[3] miyyat milyōn riyāl, w gīmat assahm fīha ɛashara alf riyāl, w ḥatistaɛmil alfulūs fi l?istirād wu ttawzīɛ bi lǰumla li kull albiḍāɛāt. kamān ḥatiftaḥ furūɛ li lbēɛ fi kull mudun almamlaka bi wāṣṭat assayyid fulān alfulāni[4] ṣāḥib ashsharika lfulāniyya bi ǰidda.

baɛd attaḥgīg allāzim ḥawalēn hāda lmawḍūɛ, ṣāḥib ashsharika ṣarraḥ innu fikrat ta?sīs hādi shsharika btadat min sanatēn, w hu ṭalab min wāḥad min almas?ulīn fi mu?assastu ɛashān yidrus hāda lmawḍūɛ wu yḥuṭ al?umūr l?asāsiyya li bad? lmashrūɛ. lākin baɛd ma gaddam mustanadāt addirāsa alli[5] kān fīha daɛawāt li lmuwāṭnīn, tashāwar ṣāḥib ashsharika maɛ alli byitɛāwanu maɛu wu garraru annu yiɛdilu ɛan fikrat ta?sīs ashsharika. w baɛdēn atlafu kull almustanadāt almazkūra. gāl innu kull alli nasharū fi ṣṣuḥuf almaḥalliyya ɛan hādi shsharika hu muǰarrad daɛwa ḍuddu sawwāha wāḥad riǰǰāl[6]. w aɛtaraf guddām mas?ūlīn bi wizārat attiǰāra annu lmu?assasa ḥaggatu mā astalamat ay mablagh min almuwāṭinīn li lmusāhama fi hādi shsharika.

binā?an[7] ɛala kull hādi ttaḥgīgāt aṣdarat wizārat attiǰāra hāda lbayān bi khuṣūṣ ashsharika lwahmiyya "sharikat attawzīɛ assuɛūdiyya."

alwizāra tibgha twaḍḍiḥ annu hādi shsharika mū mrakhkhaṣ bi ta?sīsaha fi lmamlaka. wala wāḥad min aṣḥāb alɛilāga gaddam ṭalb tarkhīṣ aw aɛṭa ismaha li ttasǰīl. hāda yuɛtabar tarwīǰ awrāg māliyya li ṣāliḥ sharika mū mawǰūda w mū mrakhshaṣa, wu hāda mukhālif li gawānīn ashsharikāt wu ttaɛlīmāt alli tinaḍḍim hādi lmawāḍīɛ. alwizāra tibgha tibayyin annu algānūn lā yismaḥ li ay sharika aw ay fard fi ta?sīs sharikāt wu istilām almusāhamāt illa baɛd[8] muwāfagat alwizāra.

alwizāra ʿammāl tinabbih kull almuwāṭinīn min makhāṭir tashghīl amwālhum fi sharikāt mū mrakhkhaṣ laha bi lʿamal fi lmamlaka, siwa kānat suʿūdiyya aw aǰnabiyya.

Vocabulary

akhad iǰrāʔāt shadīda	took strong measures
tawzīʿ *n.*	distribution; dividing; delivery (of mail, etc.); (here) wholesale
wahmi *adj.*	fictitious; imagined, hypothetical, imaginary
bi wāṣi/ṭat	by means of, through, on the part of
sharika musāhima	joint-stock company, corporation
rasmāl *n.*	capital (finance)
sham *n.pl.* ashum	share (of stock); arrow, dart
bi lǰumla	wholesale
istirād *n.*	import, importing
asāsi *adj.*	basic, fundamental, elementary, essential; chief, main, principal
mustanad *n.pl.* -āt	document; proof; legal evidence
tashāwar/yitshāwar + maʿ *v.intr.*	to consult with, to discuss with s.o.
ʿadal/yiʿdil + ʿan *v.intr.*	to give up, abandon, relinquish; to leave off; to drop
atlaf/yitlif *v.tr.*	to destroy, damage, ruin, waste
muǰarrad	mere; sheer; nothing more than; bare, naked; abstract
bināʔan ʿala	according to; in accordance with, by virtue of; thus
bayān *n.pl.* -āt	information, news; official reports, official statement
bi khuṣūṣ	concerning, regarding, with respect to
sāḥib alʿilāga	the person concerned, the person involved
murakhkhaṣ *pass.part.*	licensed, permitted, authorized
waḍḍaḥ/yiwaḍḍiḥ *v.tr.*	to clarify, clear up; to explain; to illustrate
li ttasǰīl	for registration, for recording
yuʿtabar *v.pass.*	to be considered, be regarded; to be respected
waraga *n.pl.* awrāg māliyya	bank note, paper money

li ṣāliḥ	for the-well-being (of), for the benefit (of)
mukhālif li	violating, against (a law); conflicting, contradictory
taɛlīmāt *n.*	regulations; instructions; information; directions
nabbah/yinabbih *v.tr.*	to warn, alert; to awaken; to notify
makhāṭir *n.*	risks, danger, hazards
tashghīl amwāl	investing money
siwa kān...aw	regardless; whether ... or

Notes

1. **tākhud:** *it takes.* Cf. MSA **taʔkhuðu** with the deletion of the glottal stop and the compensatory lengthening of the vowel **ā**, the common Hijazi Arabic phenomenon of changing **ð** --> **d** and the deletion of the final vowel **u**, the indicative mood marker.

2. **lissaɛ:** *still; not yet.* This is a pure Hijazi Arabic word used before a positive predicate to mean *still,* e.g., **huwwa lissaɛ nāyim**, *he is still asleep.* It is also used before a negative verb to mean *not yet,* e.g., **lissaɛ mā rāḥ almadraṣa**, *he has not gone to school yet.*

3. **rasmālha:** *its capital (finance).* Cf. MSA **raʔsamālaha** (accusative) with the deletion of the glottal stop and other vowels as well. This is a compound of **raʔs** and **māl.**

4. **fulān alfulāni:** *Mr. So-and-So.* This expression is borrowed directly from MSA.

5. **i/alli:** *which, who* (m.). This is a relative pronoun which, unlike its MSA counterpart, is not inflected for number or gender. If the clause it introduces includes a verb which takes an object, an object pronoun is also used, e.g., **alkitāb alli garētu**, *the book which I read (it).* This phenomenon which also exists in MSA, explains why, when Arabs speak English, they often add the object pronoun in relative clauses. This is what linguists refer to as interference modification (interference from the native language).

6. **wāḥa/id riJJāl:** *some man, a certain man.* The numeral **wāḥad**, *one,* is sometimes the equivalent of the English indefinite article.

7. **bināʔan ɛala:** *based on.* This expression is borrowed from MSA.

8. **illa baɛd:** *unless (lit., except after, unless after).* The word **illa** is a negative conditional particle used after a negative statment, e.g., **algānūn lā yismaḥ** li **ay fard fi taʔsīs sharika illa baɛd muwāfagat alwizāra**, *the law does not allow anyone to establish a company unless the ministry approves it (lit., until after the approval of the ministry).* illa is also used as an emphatic way of saying *yes* in response to a negative question in order to emphasize the affirmative answer, e.g., **inta mā ruḥt makka?** *Didn't you go to Mecca?* illa. *Of course.*

Selection Eighteen

assurɛa wu ttahawwur[1]

sawwāg, ēsh bak[2] musriɛ mitl assahm[3],
malḥūg willa khāyif rizgak yiṭīr?
rizgak maḥallu lō saɛētlu[4] bi lgadam,
mā hu li ghērak lō twānēt fi lmasīr.
ḥāfiḍ ɛala nafsak w ghērak wu ltazim
gaṣd almurūr[5] bi nuṣḥhum niyyat khēr
shūf illi ǰara li lghēr wu ṣḥa lā tnām
la tintaẓir yiǰīk min fiɛlak nadīr
akhāf mā yimdīk lō zal algadam
mā ɛād yinfaɛak almuwaǰǰih wu shshawīr
allāh man bayyat ɛugb nhāru ɛatm
min sabāyib[6] wāḥad rāḥ alkatīr[7]
mā trudd alḥāl min ɛugb alɛadam
sunnat lkhālig wala ɛanha maṭīr
bas mālak lō talāsha wu nhadam
dūn ḥālak gīmatu ḥabbat shaɛīr[8]
man tahawwar ḍarr ghēru lō salam
wu inn salam bākir fa ɛugbu bāsh khēr
mutōrak biamrak wala yiɛṣa lgadam
wu inn rama bīk mā yḥuss bmā yiṣīr
kull ma fi lʔamr[9] yungal li lgisim
w inta yā sātir[10] li matwāk lʔakhīr
gult ma fi khāṭri wu lgōl tamm
wu ssalām w ǰaɛl ma gaddamt khēr

Vocabulary

tahawwur *n.*	hastiness, recklessness
sahm *n.pl.* ashum, sihām	arrow, spear; share (of stock)
malḥūg *pass.part.*	in a hurry; followed
rizg *n.coll.*	livelihood
saɛa/yisɛa *v.intr.*	to seek; to walk after, to work towards
bi lgadam	on foot

twāna/yitwāna *v.intr.*	to slow down; to neglect
masīr *n.*	path; journey
altazam/yiltazim *v.intr.*	to be committed to
murūr *n.*	traffic police; passing
nuṣḥ *n.*	guidance; good advice; (here) regulation
niyya *n.pl.* -āt	intention
ǰara/yiǰri + li lghēr *v.intr.*	to happen to others
ṣaḥa/yiṣḥa *v.imp.* iṣḥa	to wake up; to be alert
nadīr *n.pl.*	warning, alarm; one who warns
amda/yimdi *v.tr.*	to last; to go far, to keep on (doing s.th.)
zall/yizill *v.intr.*	to slip; to slide off; to make a mistake
muwaǰǰih *act.part.*	guide, leader, instructor
shawīr *n.*	counselor
ɛatm *n.*	dark, darkness; (here) night
ɛadam *n.*	nonexistence; nothingness; lack, absence
sunna *n.*	law (of nature), religious law
maṭīr *n.*	(here) a way out
talāsha/yitlāsha *v.intr.*	to vanish, disappear; to be ruined; to fade
ḥabbat shaɛīr	a seed of barley; (fig.) of no value
ɛaṣa/yiɛṣa *v.tr.*	to disobey; to resist, to oppose; to defy; to rebel
yā sātir	one who covers man's shortcomings (an attribute of God)
matwāk l?akhīr	your last habitation/dwelling/place of rest
gult mā fi khāṭri	I said what is on my mind
ǰaɛl	I hope, may God

Notes

1. This poem is representative of a sort of popular verse which is a highly respected tradition in the Middle East, particularly in the Gulf area.

2. **ēsh bak:** This expression like **ēsh fīk**, means *what is wrong with you.*

3. **mitl assham:** *like an arrow.* This is a coloquial expression widely used in other Arabic dialects to show the intensity of one's speed.

4. **saɛētlu:** *went after it, walked to it.* Cf. MSA **saɛayta ilayhi** with normal Hijazi vocalic change **ay** ---> **ē** and the deletion of the final vowel of the verb. However, the major difference between the two verbs is that the MSA verb collocates with **ila** while the Hijazi verb collocates with its contracted form **-l-**.

5. **lmurūr:** *(traffic) police.* Cf. MSA **shurṭat almurūr.** This word is very common in the Gulf dialects, and even in MSA written in that region.

6. **sabāyib:** *because of (lit., reasons).* This form of plural does not occur in MSA. Cf. MSA **sabab**, pl. **asbāb**. In this case the plural form may have the force of a diminutive.

7. **rāḥ alkatīr:** *many died (lit., many went).* This expression is a euphemism for death or the loss of something.

8. **qīmatu ḥabbat shaṯīr:** *Its worth is a grain of barley i.e. it is of no value.* This expression is very common in Hijazi Arabic and in many other dialects as well.

9. **kull ma fi l?amr:** *There is no more to it than....* This construction is taken from MSA but without the final vowels, Cf. MSA **kullu mā fī l?mri.**

10. **yā sātir:** This expression refers to God. It expresses shock or dismay and is comparable to *God help us!* or *Heaven protect us!* in English. The word **sātir** means *screen, drape, cover.*

Selection Nineteen

kēf ṣār daktōr alʔādāb ṭabīb nisāʔi

ṣadīgi ddaktōr aḥmad, ustāz tārīkh fi ǰāmɛa kanadiyya. rāḥ ɛashān yizūr wāḥad min ɛashīratu fi garya nāʔiya fi balad ɛarabi. katīr min alʔahl wu lʔagārib wu lǰīrān ǰō[1] yihannūh[2] bi salāmtu. kullhum yigūlūlu, "yā ahlan wu sahlan bi lḥakīm." annās fi lgarya fahmu annu lḥakīm huwwa ṭabīb bashar, w huwwa ikhtiṣāṣi fi tawlīd anniswān[3]. w halḥīn addaktōr ḥayɛallimna[4] sālfa[5] astawat maɛā fi hadīk algarya.

fi lēla min allayāli, baɛd ma ragadt simiɛt ṭarg gawi marra ɛala bāb alghurfa. gumt minzaɛiǰ w mazɛūr gult, "khēr nshālla[6] yā ǰamāɛa, ēsh ṣār?" w nās katīr maɛ ahl addār yitraǰǰūni wu ygūlu, "dakhīlak[7] yā daktōr ilḥag!"[8]

- khēr! khēr!
- alḥurma fi lbēt...
- ay ḥurma?
- zōǰti!
- ēsh dakhkhallni bi zōǰtak?
- ɛamman[9] tiwlad!
- ṣayyaḥt, "ɛammāl tiwlad? ēsh dakhkhallni ana?"
- algābila mū mawǰuda, wu lwilāda ṣaɛba, mɛassara... dakhīlak!
- gult lahum bi hudūʔ, "yā ǰamāɛa dakhīlkum ifhamūni!"
- ɛaǰǰil, ɛaǰǰil mā rāḥ nifham
- ana daktōr tārīkh!!
- tārīkh, ǰughrāfya -- mū muhim!!
- w gabl ma akammil iɛtirāḍi ḥamalōni[10] li bēt garīb ṭāliɛ minnu ṣṣrākh, w ana shuft arriǰāl wu lḥarīm ḥawalēni yiṣayyiḥu wu ygūlu,
- khalliṣha! angidha yā ḥakīm gabl ma tmūt!
- taḍāhart anni aḥus nabaḍha w afḥaṣ ḥarāratha bi yaddi, baɛdēn gult bi ṣōt ɛāli, "ma fī sayyāra hina?"
- gālu, "ɛind fulān alfulāni, albēt ḥaggu baɛīd rubɛ sāɛa."
- yalla ilḥagūni!!

w liḥgōni li bēt rāɛi ssayyāra w ṣaḥḥōh min annōm. w ṭār fīna li makān alḥurma. ḥamalōha w ṣābagu rrīḥ li lmadīna. w hiyya tagrīban ɛala ākhir ramag. w ana lāḥighum fi lmustashfa w agūl lahum, "ṭamminu[11] bālkum, ana bi nafsi ḥaʔashrif ɛala ɛamaliyyat alwilāda."

angaḍa lʔamr ɛala khēr w laɛlaɛ ṣōt almawlūd ɛashān yiɛallimna bi ǰayyitu. halḥīn kull annās ṣāru sāktīn w tawwhum[12] yishkuru ṭabīb alwilāda lḥagīgi illi angaḍ alḥurma wu btadaw yishtumūni wu ygūlu, "mālk w māl attārīkh --- ɛishna, w shufna annu ttārīkh wu lǰughrāfya ṣār lahum dakātra."

Vocabulary

adab *n.pl.* ādāb	literature
ṭabīb *n.pl.* aṭibba	doctor, physician
ṭabīb nisāʔi	obstetrician, gynecologist
ɛashīra *n.pl.* ɛashāyir	clan, tribe, family
garya nāʔya	remote village
hanna/yihanni *v.tr.*	to congratulate
ḥakīm *n.pl.* ḥukama	physician; wise
bashar *n.coll.*	human beings
ikhtiṣāṣi *adj.*	specialized
niswān *n.*	women
tawlīd *n.*	delivering (of babies); generating
sālfa *n.pl.* sawālif	story, tale, fable
lēla min allayāli	one of those nights
ṭarg *n.*	knocking
minzaɛiǰ *pass.part.*	disturbed, bothered, annoyed
mazɛūr *pass.part.*	frightened
atraǰǰa/yitraǰǰa *v.tr.*	to beg for; to plea for s.th.
dakhīlak	if you please; I beg of you
gābila *n.pl.* -āt	midwife
muɛassara *adj.*	difficult, hard
bi hudūʔ	calmly
iɛtirāḍ *n.pl.* -āt	objection, opposition
angad/yingid *v.tr.*	to deliver, save, rescue
atḍāhar/yatḍāhar *v.intr.*	to pretend
nabaḍ *n.*	pulse
fulān alfulāni	Mr. So-and-So

ṣaḥḥa/yiṣaḥḥi *v.tr.*	to wake s.o. up
ɛala ākhir ramag	at the point of death, on one's last legs; on the verge of exhaustion
ṭammin bālak	be calm, relax, let your mind be at ease
laɛlaɛ/yilaɛliɛ *v.intr.*	to roar, resound, clang, reverberate
shatam/yishtim *v.tr.*	to curse; to vilify; to insult
mālak w māl *+n.*	what do you have to do with...?; leave alone

Notes

1. **jō:** *they came.* Cf. MSA **jāʔu.** In Hijazi Arabic this irregular verb always ends in **ō** instead of **u** in the 3rd person plural perfect.

2. **yihannūh + bi:** *they congratulate him.* Cf. MSA **yuhanniʔūnahu.** Note the deletion of the **i**, the **-na**, the final vowel, and the glottal stop.

3. **niswān:** *women.* This is the plural of **imraʔah** (pausal form). Other plural forms are **nisāʔ** and **niswa**. Although **niswān** occurs in MSA, it is not used as much as the other two forms.

4. **ḥayɛallimna:** *he will tell us.* This verb occurs in MSA but with a different meaning.

5. **sālfa:** *story.* This is a loan word from MSA. Hijazi Arabic has derived from this noun the verb **sōlaf**, impf. **yisōlif**, *to chat.*

6. **khēr nshālla:** *(I hope it is) good if God wills, I hope there is nothing wrong.* This expression is used after someone says that he has news for you. This is an optative construction expressing the wish that the news is good.

7. **dakhīlak:** *Please, I beg you.* This construction occurs with the same meaning in Hijazi Arabic as well as in many Arabic dialects.

8. **ilḥag:** *Hurry up,* imp. This verb occurs in MSA but with a different meaning. MSA **asriɛ** corresponds with this verb. **ilḥag** is also used in Hijazi Arabic to mean *follow.* See the present text for examples.

9. **ɛamman:** This particle preceding the impf. form of the verb denotes an ongoing action (progressive tense). **ɛammāl** is another varient.

10. **ḥamalōni:** *They carried me.* When a pronominal suffix is added to the 3rd person plural, perfect form of the verb, the **u** is changed to a stressed **ō** as is the case here.

11. **ṭamminu (bālkum):** *Feel at ease, don't worry.* Cf. MSA **ṭamʔinu** with the deletion of the glottal stop and the compensatory gemination of **m**.

12. **tawwhum:** This lexeme plus a pronominal suffix placed before a verb means *just* in the sense of recently completing an action.

Selection Twenty

intigād iǰtimāɛi muḍḥik[1]

ɛandi ṣadīg ismu maṭlag illi intu kullkum khābrīnu. kull ma ṣadīgi hāda yirkab assayyāra ḥaggatu yikhṭur ɛala bāli attaṣil bi winsh ɛashān yiǰi yiǰurru. marra aǰa maṭlag ɛindi, kān khāyif marra. lamma shuftu gult li nafsi, "yikfāni sharru[2], allāh yiɛlam ēsh almushkila, alyōm yōmi." lamma waṣal gultlu, "abshir, ēsh tibgha bas?" gāl, "abgha bagara." gultluh, "ēsh gult? tibgha bagara? inta tinkhāni ɛala bagara?" gāl li, "naɛm ana abgha bagara. yā rēt tshufli bagara minshān tilḥas rāsi mitl abu rās aṣlaɛ[3] illi nasharat alwikālāt ṣūratu maɛ bagara gabl yōmēn. hād hu lɛilāǰ li ṣṣalaɛ. w ana yā khūk[4] ɛindi mashrūɛ ṣalaɛ w aḥub aḥaddir alɛilāǰ gabl ma tistawi mushkila." ana ṣurt miḥtār bi amri wu ḥāwalt afahhim ṣadīgi inni mā aɛrif iza kān fī sūg li lbagar. fa ana mā aɛrif mīn ɛindu bagara mumkin yibīɛaha lana, aw yiɛīrna yāha minshān yikūn laha sharf laḥs ṣalɛat ṣadīgi maṭlag, illi lamma lwāḥad yishūfha yifakkir annha zuḥlēga[5] bi ṭṭāʔif. fa ɛashān aksab riḍāh, ḥāwalt ignaɛu bi ɛadam maɛrifti bi anwāɛ albagar. fa ṣurt adawwir ɛalēha zay tadwīrkum ɛala ṣṣudg fi lʔukkuzyōnāt[6]. igtaraḥt ɛala ṣadīgi nǰīblu ɛanza[7], min annōɛ illi byidkhul ɛalēk iza fataḥt bābak fi lḥay alfulāni. wu iza kān min aṣṣaɛb alḥuṣūl ɛala ɛanza, mumkin nidawwir ɛala tōr[8] mā yiɛrif ēsh yaɛni ishārāt almurūr.

ṣadīgi maṭlag mā agtanaɛ lā bi hāda wu lā bi hadāk. hammu lwaḥīd hu maṣlaḥat ṣalɛatu. fa gultlu, "ēsh raʔyak nidawwir ɛala bissa ɛashān tibga tilammiɛ ṣalɛatak ilēn yiṭlaɛ fīha shaɛr mitl ma byizraɛu lʔarṣifa bi lʔishārāt liktīra illi mā fī luzūm li muɛdamha." lākin ṣāḥibi mā gabal kull hādi lʔigtirāḥāt wu gāl iza biynaffiz kull hādi lʔigtrāḥāt ḥatṣīr ṣalɛatu ḥagl li taǰārib alʔalsina ṭṭawīla[9] wu lgaṣīra li makhlūgāt allāh. wu huwwa ḥayṣīr ɛindu ɛugda nafsiyya. ḥayitkhayyal annu fī lisān fōg rāsu dāyman, fēn ma rāḥ w fēn ma ǰa. maɛ innu rafaḍ kull igtrāḥāti, ana mā yiʔist zayma yiʔistu min muḥāwalat maɛrifat sir ghala lmuhūr ɛindana. yiẓhar annu mukh ṣadīgi mzargan wu mā yibgha illa lisān bagara, fa gtaraḥt ɛalē iza lāga bagara bidūn ma akūn mawǰūd, lāzim yimsaḥ rāsu gabl kull shi bi samn bagari[10] māhu mughshūsh mitl alɛāda ɛind illi yibīɛū.

Vocabulary

intigād *n.pl.* -āt	criticism; critique; satire
iǰtimāɛi *adj.*	social

muḍḥik *adj.*	funny
winsh *n.*	tow truck; winch
abshir *v.imp.*	just name it! go ahead!
nakha/yinkha *v.tr.*	to incite; to challenge, urge forcefully
laḥas/yilḥas *v.tr.*	to lick
abu rās aṣlaɛ	bald-headed person
miḥtār *adj.*	confused, bewildered
ɛār/yīɛir *v.tr.*	to lend
zuḥlēga *n.*	slippery slope
riḍa *n.*	approval, acceptance
ṣudg *n.*	truth
ukkazyōn *n.pl.* -āt	sale
igtaraḥ/yigtariḥ *v.tr.*	to suggest
ɛanza *n.pl.* -āt	goat
tōr *n.pl.* tīrān	ox
lammaɛ/yilammiɛ *v.tr.*	to shine, polish
raṣīf *n.pl.* arṣifa	sidewalk
igtirāḥ *n.pl.* -āt	suggestion
makhlūg *n.pl.* -āt	creature; created
ɛugda nafsiyya	mental/psychological complex
yiʔis/yiyʔas *v.intr.*	to give up hope, despair
mukh *n.*	brain
mzargan *adj.*	stubborn
samn bagari	clarified butter (made of cow's milk)
maghshūsh *adj.*	corrupted, debased; adulterated; cheated, fooled

Notes

1. **intigād iǰtimāɛi muḍḥik:** *a funny social satire.* One cannot criticize the government or the society openly in most Middle Eastern countries. Social satire is usually characterized by the use of a joke or of symbolism as in this selection.

2. **yikfāni sharru:** *May [God] protect me from his evil.* This expression is borrowed from MSA, and is common in most Arabic dialects.

3. **abu rās aṣlaɛ:** *the bald-headed man, (lit., the father of a bald head).* This expression is very common in Hijazi Arabic. The word **um**, *mother,* is used in the same manner.

4. **w ana yā khūk:** *and I, your brother.* The initial vowel of a noun is usually deleted when it is preceded by the vocative particle **yā**. This construction is not used in MSA, but it is very common in colloquial Arabic.

5. **zuḫlēga:** *a slippery slope.* The MSA verb **zaḫlaqa** *slide, roll,* is the source of this noun. Cf. MSA **zaḫlaqah** with the common change of **q** ---> **g** and the vocalic change of **a** ---> u and **a** ---> **ē.** Such a vocalic change is not unusual in some Arabic dialects.

6. **aṣṣudg fi lʔukkazyōnāt:** *the truth in sale (prices).* Hijazi Arabic borrowed the word **ukkazyōn** from French and gave it a regular feminine plural.

7. **ʿanza:** *goat.* In some parts of the city there are still some people who own goats and let them loose. The criticism here is quite vague, and it is not clear whether it is directed at the lack of regulations concerning this problem or at the owners themselves.

8. **tōr:** *a bull, an ox.* Cf. MSA **θawr** (pausal form) with the common change of **θ** ---> **t** and the **aw** ---> **ō.** The **tōr** is a symbol for a lack of good manners and proper etiquette. Thus the text describes the person who does not abide by the traffic regulations as being uncivil.

9. **alsina ṭawīla:** *long tongues.* The expression **lisānu ṭawīl** is also used in most other Arabic dialects to indicate a person who gossips and does not keep a secret.

10. **samn bagari:** *clarified butter.* This kind of butter is a basic ingredient in the Saudi native dish **alkabsa.** People can tell when grocers adulterate this product.

Selection Twenty-One

assāɛa lʔislāmiyya wu mazāyāha

hādi mugābala maɛ mukhtariɛ assāɛa lʔislāmiyya, addaktōr almuhandis ibrahīm ṣalāḥ.

Q. kēf atkawwanat fikrat hāda lʔikhtirāɛ, w kēf badēt[1] tanfīzha?

A. awwalan, ana insān muslim w atsharraf bi khidmat alʔislam. ɛindi[2] ɛiddat ikhtirāɛāt sābga. mawāɛīd aṣṣalā w ittijāh algibla[3] kānat mushkilat almuslimīn fi urōbba. min hina khaṭar ɛala bāli fikrat assāɛa, w badēt fi tanfīzha ɛām 1977. tḥaggagat hādi lfikra baɛd sabɛ sinīn min albuḥūt wu ttajārib almudniyya. lākin, alḥamdu li llāh tamm tasjīl hāda lʔikhtirāɛ alwaḥīd fi lɛālam, fi swīsra w ingaltra wu lyabān, w hon kong w singhafūra w fi katīr min adduwal aṣṣināɛiyya.

Q. ēsh hi fawāʔid w mumayyizāt hāda lʔikhtirāɛ?

A. assāɛa ṭāl ɛumrak[4] sahlat alʔistiɛmāl. yigdar yistaɛmilha lʔinsān alɛādi bidūn ay marjaɛ. sāɛat alʔīd hādi mbarmaja li miyyat sana[5], w tiḥtawi zākiratha ɛala miyya wa arbaɛtaɛshar dawla murattaba ḥasab alḥurūf alʔabjadiyya. bi mujarrad aḍḍaghṭ ɛala zir wāḥad bas btaɛṭīk ɛala shāshatha asāmi lbilād, w inta btikhtār albalad illi trīdu. wu btaɛṭīk utumātīkiyyan attawgīt alhijri, wu ttawgīt ashshamsi w mawāɛīd aṣṣalā w ittijāh alkaɛba lmukarrama, wu btaɛṭīk kamān mawgiɛ almakān aljughrāfi. fi nafs alwagt bitwarrīk attawgīt almaḥalli, alyōm wu shshahr wu ssana bi nniḍāmēn ashshamsi wu lgamari. hādi ssāɛa alla hadāk[6] laha fawāyid tānya li ashkhāṣ mitl aṭṭayyārīn wu lbaḥḥāra wu lfalakiyyīn, w fīha maɛlūmāt muhimma li lɛaskariyyīn wa li rijāl lʔaɛmāl fi safarhum.

Q. gullana baɛḍ almashākil wu ṣṣuɛūbāt illi wājahtaha fi taṣmīm w ṣināɛat hādi ssāɛa?

A. awwalan sawwēt sāɛa ḥaggat maktab sanat 1981 bi hādi lmuwāṣafāt, btishtaghil ɛala baṭṭāriyya, w baɛd ma najaḥat attajriba ḥaggati badēt mashrūɛ taṣmīm sāɛat lʔīd. taṣnīɛha kān aṣɛab bi katīr min sāɛat almaktab, min nāḥiyat taṣmīm kumbyūtar fīh kull hādi lḥisābāt arriyāḍiyya wu lfalakiyya lmuɛaggada yigdar yishtaghil bi baṭṭāriyya 1.5 volt w mā yiṣrif ay ṭāga tuzkar. fa lmushkila kānat fi taṣghīr alḥajm. lākin alḥamdu li llāh najaḥt fi taṣmīm alkumbyūtar w tamm taṣnīɛ assāɛa baɛd sanatēn.

Q. inta khāyif min taglīd ashsharikāt almunāfsa li hāda lʔikhtirāɛ?

A. fī ɛiddat muḥāwalāt li ttaglīd, lākin muḥtamal tākhudhum sanatēn aw talāta ḥatta yiwṣalu li asrār hādi ttaknōlōjya lmitgaddma, w maɛ hāda ḥanākhud lʔijrāʔāt alkafīla li ḥimāyat hāda lʔikhritāɛ lʔislāmi.

Q. ēsh hi umniyatak fi lḥayā?

A. annu yihdīna llāh li lkhēr dāyman, w annu tkūn ummat l?islām ṣaf wāḥad w galb wāḥad w īd wāḥda fi nashr addīn aṣṣaḥīḥ.

Vocabulary

maziyya *n.pl.* mazāya (the pl. form is more common)	merit, virtue; advantage; superiority,
algibla *n.*	direction facing the **kaʕba** in Holy Mecca. Every Muslim has to face the 'qibla' while praying
mukhtariʕ *act.part.pl.* -īn	inventor
ikhtirāʕ *n.pl.* -āt	invention
insān *n.*	human being; mankind
khaṭar ʕala bāli	occurred to my mind
tḥaggag/yitḥaggag *v.pass.*	to be fulfilled; to be achieved
baḥt *n.pl.* buḥūt	research
taǰriba *n.pl.* taǰārib	experiment; experience; temptation
muḍni *adj.*	tiring
tasǰīl *n.*	registration; recording, tape recording; (here) having an invention patented
waḥīd *adj.*	solitary, the only one
swīsra	Switzerland
singhafūra	Singapore
fāyda *n.pl.* fawāyid	benefit, gain, profit; interest (on money)
mumayyiza *n.pl.* -āt	distinguishing feature, distinctive mark
marǰaʕ *n.pl.* marāǰiʕ	reference; resource; origin
mbarmaǰ *pass.part.*	programmed
iḥtawa/yiḥtawi + ʕala *v.intr.*	to contain, include
zākira *n.*	memory
murattaba ḥasab alḥurūf l?abǰadiyya	arranged in alphabetical order
ḥarf *n.pl.* ḥurūf	edge; (here) letter of the alphabet
bi muǰarrad	as soon as, at the very moment when
zir *n.pl.* zrār	button, push button, bud (of plant)
shāsha *n.pl.* -āt	screen (of a television, a computer, a watch)
utumātīkiyyan *adv.*	automatically
ṭayyār *n.pl.* -īn	pilot
baḥḥār *n.pl.* baḥḥāra	sailor, seaman, mariner
falaki *n.pl.* -īn	astronomer; astronaut

riǰǰāl aɛmāl	businessman
taṣmīm *n.pl.* taṣāmīm	design, plan; outline; decision, resolution
muwāṣafāt *n.*	detailed description, specification
sāɛat īd	wristwatch
muɛaggad *pass.part.*	complicated, difficult
ḥisābāt riyāḍiyya	mathmatical computation
taglīd	copying, (here) imitation
munāfasa *n.*	competition, rivalry; athletic event, contest, match
sir *n.pl.* asrār	secret
iǰrāʔāt *n. in the pl. form*	measures, steps, proceedings; precautions
kafīl *n.pl.* kufala	legal guardian; (here) guaranteeing, warranty
ḥimāya *n.*	protection
umniya *n.pl.* -āt	desire, wish, ambition

Notes

1. **badēt:** *started.* The final vowel of verbs ending in **a** usually changes to **ē** in the perfect tense for the first persons and second persons as well. A similar change occurs in verbs ending in double consonants, e.g., **ḥaṭṭ**, **ḥaṭṭēt**

2. **ɛindi:** *I have.* When the preposition **ɛind** takes a pronominal suffix, it is translated into English as *have.*

3. **ittiǰāh algibla:** *direction towards which Muslims turn in praying (towards the* ***kaɛba****)*

4. **ṭāl ɛumrak:** *May (God) extend your life.* This is a common optative construction (a construction expressing a wish) often used in conversation.

5. **miyyat sana:** *hundred years.* The **tāʔ marbūṭa** in feminine nouns is not pronounced in Hijazi Arabic unless it is followed by a noun in a noun/noun construct, or by a pronominal suffix, e.g., **umniyatak**, *your goal, desire.*

6. **alla hadāk:** *May God guide you.* This is another optative construction which is often used in Hijazi Arabic and in most other Gulf dialects as well.

Selection Twenty-Two

irshādāt muhimma li lmuṣṭāfīn alkhalījiyyīn

idārat lʔiʕlām bi lʔamāna lʕāmma fi majlis attaʕāwun ḥaggat duwal alkhalīj alʕarabiyya ḥaḍḍarat naṣāyiḥ[1] li lmuṣṭāfīn alkhalījiyyīn fi urōbba wu dduwal attānya. kull wāḥad yibgha yiṣayyif lāzim yiʕrif gawānīn adduwal alli yibgha yisāfir līha, muʔakhkharan aṣdarat alʔamāna irshādāt li lmuwāṭin alkhalīji asnāʔ[2] safaru khārij adduwal alʔaʕḍāʔ, wu khāṣṣatan adduwal alʔurōbbiyya. inshālla nigdar bi nashr hādi lʔirshādāt nimakkin almuwāṭin min lʔistifāda minha, w ittibāʕha ʕashān yimaḍḍi[3] ʕuṭla ṣēfiyya khālya min almashākil wu lmatāʕib alli maʕgūl yitʕarraḍ laha lā samaḥ allāh[4]. li hāda ssabab iḥna bnitʔammal min[5] almuwāṭin alkhalīji lkarīm annu yākhud biʕēn lʔiʕtibār alʔumūr hādi.

- ʕadam rukūb sayyāra min almaṭār ghēr sayyārat lʔujra lʕādiyya lmaʕrūfa bi alwānha w ashkālha lmumayyiza.
- kull muwāṭin lāzim yiṣarriḥ ʕan almujawharāt alli maʕu w ʕan lʔawrāg almāliyya nnagdiyya, wa illa mumkin titʕarraḍ li lmuṣādara, hāda li ann fī ikhtilāfāt katīra marra bēn[6] lʔanḍima ljumrukiyya lʔurōbbiyya wu lkhalījiyya.
- alḥuṣūl ʕala taʔshīrāt addukhūl li dduwal lʔajnabiyya min albalad alli jāyīn minnu.
- lēn yiwṣal almusāfir lāzim yirājiʕ algunṣuliyya li tasjīl safaru w ʕinwānu.
- mā lāzim yiḥmil mabāligh nagdiyya kabīra aw dahab, w mā lāzim yiḥṭafiḍ fīha fi makān sakanu.
- īdāʕ jawāz assafar w tazkirat aṭṭayyāra wu lmujawharāt fi bank aw fi ṣandūg lʔamānāt almawjūd fi lfundug illi nāzil fīḥ. min lʔafḍal akhd ṣūra li ljawāz.
- saḥb almabāligh almāliyya ḥasab alḥāja. iza fī ḥāja li saḥb mablagh kabīr, lāzim yiṭlub min albank taʔmīn alfulūs li lmakān alli yibghā.
- ʕadam fatḥ bawwābāt alʕamāra lkhārijiyya li shakhṣ majhūl.
- min almufaḍḍal tajannub akhd albuzūra li ssūg.
- ḥifḍ kīs albiḍāʕa maʕ waṣl addafʕ liʔannu huwwa lʔisbāt alwaḥīd li dafʕ taman albiḍāʕa.
- min aḍḍarūri dafʕ taman albiḍāʕa fi nafs algism alkhāṣ fīha. w mā lāzim tinḥamal li agsām tānya, liʔann mumkin tisabbib attuhma bi ssirga.
- mā lāzim yifḥaṣ albiḍāʕa barra lmaḥal[7] illa baʕd izin albāyiʕ. w lāzim hu bi nafsu yākhudha li barra.
- mā lāzim tintarak[8] akyās albiḍāʕa lli nsharat min maḥallāt tānya bidūn murāgaba.
- mā tingabal ay khadamāt yigaddimha ashkhāṣ majhūlīn.

- mā yisayyib s̲h̲unaṭ lʔīd ɛala lʔarḍ aw alkarāsi bēn ma[9] yigīs almalābis wu ljizam ɛas̲h̲ān mā titɛarraḍ li nnas̲h̲l.

- min almufaḍḍal fatḥ ḥisāb fi lbunūk alɛarabiyya fi faransa.   min lʔaḥsan istiɛmāl alkartāt wu s̲h̲s̲h̲īkkāt assiyāḥiyya.

- ɛadam almubālag̲h̲a fi libs alḥula wu lmujawharāt alli tiɛarriḍ lʔinsān li lk̲h̲aṭar.

- girāyat gāyimat lʔakl gabl aṭṭalab wu ttaʔkīd min alʔasɛār wagt addafɛ w idāfat alk̲h̲idma ɛala lfātūra.

- aṭṭlab min idārat alfundug attawgīɛ ɛala kull fātūra min gibal almuṣṭāf w min gibal afrād alɛēla ḥaggatu, wu ttadgīg bi lfawātīr gabl almug̲h̲ādara.

- wu bi ma annu gawānīn assēr tik̲h̲talif fi baɛḍ albuldān, iḥna nis̲h̲addid ɛala lʔintibāh ɛala lʔaṭfāl w ɛala kubār assin lamman yiɛburu s̲h̲s̲h̲āwāriɛ ɛas̲h̲ān tajannub alḥawādis almuʔlma.

Vocabulary

irs̲h̲ād *n.pl.* -āt	instruction; guidance; information; advice
muṣṭāf *n.pl.* -īn	summer vacationer
ṣayyaf/yiṣayyif *v.intr.*	to spend the summer vacation
k̲h̲ilāl	during, through
muʔak̲h̲k̲h̲aran	lately
asnāʔ	during, while
duwal lʔaɛḍāʔ	member countries
makkan/yimakkin *v.tr.*	to enable s.o.
maḍḍa/yimaḍḍi *v.tr.*	to spend (time); to stay
k̲h̲āli *adj.*	empty; free from
matāɛib *n.pl.*	troubles, pains, discomforts; difficulties, hardships
tɛarraḍ/yitɛarraḍ li *v.intr.*	to be exposed, be subjected
atʔammal/yitʔammal *v.tr.*	to hope; to expect; to meditate
ak̲h̲ad bi ɛān lʔiɛtibār	to consider
lʔumūr hādi	the following items/matters
mujawharāt *n.*	jewelry, jewels, gems
awrāg māliyya nagdiyya	money, cash
muṣādara *n.*	confiscation, seizure
mablag̲h̲ *n.pl.* mabālig̲h̲	amount
īdāɛ *n.*	depositing, consigning
ṣandūg amānāt	safety deposit box; baggage checkroom
nāzil fi	lodging at, staying in
majhūl *pass.part. pl.* -īn	unknown

tajannub *n.*	avoiding
biḍāʕ *n.coll.pl.* -āt	goods, commodities
waṣl *n.pl.* wuṣūlāt	receipt, voucher
tuhma *n.pl.* -āt, tuham	accusation
hu bi nafsu	he himself
murāgaba *n.*	observation; supervision; surveillance, inspection; control; censorship (of the press)
bidūn murāgaba	unattended
gās/yigīs *v.tr.*	to try on, fit on
malābis *n.coll.*	clothes
nashl *n.*	snatching; stealing; extricating (from danger, difficulties, etc.)
fatḥ ḥisāb	opening a (bank) account
shēk siyāḥi	traveler's check
mubālagha *n.*	exaggeration; extravagance
ḥula *n.coll.*	jewelry
gāymat l?akl	menu
iḍāfa *n.*	adding, annexation
khidma *n.*	tip; service
fatūra *n.pl.* fawātīr	invoice, bill
min gibal	on behalf of
tadgīg *n.*	doing with precision/exactness/accuracy
intibāh *n.*	paying attention, awareness
mu?lim *adj.*	painful

Notes

1. **naṣāyiḥ:** *advices.* Cf. MSA **naṣīḥah**, pl. **naṣa?iḥ** (pausal forms). Note that the **hamza** becomes **y**, a very common phenomenon in Hijazi Arabic.

2. **asnā?:** *during.* Cf. MSA **aθnā?** with the usual Hijazi Arabic shift of **θ** ---> **s** and the deletion of the final vowel. The student should also expect to hear the MSA pronunciation.

3. **yimaḍḍi:** *spends* (time). MSA does not use this form; it uses **amḍa**, impf. **yumḍi.**

4. **lā samaḥ allāh:** *God forbid (lit., May God not permit).* This expression is used in mentioning that something bad might happen. **allāh lā yismaḥ** is also common.

5. **bnit?ammal:** *we expect (lit., we look attentively; we meditate).* The **b-** prefix is added to the indicative form of the verb when it has habitual, progressive or future meaning. MSA uses this verb form to mean *to look attentively; meditate; ponder.* The correct MSA verb form in this case is **na?malu.**

6. **bēn:** *between, among.* Cf. MSA **bayna** with the common Hijazi Arabic shift of **ay** ---> **ē** and the deletion of the final vowel. When two parties are mentioned, the word **bēn** may be used twice. Pronouns are suffixed to **bēn**, e.g., **bēnha wu bēnu**, *between her and him.*

7. **barra lmaḥal:** *outside the store.* This is a typical Hijazi Arabic construction. MSA uses **k͟hārij addukkān** (pausal form).

8. **tintarak:** *be left.* The prefixes **an-**, **in-** and **at-** are added to a perfect transitive verb to obtain the passive form of the verb. See this text for more examples.

9. **bēn ma:** *while.* Cf. MSA **baynama. ma** following the preposition **bēn** functions as a temporal conjunction.

Selection Twenty-Three

ṣadīgi lmutɛib

ɛindi ṣāḥib lā yihizzu ṭarab w lā yiɛǰibu ɛaǰab.[1] aḥkāmu fi nnās titwaggaf ɛala magāyīs mā staɛmalha min gablu w lā nāgid w lā yiftakir fīha maǰnūn w lā ɛāgil. kull ma[2] yishūfani ǰāy yibda huǰūmu ɛala ṣṣaḥāfa wu ṣṣuḥufiyyīn wu l?udaba wu lmut?addibīn. ḥāwalt ignaɛu innu ana mū ɛumda[3], wa lā nagīb fi ṣṣaḥāfa, wa lā ana min aṣḥāb almashāwir. lākin kull hāda lkalām mā nafaɛ.

marra ǰarrabt aksab wuddu a ɛaṭfu fakhtart[4] arbaɛ kutub, kull annuggād gālu innaha muhimma w tamīna. gaddamt hadōla lkutub li ṣāḥibi kahadiyya ṣaghīra w kaɛurrbūn muhādana larubbama[5] artāḥ min lisānu, w aslam min gadāyfu w nirānu, w tikhlaṣ mas?ūliyyati ɛan aṣṣaḥāfa wu ṣṣuḥufiyyīn.

astalam ṣāḥibi lkutub w gallabhum min kaf li kaf bi sukhriya, ḥassēt innu yikhtabir waznahum, w mā aktaras li ɛanāwīnhum w mā kallaf nafsu[6] yiṭalliɛ ɛala gāymat almuḥtawayāt ḥaggathum. lākinnu zamm shfāfu[7] w gawwas ḥawāǰbu w gāl, "bgullak ra?yyi bukra[8]."

ana kunt migtaniɛ innu mahma kān mawḍūɛ hadōla lkutub, alwāḥad yiḥtāǰ li ɛiddat ayyām ɛashān yigrāhum. wa lākin asharēt alyōm bi bukra. fabkhalliṣ bi nafsi lyōm, w khalli ykūn fi bukra illi ykūn.

w aǰa bukra, w aǰa ṣāḥibi ḥāmil l?arbaɛ kutub. wu ttaham zōgi[9] bi ttakhalluf w innu tagāfati saṭḥiyya, w ɛād min ǰadīd ?uṣṭuwānat aṣṣaḥāfa wu ṣṣuḥufiyyīn. w astashhad bi tafāhat lli katabūhum "sālim" aw "sālmīn."

halḥīn aɛtarif inni tashakkakt fi aḥkāmi ssābga ɛala shakhṣiyyat arriǰǰāl. kān ɛindi taraddud, "yā tura huwwa mutaggaf shāyif ḥālu[10], aw ǰāhil ɛāmil ḥālu[11] fahmān?" w ɛashān arayyiḥ w astarīḥ qarrart aɛzumu li lkitāba. w ǰā baɛd ayyām yiḥmil almagāl ḥaggu "alyatīm" baɛd ma ṣawwaru, li annu khāf yiḍīɛ aw ana ahmilu "lā samaḥ llāh." w yikfi innu ɛunwān almagāl ykūn "mīn ashǰaɛ abu zēd aw ɛantara." li hāda ssabab garrart anni akūn ashǰaɛ min l?itnēn w aktub kull gisṣati maƹu. rubbama girāyatha ḥatinfaƹ mawḍūƹ ta?ammulāt ƹālim mutǰāhil aw ǰāhil mutaƹālim. w lak allāh yalli abtalāk azzamān bi mitl ṣāḥibi.

Vocabulary

hazz/yihuzz *v.tr.*	to shake
ṭarab *n.*	music; delight, pleasure
ƹaǰab *n.*	wonder, astonishment
atwaggaf/yitwaggaf + ƹala *v.intr.*	to depend on, be based on
magāyīs *n.*	measures, standards
nāgid *act.part.pl.* nuggād	critic
maǰnūn *adj.pl.* maǰānīn	crazy; fool
ƹāgil *adj.*	wise
huǰūm *n.*	attack, raid
ṣaḥāfa *n.*	journalism
adīb *n.pl.* udaba	scholar, one who is learned (in literature); (here) author
ma<u>sh</u>āwir *n.*	consultation
kasab/yiksab *v.tr.*	to win, gain
wudd *n.*	friendship, amity
ƹaṭf *n.*	sympathy
tamīn *adj.*	valuable
hadiyya *n.pl.* hadāya	gift
ƹurbūn *n.*	token, symbol, pledge
muhādana *n.*	truce, suspension of hostilities, armistice
rubbama *adv.*	maybe, perhaps
artāḥ/yirtāḥ *v.intr*	to rest
gadīfa *n.pl.* gadāyif	missile, projectile, rocket
gallab/yigallib *v.tr.*	to turn, turn over
kaff *n.pl.* kufūf	palm; glove; (here) hand
su<u>kh</u>riya *n.*	sarcasm
wazn *n.pl.* awzān	weight
aktaras/yiktaris + li *v.intr.*	to care for; to pay attention to
kallaf nafsu	to take the trouble to do
gāymat almuḥtawayāt	table of contents
zamm/yizimm *v.tr.*	to purse (the lips); to tie up, fasten, tighten
gawwas/yigawwis *v.tr.*	to bend, curve; to arch (the eyebrow)
ḥāǰib *n.pl.* ḥawāǰib	eyebrow

mugtaniʕ *adj.*	convinced
mahma	whatever, no matter what
attaham/yattahim *v.tr.*	to accuse
zōg *n.*	taste, inclination, liking
takhalluf *n.*	backwardness, underdevelopment
saṭḥiyya *adj.*	superficial, external, on the surface
ʔuṣṭuwāna *n.*	(phonograph) record; cylinder (of an engine)
astashhad/yastashhid + bi *v.intr.*	to quote; to refer to; to die as a martyr, a hero
tafāha *n.*	silliness, stupidity, insignificance, paltriness, tastelessness
sālim aw sālmīn	whoever they are, whether this or that
tashakkak/yitshakkak + bi *v.intr.*	to doubt, be skeptical
shakhṣiyya *n.*	personality
taraddud *n.*	hesitation, hesitance
yā tura	I wonder if...
shāyif ḥālu	conceited
ǰāhil *adj.*	ignorant
ʕāmil ḥālu fahmān	acting clever, pretending to be intelligent
garrar/yigarrir *v.tr.*	to decide
ʕazam/yiʕzim *v.tr.*	to invite
yatīm *n.pl.* aytām	orphan
ṣawwar/yiṣawwir *v.tr.*	to make copies of; to draw; to take a picture of
ḍāʕ/yiḍīʕ *v.intr.*	to be lost
hamal/yihmil *v.tr.*	to ignore, neglect
lā samaḥ allāh	God does not permit, God forbid
ashǰaʕ *adj.comp.*	more courageous
rubbama *adv.*	maybe
taʔammul *n.pl.* -āt	devotion, hope; inspiration
ʕālim *n.pl.* ʕulama	scientist, scholar, learned person
abtala/yibtali + bi *v.intr.*	to be afflicted, plagued

Notes

1. **lā yihizziu ṭarab w lā yiʕǰibu ʕaǰab:** *nothing pleases him (lit., music does not move him and wonders do not please him).* This expression is very common in Hijazi Arabic and in other Arabic dialects as well. It is used to describe a person who is very hard to please.

2. **kull ma:** *whenever.* When **kull** is followed by **ma,** it functions as a subordinating conjunction and may only be followed by a verbal clause, e.g., **kull ma yishūfani Jāy yibda huJūmu,** *whenever he sees me coming he starts his attack.*

3. **ana mū ɛumda:** *I am not someone important.* This expression is very common in Saudi Arabia. For example, **ahlan wu sahlan bi lɛumda,** *welcome honorable sir.*

4. **fakhtart:** *I chose.* Cf. MSA **fakhtartu** with the deletion of the final vowel. The particle of classification or gradation **fa** indicates coordination together with the idea of development in the narrative. Many educated Saudis use **fa** when talking about an event or telling a story.

5. **larubbama:** *maybe.* This is a loanword from MSA (The narrator of the story is an educated Saudi.) The particle **la** is often prefixed to **rubbama** to imply a greater probability or a stronger expression of a wish.

6. **mā kallaf nafsu:** *he didn't even bother to, he didn't take the trouble to...* This expression is very common in most Arabic dialects.

7. **zamm shfāfu:** *He pursed his lips.* With respect to the parts of the body that occur in "pairs", most Arabic dialects refer to them by the plural form, not by the dual, i.e., **shfāfu** for **shafatē, ḥawāJbu** for **ḥāJibē** and **kfūfu** for **kaffē**. MSA pl. form of **shafah** is **shifāh.** Note that in Hijazi Arabic the **h** is substituted for **f** before the pronominal suffix.

8. **bukra:** *tomorrow.* This word is often used loosely in Arabic dialects. Most speakers use it to imply *some time in the future.* This word occurs in MSA, but there it means *early in the morning,* e.g., **ataytuka bukratan,** *I came to you early in the morning.*

9. **zōgi:** *my taste.* Cf. MSA **ðawqi** with the common Hijazi Arabic changes of **ð** ---> **z, aw** ---> **ō** and **q** ---> **g.**

10. **shāyif ḥālu:** *conceited.* This expression is pure colloquial Arabic. **shāyif** is the active participle of the verb **shāf.** MSA uses **mutakabbiru** instead.

11. **ɛāmil ḥālu (fahmān):** *He thinks he is clever, intelligent.* This is another pure colloquial Arabic expression. It is used when someone pretends to be something he is not. MSA uses **yataẓāharu bi annahu fahīmun.**

Selection Twenty-Four

aghrab[1] giṣaṣ almukhaddirāt fi lmamlaka

ǰarīda suɛūdiyya nasharat giṣaṣ gharība ɛan mushkilat almukhaddirāt fi lmamlaka. giṣṣa ɛan sawwāg siyyāra gatal talatīn ḥaǰǰ. wu ttānya ɛan wāḥad sabbab harq ɛarīs wu ɛarūsatu wu garāyibhum fi lēlat azzafāf. wu ttālta ɛan riǰǰāl yiɛtadi ɛala ɛarḍ karīmatu wu yitɛarraḍ li ɛugūbat alʔiɛdām, wu lgiṣṣa arrābɛa ɛan riǰǰāl ḥaṭ mukhaddir fi kubbāyāt[2] khamr wu gatal aṣdigāʔu wu shurakāʔu fi hadīk alǰalsa.

kull hadōl algiṣaṣ mū humma riwāyāt min asāṭīr shaɛbiyya, wu mū min ḥikāyāt alǰadda illi tiḥkīha li ḥafīdha ɛashān yinām. lākin hādi ṣuwar ḥagīgiyya li lmaʔās illi nataǰat min tafashshi akhd almukhaddirāt bēn ǰamāɛāt min afrād muǰtamaɛna lli ɛāsh li fatra min azzaman sālim min hādi ssumūm algattāla[3].

alliwāʔ muḥammad huwwa ḥayǰāwib kull alʔasʔila ɛan mushkilat almukhaddirāt fi lmamlaka. huwwa aɛṭāna furṣa ɛashān nitḥāwar maɛ ɛadad min almasǰūnīn bi sabab gaḍāya lmukhaddirāt ɛala ikhtilāf tawarruṭhum fīha. minhum kānu muharribīn wu minhum murawwiǰīn, wu minhum mustaɛmilīn wu wuṣaṭa[4]. iḥna ḥaniɛruḍ algaḍiyya guddām ashshaɛb, wu inshāʔ allāh bi hād almaǰhūd ḥanɛarrif arraʔiy alɛām ɛan annatāyǰ alkhaṭīra wu lʔaḍrār annātǰa min taɛāṭi lmukhaddirāt

- saɛādat alliwāʔ, kēf mumkin tintashir almukhaddirāt bi hādi ṣṣūra bi rrughm min attashdīd ɛala gafl mawāniʔ lmamlaka lbaḥriyya wu lbarriyya wu lǰawwiyya fi waǰh almuharribīn?
- awwalan ana aftakhir wu aɛtazz bi kull ǰuhūd riǰāl alǰamārik wu silāḥ alḥudūd li tawgīf ɛamaliyyāt attahrīb bi kull ḥazm wu guwwa. lākin ǰarīmat almukhaddirāt hiyya ǰarīma munaẓẓama, wu illi yirtikbūha byilɛabu adwār mutaɛaddida wu btitghayyar bi ṣūra mustamirra. mitl ma ygūl almatal, "alḥāǰa umm alʔikhtirāɛ." fa binshūf ɛiṣābāt attahrīb bitsawwi kull alʔasālīb wu ṭṭurug illi timakkinhum min tadkhīl hādi ssumūm ila lmamlaka.

dalḥīn khallīna nitkallam ɛan fiʔāt almutɛāmilīn bi lmukhaddirāt wu lɛugūbāt aṣṣārma ḥaggōnhum.

1. almumawwil huwwa illi yistakhdim zakāh[5] wu mālu ɛashān yimawwil ɛamaliyyāt attahrīb bi ǰamīɛ alʔighrāʔāt almukhtalfa ɛashān yiḥaggig ahdāfu lmāddiyya. almumawwil yuɛtabar rās alḥayya.

2. almuharrib huwwa illi yitwalla ɛamaliyyāt nagl wu idkhāl almukhaddirāt li lmanāṭig. hāda yuɛtabar ǰisr ashshar. hadōl alʔitnēn ɛugūbathum khamstaɛsh sana siǰn, wu gharāma ɛashara alf riyāl maɛ ɛugūbat alǰald.

3. sharīk almuharrib huwwa illi yisāɛid wu yitɛāwan maɛ almuharrib fi ɛamaliyyāt attahrīb. hāda shshakhṣ ɛugūbatu sabɛa sinīn siǰn wu lfaṣl min alkhidma iza kān muwaẓẓaf.

4. almuhdi huwwa aṣṣadīg alɛaduw illi yitzayyin li aṣḥābu ɛashān yishaǰǰiɛhum ḥatta yitɛāṭu hādi ssumūm alfattāka wu yihdīhum yāha bidūn mugābil. hāda huwwa ǰalīs assūʔ wu yuɛtabar akhṭar min almurawwiǰ. ɛugūbat almuhdi khams sinīn siǰn wu gharāma ɛashara alf riyāl maɛ ɛugūbat alǰald.

5. almurawwiǰ huwwa illi yilɛab dōr attāǰir wu lmuwazziɛ li hādi ssumūm wu yuɛtabar almumawwil alhaddām. wu yiɛāgbūh zay ma yiɛāgibu almuhdi.

6. almutaɛāṭi huwwa lhadaf alwaḥīd ḥag ɛamaliyyāt attahrīb, wu fi lghālib yikūn shakhṣ marīḍ aw mughra. hada yinsaǰan sanatīn maɛ ɛugūbat alǰald illi yigarrirha lḥākim ashsharɛi.

khallīni agūl innu ṣadar amr min ṣāḥib assumuw almalaki nāʔib wazīr addākhiliyya bi tashhīr almuharribīn wu lmurawwiǰīn bi nashr ṣuwarhum fi ṣṣuḥuf almaḥalliyya wu tanfīz ɛugūbat alǰald ɛalēhum ɛalanan fi amākin ɛāmma minshān yikūnu ɛibra li kull wāḥad yifakkir bi hāda lɛamal alʔiǰrāmi.

Vocabulary

aghrab *adj.*	stranger, strangest
giṣṣa *n.pl.* giṣaṣ	story, tale; problem
mukhaddirāt *n.*	drugs, narcotics; anesthetics, painkillers, tranquilizers
ḥaǰǰ *n.pl.* ḥuǰǰāǰ	pilgrim
lēlat azzafāf	wedding night
aɛtada/yiɛtadi + ɛala *v.intr.*	to rape; to assault
ɛarḍ *n.*	honor; width; exhibit
karīma *n.adj.*	daughter; precious; generous
iɛdām *n.*	execution, death sentence
sharīk *n.pl.* shuraka	companion; partner
khamr *n.coll.pl.* khumūr	wine, alcoholic beverage
riwāya *n.pl.* -āt	story; drama, play

usṭūra *n.pl.* asāṭīr	myth; fable, fairy tale
ǰadda *n.pl.* -āt	grandmother
ḥaka/yiḥki *v.tr.*	to tell (a story); speak
ḥafīd *n.pl.* aḥfād	grandson
maʔsāt *n.pl.* maʔāsi	tragedy; misery
tafa<u>shsh</u>i *n.*	spreading, outbreak
samm *n.coll.pl.* sumūm	poison
liwāʔ *n.*	major general
atḥāwar/yitḥāwar + maʕ *v.intr.*	to debate; to interview; to talk
tawarruṭ *n.*	being in a bad situation/in a bad fix/in a dilemma
muharrib *act.part.pl.* -īn	smuggler
murawwiǰ *act.part.pl.* -īn	marketer, pusher (of drugs)
waṣīṭ *n.pl.* wuṣaṭa	mediator, middleman
raʔiy ʕām	public opinion
saʕādat	your excellency; happiness
bi rru<u>gh</u>m	in spite of
mīna *n.pl.* mawāniʔ	harbor, port
baḥriyya *adj.*	sea
barriyya *adj.*	land
ǰawwiyya *adj.*	air
afta<u>kh</u>ar/yifta<u>kh</u>ir + bi *v.intr.*	to be proud of, take pride in
aʕtazz/yiʕtazz + bi *v.intr.*	to be proud of, take pride in
riǰāl alǰamārik	custom officers
silāḥ alḥudūd	border defense forces
ḥazm *n.*	strictness; strength
ǰarīma munaẓẓama	organized crime
artakab/yirtakib *v.tr.*	to commit a crime or offense, engage in criminal activity
dōr *n.pl.* adwār mutaʕaddida	numerous roles
i<u>kh</u>tarāʕ *n.pl.* -āt	invention
ʕugūba *n.pl.* -āt	punishment
ʕiṣāba *n.pl.* -āt	gang
ʔuslūb *n.pl.* asālīb	method, style, way
ṣārma *adj.*	severe, fierce; strict
zaka *n.*	intelligence, cleverness
mawwal/yimawwil *v.tr.*	to supply; to finance
ḥayya *n.pl.* -āt	snake

ǰisr *n.pl.* ǰusūr	bridge
g͟harāma *n.*	a fine, money imposed as penalty for an offense
ǰald *n.*	lashing
faṣl min alk͟hidma	discharge from the service
atzayyan/yitzayyan + li *v.intr.*	to be adorned, be made attractive; (here) to seduce
fattāka *adj.*	devastating
muwazziɛ *act.part.pl.* -īn	distributer
mutɛāṭi *act.part.pl.* -īn	user
mug͟hra *pass.part.*	deluded; tempted, attracted, seduced
tas͟hhīr *n.*	exposition, exposé, exposure of something discreditable

Notes

1. **ag͟hrab** comp., super. of **g͟harīb:** *stranger; strangest.* Hijazi Arabic uses the pattern aCCaC for forming comparative and superlative adjectives. The comparative adjective is followed by **min** while the superlative adjective is usually followed by a noun, e.g., **aḥmad akbar min ɛali**, *Ahmad is older than Ali;* **aḥmad huwwa akbar walad**, *Ahmad is the oldest boy.* Hijazi Arabic also uses the MSA superlative form which consists of the comparative with the definite article **al-**, e.g., **aḥmad huwwa alʔakbar**, *Ahmad is the oldest.*

2. **kubbāya:** *(a drinking) glass.* This is strictly a colloquial word which is used in many Arabic dialects. MSA **kūb**, pl. **akwāb** or **kaʔs**, pl. **kuʔūs** correspond to this word.

3. **sumūm gattāla:** *deadly/lethal poison.* Cf. MSA **sumūmun qattālatun** (fully vocalized). This expression is commonly used to describe harmful affects of a physical substance or of an idea on the society.

4. **wuṣaṭa** pl. of **waṣīṭ:** *middleman; mediator.* Cf. MSA **wusaṭāʔu** with the deletion of the glottal stop and the final vowel. Note the regressive assimilation of **s** to **ṣ**.

5. **zakāh:** *his intelligence.* Cf. MSA **ðakāʔahu** with the common change of **ð** to **z**, and the deletion of the glottal stop and the final vowel.

6. **yāha:** *it.* MSA **iyyāha** is the cognate of this word with the deletion of the first vowel and the degemination of **y**. When a verb takes two objects in the form of pronominal suffixes, the pronoun of the first person is suffixed to the verb and the other to the particle **iyya-** which immediately follows the verb, e.g., **aɛṭāni yyāha**, *he gave it to me.*

Selection Twenty-Five

mugābala maɛ murawwiǰ mukhaddirāt

- ēsh ismak?[1]
- ṣāliḥ.
- ēsh hiyya ǰinsiyyatak?
- yamāni.
- ēsh hiyya asbāb tawgīfak?
- (gāl bi ṣōt tikhnugu ɛibārāt alḥuzn) lā ḥawala wala quwwata illa bi llāh[2]. gabaḍu ɛalay li anni arawwiǰ alḥubūb almusahhira. alḥagīga anni adnabt w ǰanēt ɛala nnās w ɛala[3] nafsi. alkalām mā yinfaɛ dalḥīn, lākin khallīni agullak anni nadmān ɛala lli sawwētu w ana rāǰiɛ ila llāh aṭlub minnu lluṭf wu rraḥma.
- inta kunt tiɛrif innu hādi lḥubūb mamnūɛa wu fī ɛugūbāt shadīda li tarwīǰha?
- naɛam kunt ɛarfān wu lākin ashshēṭān wu ǰulasa ssū? aghwūni wu nassūni guwwat alɛugūba.
- ēsh alli khallāk tibīɛ alḥubūb?
- abadan wala shay ghēr alkasb almāddi.
- bi gaddēsh[4] kunt tishtari lḥabba w bi gaddēsh kunt tibīɛha?
- kunt ashtari lɛulba bi miyyat riyāl w abīɛha bi miyya wa khamsīn riyāl.
- izan kunt tirbaḥ khamsīn riyāl bi lɛulba?
- naɛam, lākin ṣaddigni rribḥ alḥarām yiṭīr bidūn istifāda minnu w bidūn ma tḥuss. yrūḥ wu yrūḥ maɛu rrātib alli atgāḍā min almuʔassasa lli ashtaghil fīha. lamma yikhtaliṭ alḥalāl bi lḥarām, tnēnāthum yrūḥu ɛa lḥarām.
- mata badēt tbīɛ hādi lḥubūb, w kunt inta tistaɛmilha?
- kunt abīɛha li muddat shahr gabl ma algu lgabḍ ɛalay, wu lākin mā kunt astaɛmilha li annha tḍurr aṣṣiḥḥa wu lɛagl.
- mā dāmak tiɛrif innaha tḍurr aṣṣiḥḥa wu lɛagl lēsh tibīɛha?
- gult lak innu shshēṭān aghwāni w ana nadmān ɛala lli ɛamiltu.
- mīn humma lʔashkhāṣ alli tibīɛhum?
- aghlab zabāyni sawwāgīn shāḥināt kabīra wu gallābiyyāt.
- kēf khaṭarat ɛala bālak fikrat bēɛ almukhaddirāt?
- taɛarraft ɛala shakhṣ kān yishtaghil bi hādi ttiǰāra lkhāsra w aghrāni kalāmu
- khabbart idārat mukāfaḥat almukhaddirāt ɛan ṣāḥbak hāda?

- naɛam w humma baɛdhum yidawwirū ɛalē[5]

- w khabbarthum ɛan zabāyinak?

- naɛam khabbart alʔidāra ɛanhum.

- biwuddak[6] tgūl ay shi tāni?

- naɛam biwuddi agūl anni nādim ǰiddan wa tubt li llāh. wa anṣaḥ akhwāni lmuslimīn, wu khāṣṣatan akhwāni lyamāniyyīn alli taraku waṭanhum wu tagharrabu, w ǰō lmamlaka minshān yiḥaṣṣilu maɛīshathum bilḥalāl, ḥatta yibtaɛdu ɛan bēɛ hādi lḥubūb w ɛan ay rizg mū ḥalāl, li annahum iza sawwu hāda nihāyathum ḥatkūn mitl nihāyati, wagtha[7] mā yinfaɛ annadam.

Vocabulary

mugābala *n.pl.* -āt	meeting; gathering; interview
yamāni *adj.*	Yemeni
tawgīf *n.*	arrest; stopping
khanag/yikhnug *v.tr.*	to choke, suffocate
ɛibāra *n.pl.* -āt	expression
ḥuzn *n.*	sadness
gabaḍ/yigbaḍ + ɛala *v.intr.*	to arrest, catch, capture
ḥabba *n.pl.* ḥubūb	pill, tablet; one piece (of fruit)
musahhir *adj.*	stimulant, something that makes one stay up and lose sleep.
ḥubūb musahhira	amphetamine
adnab/yidnib *v.intr.*	to commit an offense, be at fault, do something wrong
ǰana/yiǰni + ɛala *v.intr.*	to offend, sin (against); to harm; to hurt
nadmān *act.part.*	regretful, repentant
luṭf *n.*	kindness, goodness
raḥma *n.*	mercy
shēṭān *n.pl.* shayāṭīn	devil, Satan
ǰalīs *n.pl.* ǰulasa	companion, friend
sūʔ *n.*	bad, evil
abadan	absolutely not
kasb *n.*	gain, earning; winning, profiting
māddi *adj.*	material; financial, monetary
ashtara/yishtari *v.tr.*	to buy
bāɛ/yibīɛ *v.tr.*	to sell
ɛulba *n.pl.* ɛulab	box
izan	therefore

rabaḥ/yirbaḥ *v.tr.*	to profit; to win, earn; to benefit
ṣaddigni *v.imp.*	believe me
ribḥ alḥarām	unlawful profit, illegal profit
ṭār/yiṭīr *v.intr.*	to fly ;(here) fly away, disappear
istifāda *n.*	profiting, gaining
rātib *n.pl.* rawātib	salary
atgāḍa/yitgāḍa *v.tr.*	to be paid
akhtalaṭ/yikhtaliṭ *v.intr.*	to be mixed
ḍarr/yiḍurr *v.tr.*	to harm
ɛagl *n.pl.* ɛugūl	mind, brain
zabūn *n.pl.* zabāyin	customer, client
shāḥina *n.pl.* -āt	truck
gallābiyya *n.pl.* -āt	bulldozer, tractor
khaṭar ɛala bāl + *obj.pron.*	it occurs to the mind
fikra *n.*	idea, thought
tījāra *n.*	trade, commerce, business
khāsra *adj.*	losing
mukāfaḥa *n.*	fighting; stopping
idārat mukāfaḥat almukhaddirāt	Drug Enforcement Administration
khabbar/yikhbbir *v.tr.*	to tell, inform
bi wuddak	would you like, do you desire
tāb/yitūb *v.intr.*	to repent, turn to God
naṣaḥ/yinṣaḥ *v.tr.*	to advise
tagharrab/yitgharrab *v.intr.*	to go west, to go abroad; to immigrate; to emigrate
maɛīsha *n.*	living, livelihood
ḥalāl *adj.*	lawful, according to God's will
abtaɛad/yibtaɛid + ɛan *v.intr.*	to be far from; to avoid
rizg *n.pl.* arzāg	earnings; means of making a living, livelihood
nihāya *n.pl.* -āt	end

Notes

1. **ēsh ismak:** *What is your name?* This is an example of an equational sentence. In an equational sentence the verb is not expressed. The subject is equated with a non-verbial predicate, and when translated into English, the verb *to be* or *to have,* is used.

2. **lā ḥawla wala qunwata illa bi llāh:** *There is no power and no strength save in God.* This expression is borrowed from MSA. It is used when one wishes to say that he is completely powerless.

3. **ǰanēt ɛala:** *I harmed, hurt.* Cf. MSA **ǰanaytu** with the common change of **ay** ---> **ē** and the deletion of the final vowel. Note that when this verb takes a direct object it means *to reap, harvest.*

4. **bi gaddēsh:** *How much?* This phrase is pure colloquial Arabic and is used to refer to *time, price, amounts, weight and length,* e.g., **gaddēsh assāɛa?** *What time is it?* **gaddēsh ashtarēt?** *How much did you buy?* **gaddēsh ṭūlak?** *How tall are you?* Note that when asking about prices, the word **gaddēsh** is proceeded by the preposition **bi.**

5. **yidawwiru ɛalē:** *They are looking for him.* MSA does not use this verb; it uses **baḥaθ**, impf. **yabḥaθu.** When this verb takes a direct object, it means *to make s.th. round.*

6. **b(i)wuddak:** *do you wish, desire.* This expression is borrowed from MSA, and is widely used in the Gulf dialects.

7. **wagtha:** *then, at that time, (lit., its time).* Cf. MSA **waqtaʔiðin**. Hijazi Arabic adds the pronominal suffix **-ha** to any noun denoting time, such as, **yōm**, *day;* **lēla**, *night;* **sāɛa**, *hour* to denote *at that day, night, hour.*

Selection Twenty-Six

ḥiwār maɛ ṣāḥib istudyō yitɛāṭa lmukhaddirāt

- mumkin aɛrif ismak?
- ismi lʔawwal ɛabdallah wu mā aḍunn innu fī ḥāǰa li maɛrifat ismi lkāmil.
- yā akh, ēsh huwwa sabab siǰnak?
- tawarraṭṭ[1] fi taɛāṭi lḥubūb almusahhira.
- kēf wagaɛt fi hāda shsharak?
- fi lbidāya gharrani wāḥad min rifāg assūʔ "wu mā aktarhum[2]" minshān astaɛmil alḥubūb almusahhira.
- hall admant ɛala lḥubūb almusahhira?
- naɛam.
- min mata?
- min gabl siǰni bi shahr.
- ēsh hiyya ṭabīɛat shughlak illi khallatak tiḍṭarr tākhud alḥubūb almusahhira?
- ana ɛindi istudyō taṣwīr wu lāzim ashar fi muɛḍam alwagt.
- li annak mudmin lā budd innak titḍāyag min baɛḍ lʔaɛrāḍ bi sabab ingṭāɛak ɛan almukhaddirāt. ṣaḥ?
- fi lbidāya shaɛart bi alam shadīd wu ḍīg wu iktiʔāb w tawattur ɛaṣabi wu hāda kān fi awwal yōmēn min siǰni. wu lākin ṣiḥḥati ṣārat titḥassan baɛd akhd alɛilāǰ.
- hal assarat almukhaddirāt ɛala muɛāmaltak maɛ annās?
- naɛam kunt lamma ākhud alḥubūb aṣīr mutawattir alʔaɛṣāb yaɛni mitnarfiz[3] w aghḍab min ay shi, wu ashɛur innu lāzim aɛtadi ɛala lli yitḥarrash biyya[4].
- ṣār maɛak ḥādis sayyāra bi sabab almukhaddir?
- lā alḥamdu li llāh. kunt atǰannab swāgat assayyāra wagt ma ākhud alḥubūb.
- ēsh tḥus dalḥīn min baɛd ma masakūk wu ḥaṭṭūk fi hāda lmakān?
- ashɛur inni adnabt fi ḥag nafsi[5] wu ahli wu awlādi. wu ashɛur bi lḥufra lwiskha lli gādani ilha[6] rafīg assūʔ, lā waffagu llāh. ana lʔān tāyib ila llāh subḥānahu wa taɛāla, wu aṭlub minnu lɛafu wu lmaghfira.
- gaddēsh kunt tiṣrif ɛala lmukhaddirāt?
- kunt aṣrif ḥawāli talāt miyyat riyāl yōmiyyan.
- kunt tiɛrif ɛigāb taɛāṭi lmukhaddirāt?
- kunt arɛrif innu fi ɛugūba wu lākin mā aɛrif innaha bi hādi/ṣṣūra.

- kēf nōɛ arriɛāya lli tlāgīha fi ssiǰn?

- arriɛāya ṭayyiba wu lmaɛīsha ǰayyida, wu lʔahamm min kull shay huwwa alli nitɛallamu min attawɛiya ddīniyya, wu idāʔ ṣṣalāt maɛ alǰamāɛa, wu lʔistifāda min almawāɛiḍ wu grāyat alkutub annāfɛa lmawǰūda fi maktabat attawgīf.

Vocabulary

ḥiwār *n.*	dialogue, text (of a play); talk, conversation; (here) interview
istudyō *n.*	studio
kāmil *adj.*	complete
tawarraṭ/yitwarraṭ + fi or bi *v.intr.*	to be put in an unpleasant situation, be in a bad fix, be in a dilemma
gharr/yighurr *v.tr.*	to deceive, trick, mislead, seduce; to dazzle
adman/yudmin + ɛala *v.intr.*	to be addicted
aḍṭarr/yiḍṭarr *v.intr.*	to have to do something, find it necessary to do something
taṣwīr *n.*	photography, drawing
sahar/yishar *v.tr.*	to stay up late
taḍāyag/yitḍāyag + min *v.intr.*	to be bothered by, suffer from
aɛrāḍ *n.*	symptoms
shaɛar/yishɛur + bi *v.intr.*	to feel
alam *n.pl.* ālām	pain
ḍīg *n.*	tightness
iktiʔāb *n.*	depression
tawattur ɛaṣabi	nervousness, nervous tension
ɛilāǰ *n.pl.* -āt	treatment
mitnarfiz *adj.*	nervous, edgy
ghaḍab/yighḍab *v.intr.*	to be angry, mad; to become upset
taḥarrash/yitḥarrash + bi *v.intr.*	to meddle with, interfere with, provoke
atǰannab/yitǰannab *v.tr.*	to avoid
ḥufra *n.pl.* ḥufar	hole; (here) trap
wisikh *adj.*	dirty
lā waffagu llāh	may God not grant him success
subḥānahu wa taɛāla	God to whom be ascribed perfection and majesty
ɛafu *n.*	pardon
maghfira *n.*	forgiveness

tawɛiya *n.*	awareness, awakening, enlightenment
idāʔ *n.*	fulfilling (a prayer obligation); accomplishment (of a task)
mawɛiḍa *n.pl.* mawāɛiḍ	sermon, religious exhortation, spiritual counsel

Notes

1. **t(a)warraṭṭ:** *I was entangled, embroiled, involved.* Cf. MSA **tawarraṭtu** with the deletion of the final vowel and the change of **t** ---> **ṭ** via progressive assimilation.

2. **mā aktarhum:** *How numerous they are!* Note that **mā** here is as an exclamatory particle. Although this usage is strictly MSA, it is often used in Hijazi Arabic and in many other Arabic dialects as well.

3. **mitnarfiz:** *nervous.* This is a loanword from English. The word **ḥamūgi** is also used.

4. **yitḥarra<u>sh</u> biyya:** *He provokes me.* This is an MSA verb with the common Hijazi Arabic vocalic change and deletion. The Hijazi Arabic form collocates with **biyya** or **fiyya** instead of MSA **bī**.

5. **adnabt fi ḥag nafsi:** *I sinned against myself, I have been unjust to myself.* This is a very common expression in many Arabic dialects. The word **ḥag** here expresses possession.

6. **ilha:** *to it.* Cf. MSA **ilayha** with the deletion of the diphthong **-ay-**.

Selection Twenty-Seven

nahḍa ḥaḍāriyya shāmla fi lmamlaka

inta ɛammāl tisʔalni ɛan attagaddum alḥaḍāri fi lmamlaka. ṣarāḥa, mā aɛrif min fēn abda[1]. almamlaka, ṭāl ɛumrak, halḥīn tiɛīsh marḥala shāmla min attagaddum alḥaḍāri wu lʔinǰāzāt[2] alhāyla fi kull maǰālāt attanmiya wu ttaṭawwur. fa bitlāḥiẓ innu lmamlaka tagaddamat tagaddum ɛaẓīm fi fatra giyāsiyya mā tizīd ɛan ɛashr sinīn. alḥagīga, agdar agūl annu ḥaggagna munǰazāt wu mashārīɛ mā tḥaṣṣilha buldān tānya bi miyyat sana. aṭṭawwarat almamlaka bi shakl ɛaẓīm[3]. bidūn shak, hadōla ssinīn alɛashara lmāḍya kānu zay taḥaddi li ḥukūmatna lgawiyya. lākin alḥamdu lillāh bi giyādat malikna almufadda gidrat almamlaka tiḥaggig ahdāf marḥalat attanmiya shshāmla hādi. fa bitlāgi inǰāzāt ḍakhma fi kull almaǰālāt aṣṣināɛiyya wu zzirāɛiyya wu ttaɛlīmiyya wu ṣṣiḥḥiyya wu lʔiǰtimāɛiyya wu lɛumrāniyya.

mā lāzim ninsa annu lmamlaka bazalat ǰuhūd katīra li buna shakhṣiyyat almuwāṭin assuɛudi awwal shay. mumkin nigūl annu hādi lǰuhūd kānat timshi īd bi īd[4] maɛ ǰuhūd attanmiya wu ttaṭawwur. ihtammat almamlaka bi taḥḍīr ǰīl mutaggaf. fa binshūf annu alḥukūma assasat ālāf almadāris wu miyyāt almaɛāhid wu sabɛ ǰāmiɛāt kabīra fīha ɛasharāt alkulliyyāt.

daḥḥīn fī aktar min malyōnēn ṭālib wu ṭālba fi marāḥil attaɛlīm alʔibtidāʔi wu lmutawaṣṣiṭ wu ttanawi wu lǰāmiɛi. ṣār fī madāris fi lgura wu fi kull alʔamākin arrīfiyya. wu bi nnisba li lmustashfayāt, fī mustashfayāt ḥadīsa wu khadamāt tānya alli twaffirha ddōla li lmuwāṭin assuɛūdi minshān saɛādatu wu rāḥatu wu rafāhiyyatu. binshūf innu ashshabāb assuɛūdiyyīn ḥaṣṣalu daraǰāt ɛilmiyya ɛālya dākhil almamlaka wu kamān bi wāṣṭat[5] albiɛsāt fu lkhāriǰ. humma daḥḥīn mutḥammlīn masʔūliyyāt ḍakhma fi lmadāris wu fi lmaṣāniɛ wu fi lmazāriɛ.

iḥna niftakhir katīr lamma tiḥtafil ǰāmɛat almalik fēṣal bi shshargiyya bi takhrīǰ dafɛa min shabābna illi takhaṣṣaṣu fi maǰāl aṭṭub wu asbatu bi kafāʔāthum wu magdirāthum innhum lā yigillu ɛan illi takharraǰu min ǰāmiɛāt albilād almitgaddma.

Vocabulary

nahḍa *n.pl.* -āt	boom; growth, rise, awakening; progress
ḥaḍāriyya *adj.*	modernizing
shāmil *adj.*	comprehensive, exhaustive, general, overall; complete
ṣarāḥa *n.*	frankness, frankly
ṭāl ɛumrak	may God prolong your life
marḥala *n.pl.* marāḥil	period, level, stage
inǰāz *n.pl.* -āt	achievement, accomplishment
tanmiya *n.*	expansion, advancement; growth
taṭawwur *n.*	development, progress; evolution
fatra giyāsiyya	record breaking period, record time
taḥaddi *n.*	challenge
bi giyādat	under the leadership
ɛumrāniyya *adj.*	(relating to the) infrastructure/cultural development
bazal/yibzil *v.tr.*	make (an effort); to spend; to sacrifice
timshi īd bi īd	to go hand in hand
ǰīl *n.coll.pl.* aǰyāl	generation
assas/yiʔassis *v.tr.*	to establish
kulliyya *n.pl.* -āt	college (within a university); department
ibtidāʔi *adj.*	elementary
mutawaṣṣiṭ *adj.*	junior high
tānawi *adj.*	secondary (high school)
amākin rīfiyya	rural areas
ḥadīsa *adj.*	modern
waffar/yiwaffir *v.tr.*	to provide, make available; save(money)
saɛāda *n.*	happiness
rāḥa *n.*	rest, comfort
rafāhiyya *n.*	luxury, leisure
i/aftakhar/yiftakhir + bi *v.intr.*	to take pride in
biɛsa *n.pl.* -āt	mission; delegation; expedition; student exchange
takhaṣṣaṣ/yitkhaṣṣaṣ *v.intr.*	to specialize

Notes

1. **min fēn abda:** *from where I (am to) start.* Cf. MSA **min ayna abdaʔu.**

2. **injāzāt hāyla:** *great accomplishments.* Cf. MSA **injāzātun hāʔilatun** (fully vocalized). Besides the deletion of the final vowels and the change of the glottal stop to a **y**, inanimate plural nouns take singular concord as is the case here.

3. **tagaddamat tagaddum ʕaẓīm:** *It advanced greatly.* All verbs whether transitive or intransitive may take their own verbal noun as an object. This is commonly called the cognate or absolute accusative, **almafʕūlu almuṭlaqu.** It is normally used for emphasizing, **liltaʔkīdi** or for magnifying, **liltaʕẓīmi**, the idea expressed by the verb. The cognate accusative often is replaced by its modifying adjective, e.g., **tagaddamat katīr marra**, *it advanced very much.*

4. **īd bi īd:** *hand in hand.* Cf. MSA **yadan bi yadin** (fully vocalized). This expression is very common in many Arabic dialects.

5. **bi wāṣṭat:** *by means of.* Note the regressive assimilation, i.e., the affect of **ṭ** on the **s** before it.

   General Note: The language of this selection is affected to a great extent by the industrial development in the area.

Selection Twenty-Eight

azzuwāǰ

Part One

alwālda aǰat tigulli[1], "ana shuftillak ɛarūsa. wu hi tiɛǰibni fi ṭabīɛt lḥāl." fa ɛaraḍat ɛalay almawḍūɛ, wu ṣarāḥa mā kān ɛindi ay māniɛ, lanni ḥassēt[2] innu yaɛni mumkin atḥammal masʔūliyya. fa gult li ummi wu abūy, "khalāṣ tgaddamu intu wu shūfu lmawḍūɛ wu raǰǰiɛūli khabar." alɛādāt ɛindana alwālid wa lwālda yirūḥu yitgaddamu li ahl albint. ygūlūlhum bi ṭarīga ɛan waladhum wu shaghghāl fi lmakān alfulāni[3], wu ēsh hi ṭabīɛat ɛamalu, yaɛni kull alḥāǰāt ɛannu, wu baɛdēn ygūlu, "bi wuddana[4] nikhṭub bintakum li waladna". ṭabɛan ḥāyiǰi rrad bi lmuwāfaga aw bi rrafḍ.

ilmuhim riǰɛat alwālda lī ana w gālatli annu wāfagu lǰamāɛa. w gālatli ṭabɛan mīn hi lbint, min bēt mīn, wu bint mīn. waṣafatli yyāha tamāman. fa ṭabɛan ana ḥabbēt ashūfha, wu hāda shay ṣaɛb ɛindana. fa shuftaha bi ṭarīga aw bi ʔukhra, bas almuhim innu hi mā tidri. ɛindana aktar annās tikūn mitmassika innu zōǰha mā yishūfaha gabl azzawāǰ. ana shuftaha. w ɛaǰabatni lbint. aɛṭēt li ummi kilma gultillha annani muwāfig ɛalēha. khalāṣ alʔum tirfaɛ yaddaha[5] min almawḍūɛ, wa yiddakhkhal[6] alwālid.

alwālda aɛṭathum khabar, gālatlhum innu abūya inshālla ḥayitgaddam lahum. rāḥ abūy wu tkallam maɛ abu lɛarūsa wu wāfagu, wu ṭabɛan giryu lfātiḥa[7], lli hi ɛindana tagrīban almuwāfaga ɛala zzawāǰ, muwāfaga mabdaʔiyya. baɛd kida yaɛṭūk fatra ɛashān tiʔahhil nafsak. lamma tiǰi lkhuṭba lāzim tiǰīb addibal. dibla li lɛarūsa wu dibla li lɛarīs. ɛādatan iḥna lāzim tikūn addibal ɛa blāltīn abyaḍ[8] mush dahab, liʔannu ḥarām ɛindana. khuṣūṣan addibla ḥaggat arriǰǰāl lāzīm tikūn bēḍa, wu ḥaggat assit mush muhim. fī aghrāḍ tānya lāzim niǰībha. nisawwi ɛarabiyya min maǰmūɛat ɛuṭūr wu fi nafs alwagt nigaddim mikyāǰ ḥag alwaǰh wu manākīr wu bakhkhūr. fī anwāɛ bakhkhūr, wu lubān wu hēl wu sukkar nabāt. ḥāǰāt yaɛni zay kida fa tiɛmal ɛarabiyya muzayyana bi kull hādi lḥāǰāt wu trūḥ tigaddimhum.

fī mudda mḥaddada bēn alkhuṭba wu bēn ashshabka[9]. lamma yiǰi wagt ashshabka, alʔahl yittaṣlu bi ahl alɛarūsa wu ygūlu iḥna ḥaddadna wagt ashshabka, masalan alǰumɛa alǰāya. fa byiɛzimu ahl alɛarīs wu bisīr iḥtifāl. yirūḥ alɛarīs ʕashān yilabbis alʕarūsa ddibla. addibla bitkūn fi yad alyamīn fi ayyām ashshabka. kamān fī mudda bēn ashshabka wu bēn azzawāǰ. ʕashān alʕarusēn yākhdu fikra ʕan baʕḍ. masalan yimkin fi lfatra hādi shshāb yishūf innu akhlāg albint mā hi kwayyisa, aw ṭarīgatha fi lmuʕāmala māhi mumtāza, māhi mutaʕallima zay māhu yibgha. wa nafs ashshay hi tishūf alʔikhtilāf illi fīh. ǰāyiz innaha mā tibghāk. hu ǰāyiz yikūn gaṣīr, dabdub/matīn[10]. fi lfatra hādi yikhtabru baʕḍahum. almuhim hi tishūf alḥāǰāt aṭṭayyiba illi fīh aw alḥāǰāt albaṭṭāla, bas innu mā fī intigādāt, hu yiḥāwil yighayyir shay minnaha, w hiyya bi nafs alwagt tighayyir shay minnu hu.

Vocabulary

ʕaraḍ/yiʕriḍ + ʕala *v.intr.*	to bring up; to suggest; to offer, propose
māniʕ *n.pl.* mawāniʕ	objection; obstacle; hindering
masʔūliyya *n.pl.* -āt	responsibility
tgaddam/yitgaddam + li *v.intr.*	to ask for a girl's hand, propose marriage
muwāfaga *n.pl.* -āt	approval; agreement, conformity
rafḍ *n.*	rejection, refusal
waṣaf/yūṣif *v.tr.*	to describe
rafaʕ/yirfaʕ yaddu *v.tr.*	to refrain from s.th.
ahhal/yiʔahhil nafsu *v.tr.*	to prepare oneself; to be qualified; to enable
dibla *n.pl.* dibal	wedding band
blātīn *n.coll.*	platinum; white gold
gharaḍ *n.pl.* aghrāḍ	articles of everyday use, odd and ends, things
ʕarabiyya *n.pl.* -āt	carriage, cart
mikyāǰ *n.coll.*	cosmetics, make-up
manākīr *n.coll.*	nail polish
bakhkhūr *n.coll.*	incense
lubān *n.coll.*	frankincense, olibanum, gum resin
hēl *n.coll.*	cardamom
sukkar nabāt	rock candy
muzayyana *adj.*	decorated, adorned, ornamented
akhlāg *n.*	manners
ǰāyiz *adj.*	possible
dabdūb *adj.*	fat
matīn *adj.*	fat
intigād *n.pl.* -āt	criticism; objection

Notes

1. **tigulli:** *She says to me.* Cf. MSA **taqūlu lī**. Hijazi Arabic changes the preformative vowel **a --> i** after the **y, t, n** of an imperfect marker. However, many speakers do not pronounce this vowel in rapid speech. The prepositional phrase **lī** is suffixed to the verb, causing the shortening of the vowel **u**. This development never happens in MSA.

2. **ḥass, ḥassēt:** *I felt.* Arab grammarians refer to this type of verb as **alfiʕlu almuḍāʕafu**, *the doubled verb* or **alfiʕlu alʔṣammu**, *the solid verb.* Note that in Hijazi Arabic the third radical is joined with the second, and the vowel **ē** is inserted before the pronominal suffixes of the first and second persons singular and plural.

3. **shaghghāl fi lmakān alfulāni:** *He works at such and such a place.* It is quite common in MSA to derive the adjective form **faʕʕāl** from the active participle **fāʕil**. This form usually conveys the notion of intensity or habitual action. It is called in Arabic, **ismu lmubālaghah**, *the noun of intensiveness,* e.g., **ʕālimun**, *knowing, learned,* **ʕallāmun**, *very learned, completely familiar (with).* Most nouns designating professions and trades have the form of **faʕʕāl**, e.g., **ṭabbākh**, *cook,* **najjār**, *carpenter.* However, the use of **shaghghāl**, meaning worker, is very rare in MSA. Hijazi Arabic uses this word to describe something in operation, e.g., **assayyāra shaghghāla**, *the car is running* or *it is in working condition.*

4. **bi wuddana:** *we want.* This expression is borrowed from MSA.

5. **tirfaʕ yaddaha min:** *she refrains from (lit., she lifts her hand from).* This expression is very common in many Arabic dialects. It is used when someone stops being involved in something, or when one is asked to refrain from further involvement.

6. **yiddakhkhal:** *gets involved, interferes, takes over.* This is an assimilated form of **yitdakhkhal**, per. **tdakhkhal.** The consonant **t** triggered this assimilation, which often occurs with the third person singular and plural.

7. **giryu lfātiḥa:** *They read the first chapter of the Qur'an.* Cf. MSA **qaraʔū alfātiḥata**. Reading Al-Fatiha after an agreement between two parties has always been practiced in the Islamic world. It symbolizes the seal of approval of the people concerned and their blessing on what has been agreed upon.

8. **addibal ʕa blātīn abyaḍ:** *the wedding rings are of white gold (lit., platinum).* The preposition **ʕa** is the contraction of **ʕala**, a common practice when used with colors. Islam forbids men from wearing gold and silk. Note that the word **dibla**, pl. **dibal** is not used in MSA.

9. **ashshabka:** *engagement party.* The MSA cognate of this word is **shubkah** meaning *kinship,* e.g., **bayni wa baynahu shubkatun**, *there is kinship between me and him.*

10. **dabdūb:** *fat.* This word does not occur in MSA, but it could be a semantic extension of the word **dub**, *bear,* which is used in some Arabic dialects to mean a big fat person. The MSA word **dabūb** is another possible cognate of this word. It is used for fat animals, e.g., **nāqatun dabūbun takādu lā tamshi min kaθrati laḥmiha**, *the fat camel almost cannot walk because of its excessive flesh*

azzuwāǰ

Part Two

fi ayyām ashshabka hi tiḥāwil taɛrif kull ẓaghīra wu kabīra[1] ɛannu ka zōǰ. lāzim tikūn ɛārfa aklātu lmufaḍḍala, libsu, kēf yiḥub yilbas, iza yiḥub yikhruǰ katīr, mā yiḥub yiṭlaɛ, aṣḥābu yizūrū katīr willa hu yizūrhum katīr, yiḥub albuzūra[2], ṭarīgatu wagt al?infiɛāl. yaɛni lā bud innu fi shay biykhalli l?insān yinfaɛil, wu hi bitḥub taɛrif ṭarīgatu ɛashān titǰannabha. azzōǰa tagrīban ɛindana iḥna tikun ḥarīṣa aktar shay ɛala innaha mā tkhallīh yinfiɛil. fa fi lfatra hādi kull wāḥad yidrus attāni, fa iza kān nāsabatuh biyḥaddid mōɛid azzawāǰ. w iza kān mā nāsabatuh, lissaɛ yaɛni mā yiḥṣal bēnu w bēnha ay tagārub. mā yiḥṣal ay shay ghēr alǰalsa, kalām, iḥtirām, yaɛni bas muǰarrad innu ēsh mukhāṭaba ɛādiyya. mā yiḥṣal bēnhum ay shay, rughm innaha ḥalālu linnha aṣbaḥat zōǰatu. li?ann fi shshabka yiǰi lma?zūn w yinɛaqid alɛaqd ɛala sunnat allāh wa rasūlu. muǰarrad ma yiɛaddi wu ygābilha yōm ashshabka aṣbaḥat ḥalāluh, zōǰa sharɛiyya.

lamma yiǰi lma?zūn ṭabɛan yiǰi abu lɛarīs wu abu lɛarūsa w yiǰlisu. alma?zūn yis?al mīn alwakīl ḥag alɛarūsa wu lwakīl ḥag alɛarīs. ṭabɛan abūh wu abūha hum alwukala ɛindana, fa hu byis?al abu lɛarūsa iza mwāfig yizawwiǰ bintu. ḥaygūl naɛam wāfagt. alma?zūn yis?al, "almahr gaddēsh?" fa byaɛṭīh mablagh ɛashr ālāf, ɛishrīn alf ḥasab almahr illi wāfagu ɛalē. aḥyānān yikūn fī shurūṭ, maṣalan mā yisaffir bintu barra, aw mā yisāfir wu ykhallīha. masalan mā yibghāha tiskun baɛīda ɛan manṭagatu. baɛd ma yintahi yis?al abu lɛarīs iza maɛāh almahr. baɛḍ awgāt yiṣīr ṭaslīm almahr guddām alma?zūn. aḥyānan alma?zūn yiḥub yismaɛ min fum alɛarūsa yigullaha, "inti muwāfga tākhudi hāda ka zōǰ laki." li?ann aḥyānan fī banāt ɛammāl bīkūnu murghamīn yitzawwaǰu awlād ɛammahum. ɛindana nās lā zāl mutmassikīn bi lɛādāt. fa masalan ana ɛindi walad wu akhi ɛindu bint lāzim niǰburhum yitzawwaǰu baɛḍ. ayyām zamān kānu yisammu hāda bi ttaslīm.

li yōm alfaraḥ niḥaddid almakān wu lwagt. ṭabɛan lāzim yikūn almakān kabīr linnu fi maɛāzīm katīr. iḥna niɛzim khams miyya, sit miyyat shakhṣ, riǰāl wu ḥarīm. lāzim yikūn fī dabāyiḥ[3] li rriǰāl. binǰīb khirfān w nidbaḥha. wu li lḥarīm mumkin nisawwīlhum būfē.

yōm alfaraḥ ahl alɛarīs yirūḥu wu yǰību lɛarūsa. alɛarīs yikūn fi makān alfaraḥ ɛashān yistagbil almaɛāzīm wu yhannūh. lamma tiǰi lɛarūsa yiǰi maɛāha ṭṭīrān. timshi hi wu lɛarīs min awwal almadkhal ḥag alḥarīm. yimshu mashya baṭīʔa ǰiddan, yaɛni yā dūb[4] bas yiḥarriku riǰl waḥda w baɛdaha ttānya. alḥaraka baṭīʔa marra. w humma yighannu li ḥad ma tūṣal almakān. wu lamma yiǰlisu yibda ghuna tāni liʔannu fī ghuna khāṣ bi zzaffa wu ydiggu ṭṭīrān. baɛdēn yikhushshu yiǰlisu fi maḥal alkūsha. alkūsha hiyya lmakān alli yiǰlisu fīh alḥarīm wu fī muṭribīn. yigɛudu nuṣ sāɛa, sāɛa, yighaṭrifu lḥarīm wu yighannu. baɛdēn alɛarīs yākhud ɛarūsatu ila bētu. ākhir shay bi wuddi agūl innu hādi lɛadāt tikhtalif min makān li makān w min ɛāyila li ɛāyila.

Vocabulary

a/infaɛal/yinfaɛil *v.intr.*	to react; to be irritated, be upset, be angry
atǰannab/yitǰannab *v.tr.*	to avoid
ḥarīṣa *adj.*	careful, cautious
nāsab/yināsib *v.tr.*	to suit, fit, be in agreement/in conformity, with
iḥtirām *n.*	respect
muǰarrad *adj.*	as soon as; nothing more than; mere
mukhāṭaba *n.*	conversation, talk
rughm *prep.*	in spite of, despite
maʔzūn *n.*	clergyman authorized to perform marriages
sunnat allāh	God's law
wakīl *n.pl.* wukala	trustee; guardian; agent
mablagh *n.pl.* mabāligh	amount
taslīm *n.*	handing over; delivery; surrender, submission
murgham *pass.part.*	forced, compeled, coerced
aǰbar/yiǰbu/ir *v.tr.*	to force, obligate, compel
yōm alfaraḥ	wedding day
maɛāzīm *adj.*	invited guests
dabīḥa *n.pl.* dabāyiḥ	slaughtered animal; sacrifice
kharūf *n.pl.* khirfān	lamb
būfē *n.pl.* -yāt	buffet
hanna/yihanni *v.tr.*	to congratulate
ṭāra *n.pl.* ṭīrān	tambourine

yā dūb	barely, hardly
kū<u>sh</u>a *n.*	the place where women sit during the wedding and where the bride and groom enter for the final wedding procession
muṭrib *n.pl.* -īn	(professional) singer
<u>gh</u>aṭraf/yi<u>gh</u>aṭrif *v.intr.*	to utter shrill, long-drawn-out trilling sounds (as a manifestion of joy by Arab women)

Notes

1. **kull za<u>gh</u>īra wu kabīra:** *every little and big thing.* This expression is very common in Hijazi Arabic and in many Arabic dialects as well. MSA also uses the same expression.

2. **buzūra** s. **bizra:** *Children.* It is possible that MSA **bizra**, *seed,* is the cognate of this word.

3. **dabāyiḥ**: *slaughtered animal.* Cf. MSA **ðabāʔiḥ** (pausal form) with the change of **ð** ---> **d** and the glottal stop to **y**. It is noteworthy that killing a lamb in honor of a guest is a sign of Arab hospitality.

4. **yā dūb:** *barely; just.* This expression is used before a verb to stress the slowness of an action, as illustrated in this text. It is also used with the meaning of *just* in the sense of having recently completed an action.

Selection Twenty-Nine

addīn wu ddōla

giṣṣat infiṣāl addīn ʿan addōla hāda shay mā yimshi ʿindana[1]. hāda shay gharbi mā yinṭabig ʿala dduwal alʔislāmiyya abadan. ʿindana addīn hu asās kull shay. iḥna niʿtabir annu addīn alʔislāmi hu ṭarīgat ḥayā yōmiyya li kull muslim min ayyām annabi muḥammad ṣalla llāh ʿalē wu sallam li hāda lwagt. fa libsana wu aklana wu shughlana wu gawānīnana wu siyāsatna kullaha murtabṭa bi ddīn. almalik assuʿūdi yiʿtabir nafsu khādim alḥaramēn[2], wu hu qāʔid siyāsi wu dīni fi nafs alwagt, wu dastūr addōla hu shsharīʿa, alqurʔān alkarīm.

assuʿūdiyya tiʿtabir innu sharaf laha wu min wājbātha innu tihtam bi kull lʔumūr almitʿallga bi nnawāḥi ddīniyya. fa bi nnisba li lḥaj masalan binshūf innu alḥukūma banat mabāni ḍakhma fi madīnat alḥujjāj fi jidda. hināk byijlisu[3] lḥujjāj lēn yiḥaḍḍiru kull shay gabl ma yibdu riḥlathum li makka lmukarrama. ḥukkām almanṭiga byiṭlubu min kull ḥaj innu yidfaʿ rasm māli basīṭ, bas li taghṭiyat almaṣārīf ḥaggathum. ayyām zamān tagrīban kān alḥaj akbar madkhūl li ssuʿūdiyya, wa lākin daḥḥīn māhu illa mujarrad rasm basīṭ[4]. almamlaka ʿindaha fulūs kāfya min albatrōl ḥaggaha ʿalashān tidfaʿ muʿẓam maṣārīf alḥaj wu ṣiyānat alḥaramēn. alḥukūma tiṣruf min fulūsha ʿala khidmat alʔislām wu lmuslimīn wu ʿala nashr alqurʔān fi kull alʿalam.

alḥukūma asuʿūdiyya btibzul majhūdāt kabīra in kān fi shag aṭṭurug aw fi tawfīr almuwāṣalāt li malayīn alḥujjāj. assuʿūdiyya btishtari aḥdas almaʿddāt minshān tiʔammin rāḥat alḥujjāj wu tsahhil lahum hāda lmasʿa[5] lkarīm. alḥukūma bitʔammin aʿdād kabīra min almuwaẓẓafīn in kān min aṭibba aw mumarriḍīn wu fanniyyīn wu shurṭa wu sawwāgīn alli byishtaghlu lēl nhār fi ayyām alḥaj. fa bidūn hādi lmajhūdāt mustaḥīl innu lḥaj yistawʿib malāyīn alḥujjāj. assuʿūdiyya btishʿur annu min wājbātha annu tgaddim kull hādi ttashīlāt li lʿālam alʔislāmi minshān yiḥaggigu hādi lfarīḍa illi allāh subḥānu wa taʿāla ḥaṭṭaha rukn min arkān alʔislām.

ʿindana fi ssuʿūdiyya ṭāl ʿumrak, addīn hu assās kull shay fi lmujtamaʿ. fa masalan alḥukūma btijburak tṣūm shar ramaḍān, ʿala sharṭ innu mā yikūn ʿindak ay māniʿ ṣiḥḥi aw iza kunt msāfir, bas alḥālāt illi byismaḥ fīha lqurʔān. fa mā bījūz lak tākul[6] wu tishrab wu tdakhkhin guddām annās aṣṣāymīn, aw fi amākin ʿāmma.

mumkin almuṭawwiɛ[7] yiwaggifak. khallīni aɛṭīk masal tāni, ɛindana ddīn bīḥarrim almuskir, fa izan ṣār assukr ḍud alqānūn. assuɛūdiyya balad islāmi. mustaḥīl yifṣil addīn ɛan addōla. makka hi madīnat alʔislām fi kull alɛālam wu fīha albēt alḥarām. hināk wulid annabi muḥammad wu hināk nizil ɛalē awwal waḥy, wu hināk rufiɛ shiɛār alʔislām illi hu lā ilāha illa llāh wu muḥammad rasūlu llāh. fa hādi shshihāda hi shiɛārana wu ɛalamana. fa iḥna māshyīn ɛala sunnat allāh wu rasūlu.

Vocabulary

infiṣāl *v.n.*	separation; disengagement
anṭabag/yinṭabig + ɛala *v.pass.*	to be applicable; to correspond
ṣalla llāh ɛalē wu sallam	God bless him and grant him salvation
ashsharīɛa *n.*	Islamic law, the Shari'a
sharaf *n.*	honor
ihtam/yihtam + bi *v.intr.*	to be concerned, take an interest; to go to the trouble
mabna *n.pl.* mabāni	building
ḍakhma *adj.*	huge, big
ḥākim *n.pl.* ḥukkām	governor, ruler
rasm *n.pl.* rusūm	fee, tax; drawing; picture
taghṭiya *n.*	covering
maṣrūf *n.pl.* maṣārīf	expenditure, expenses, costs
madkhūl *n.*	income
muǰarrad	nothing more than, mere; bare, naked
ṣiyāna *n.*	maintenance, upkeep; protection
nashr *v.n.*	spreading; publishing
maǰhūd *n.pl.* maǰhūdāt	effort
shag aṭṭurg	opening up roads
aḥdas almaɛaddāt	the most modern equipment
rāḥa *n.*	comfort, rest
masɛa *n.pl.* masāɛi	endeavor, effort
mustaḥīl *adj.*	impossible
astawɛab/yistawɛib *v.tr.*	to contain; to have room; to comprehend
farīḍa *n.pl.* farāy/ʔiḍ	religious duty; ordinance of God
rukn *n.pl.* arkān	pillar (of Islam); corner; basis
aǰbar/yiǰbur *v.tr.*	to force, oblige
muṭawwiɛ *act.part.pl.* -īn	religious police
waḥy *n.*	revelation; inspiration

shiɛār *n.pl.* -āt	credo; emblem; slogan; motto
ɛalam *n.pl.* aɛlām	flag
sunnat allāh	God's law

Notes

1. **mā yimshi ɛindana:** *It is not practiced/it does not hold true in our country.* The verb **yimshi**, *walk* is often used in Hijazi Arabic to denote validity or applicability. The active participle **māshi** is used for the same purpose, e.g., **hāda shay mū māshi ɛindana**, *this is something which is not practiced/is not valid in our country.*

2. **khādim alḥaramēn:** *the custodian of the two holy mosques (Mecca and Medina).* Since there is no separation of religion and state in Saudi Arabia, the king is considered the spiritual leader as well as the head of state.

3. **byiJlisu:** *they stay.* As has been noted before, the suffix **-b** is added to an impf. verb to express a habitual action. The verb **Jalas**, impf. **yiJlis**, *to sit,* in Hijazi Arabic means *stay*, e.g., **assana lmāḍya ruḥt arriyāḍ wu Jalast hināk usbūɛēn**, *I went to Riyadh last year and I stayed there two weeks.*

4. **baṣīṭ:** *simple; small; naive.* Note that the **s** here becomes emphatic, caused by a regressive assimilation since it is followed by the emphatic **ṭ**.

5. **masɛa:** *endeavor, effort.* This word is borrowed from MSA and is often used in the Hijazi dialect.

6. **tākul:** *you eat.* Cf. MSA **ta?kulu.** Note the deletion of the glottal stop and the compensatory lengthening of the vowel **a**.

7. **muṭawwiɛ:** *religious police.* The **muṭawwiɛ** is hired by the government to enforce the **sharīɛa** since Islam is an integral part of a Muslim's social life.

Selection Thirty

alḥaǰ[1]

"labbayka allāhumma labbayk[2], labbayka lā sharīka laka labbayk, inna lḥamda wa nniɛmata laka wa lmulk, lā sharīka laka labbayk." malāyīn alḥuǰǰāǰ min kull buldān alɛālam btismaɛhum biraddidu hāda nnidāʔ w humma dākhlīn makka lmukarrama.

alḥaǰ hu rukn min arkān alʔislām alkhamsa. kānu lḥuǰǰāǰ min zamān yitḥammalu mashaggāt wu matāɛib katīra minshān yiǰu lḥaǰ. katīr minhum mātu ɛala ṭarīg alḥaǰ min assafar bi lbar wu lḥar wu lɛaṭash. wu lākin daḥḥīn taghayyarat alʔaḥwāl, wu lmuwāṣalāt ṣārat sahla wu mutwaffra in kān bi lǰaw aw bi lbaḥr aw bi lbar. fa bitshūf miyyāt alʔālāf min alḥuǰǰāǰ fi maṭār ǰidda wu fi lmīna ḥaggaha kamān, kulluhum mintaẓrīn albāṣāt ɛashān tākhudhum ila makka. ɛādatan bīkūn fī zaḥma hāyla fi ǰidda fi lʔayyām alʔūla min shahr zu lḥiǰǰa. ḥawāli miyyat alf bāṣ wu sayyāra msāfrīn fi nafs alwagt wu fi ittiǰāh wāḥid. alqurʔān lā yismaḥ li ghēr almuslimīn yidkhulu makka. gabl ḥudūd makka fi maḥaṭṭat shurṭa minshān yitʔakkadu min ǰawazāt assafar. kull ḥaǰ lāzim yibarhin innu muslim ɛashān yiḥṣal ɛala fīzat alḥaǰ[3]. daḥḥīn fī ṭarīg khuṣūṣi li ghēr almuslimīn lāzim yifrugu ɛalēha gabl ḥudūd makka bi arbaɛtaɛshar mīl.

alḥukūma ssuɛūdiyya btihtam bi lḥuǰǰāǰ min sāɛat ma yiwṣalu li ssuɛūdiyya. fī wikāla ḥukūmiyya bitgūd alḥuǰǰāǰ fi kull marāḥil alḥaǰ. humma byihtammu bi lmuwāṣalāt wu bi khiyam assakan minshān yitʔakkadu innu kull ḥaǰ ɛammāl yiṭabbig kull marāsīm alḥaǰ allāzama. kull alḥuǰǰāǰ byidkhulu makka lābsīn nafs allibās, giṭɛatēn min algumāsh alʔabyaḍ bidūn khiyāṭa. hāda llibās yusamma alʔiḥrām[4]. hāda shshay bīwarri innu kullahum mitsāwyīn, wu innahum bi ḥāla ṭāhra wu hum mutgaddimīn ila llāh. lamma yikūn alʔinsān fi ḥālat alʔiḥrām lāzim yitwaggaf ɛan ashya katīra, zay alǰimāɛ, wu lmukhāṣama, libs ay shay mkhayyaṭ, gaṣṣ ashshaɛr wu lʔaḍāfir wu ashya tānya.

gabl dukhūl makka lāzim kull wāḥad yitwaḍḍa, liʔann hāda shay mafrūḍ gabl aṣṣalā. alwuḍūʔ fi makka shay muhim ǰiddan liʔann almūya maʔkhūda min bīr zamzam[5]. lamma yiwṣalu makka lāzim yirūḥu mubāsharatan li lmasǰid alḥarām. alkaɛba mawǰūda fi waṣaṭ almasǰid. alkaɛba mghaṭṭāya bi lkiswa illi mṭarraz ɛalēha bi ddahab wu lfiḍḍa āyāt qurʔāniyya. lāzim almuʔmin yidkhul alkaɛba bi tawāḍuɛ wu khushūɛ wu huwwa ɛammāl yidɛi hāda dduɛāʔ, "allāhumma ighfir lī dunūbi wa iftaḥ lī abwāb raḥmatak."

yibda lḥaǰ bi ṭṭawāf[6] sabɛ marrāt dākhil almasǰid wara ḥaǰar ismāɛīl (alḥaǰar alʔaswad)[7]. baɛdēn bīkūn assaɛy bēn aṣṣafa wu lmarwa[8] sabɛ marrāt. lāzim yibda ssaɛy fi ṣṣafa wu yintahi bi lmarwa. baɛd assaɛy, fi lyōm attāmin min zu lḥiǰǰa lāzim yirūḥu lḥuǰǰāǰ ila ɛarafa, ḥawāli ɛashr amyāl min makka, wu yibātu hināk li ṣṣubḥ. fi lyōm attāsiɛ fi ṣṣubḥ badri lāzim yitim alwugūf fi ɛarafa wu byiṭlubu rraḥma wu lghufrān min allāh. baɛd ṣalāt lmaghrib lāzim yirūḥu ila lmuzdalifa wu hināk kull wāḥad bīǰammiɛ tisɛa wu arbaɛīn ḥaǰar. fi lyōm attāni bīrūḥu ila lmīna. yōm annaḥr[9] alli hu yōm alɛīd fi ɛashara zu lḥiǰǰa. fi lmīna byirǰumu shshēṭān. kull yōm lāzim yirmu ɛadad muɛayyan min alḥiǰāra. kull wāḥad lāzim yigaddim ḍaḥiyya, byākull nuṣṣha wu byaɛṭi nuṣṣha li lfugara.

ākhir shay kull ḥaǰ lāzim yirǰaɛ ila makka ɛashān yiṭūf sabɛ ashwāṭ wu yisɛa sabɛ ashwāṭ kamān. baɛd kida byintahi alḥaǰ, ḥaǰ mabrūr wu saɛy mashkūr wu zanb maghfūr.

Vocabulary

labbayka	here I am! At your service!
niɛma *n.pl.* -āt, niɛam	grace, blessing
nidāʔ *n.*	appeal, proclamation; call
rukn *n.pl.* arkān	pillar; corner; basis
mashagga *n.pl.* -āt	hardship, toil, trouble
matāɛib *n.*	troubles, hardships, difficulties
ɛaṭash *n.*	thirst
ɛādatan *adv.*	usually
ittiǰāh *n.*	direction
atʔakkad/yitʔakkad + min *v.intr.*	to be sure of, make sure of, verify
barhan/yibarhin *v.tr.*	to prove
farag/yifrug *v.intr.*	to exit, part
marāsīm alḥaǰ	the hajj rituals, the rites of the pilgrimage
mitsāwi *pl.* -īn	equal
ṭāhra *adj.*	pure, clean
alǰimāɛ *n.*	sexual intercourse

ḍafr *n.pl.* aḍāfir	fingernail, toenail
atwaḍḍa/yitwaḍḍa *v.intr.*	to perform the ritual ablution before prayer
wuḍūʔ *n.*	ablution
bīr zamzam	Zamzam Well
almasǰid alḥarām	the Holy Mosque in Mecca
alkiswa *n.*	the covering of the Ka'aba
mṭarraz *adj.*	embroidered
āya *n.pl.* -āt	Qor'anic verse; miracle
tawāḍuɛ *n.*	humbleness; modesty
khushūɛ *n.*	submission, humility
ð/zanb *n.pl.* zunūb	sin, offense, crime, misdeed
raḥma *n.*	mercy, sympathy
bāt/yibīt *v.intr.*	to spend the night
ǰammaɛ/yiǰammiɛ *v.tr.*	to gather, collect
yōm annaḥr	the Day of Immolation (on the 10th of zu lḥiǰǰa)
raǰam/yirǰim *v.tr.*	to stone
ḍaḥiyya *n.pl.* -āt, ḍaḥāya	blood sacrifice; victim
shōṭ *n.pl.* ashwāṭ	round
saɛa/yisɛa *v.intr.*	to run; to strive

Notes

1. **alḥaǰ:** *the pilgrimage.* The hajj is one of the Five Pillars of Islam. The annual pilgrimage to Mecca is an obligation only for those who are physically able to perform it. The main rites of the hajj are concentrated on the first ten days of **zu lḥiǰǰa**, the last month of the Islamic year.

2. **labbayka allāhumma labbayk:** *Here I am in answer to thy call, O God!* All the pilgrims repeat this prayer as they enter Mecca and as they circle the Ka'aba.

3. **fīzat alḥaǰ:** *a visa to enter Mecca.* The MSA **taʔshīrat dukhūl** is used also. Since non-Muslims cannot enter Mecca, one has to prove that he or she is a Muslim.

4. **alʔiḥrām:** Each male pilgrim puts on a simple garment of unsewn cloth in two pieces before he gets to Mecca. When a pilgrim puts on the **iḥrām**, he is then renouncing the vanities of the world. After this and until the end of the pilgrimage he must not wear other clothes or ornaments, anoint his hair, use perfumes, hunt, or do other prohibited acts. Upon the completion of the pilgrimage, men shave their heads and women cut off a few locks of their hair, and then they take off the **iḥrām**.

5. **bīr zamzam:** *the Well of Zamzam.* Cf. MSA **biʔr zamzam** (pausal form). Note the deletion of the glottal stop and the lengthening of the vowel i. Hagar, the mother of Ismail, was wandering in the desert searching for water. She prayed for water, and in her eager quest around the hills, her prayers were answered and she saw the Well of Zamzam.

6. **aṭṭawāf:** *circumambulation of the Ka'aba; circuit.* **aṭṭuwāf** is circling the Ka'aba seven times.

7. **alḥaJar al?aswad:** *the black stone.* This stone is also known as the Stone of Ismail. Each round of circling the Ka'aba should start and end at this black stone. It is believed that this stone is a remnant of the altar which Abraham and his son Ismail built for the sacrifice.

8. **assaʕy bēn aṣṣafa wu lmarwa:** *running between Safa and Marwa.* Each pilgrim is supposed to run about a mile and a half between the two hills of Safa and Marwa seven times. It is believed that Hagar in her search for water ran between these two hills.

9. **yōm annaḥr:** *the Day of Immolation.* This takes place in Mina on the tenth day of **zu lḥiJJa**, which is known as the *Day of Sacrifice.* Each pilgrim offers a sacrifice, then the symbolic ceremony of casting seven stones at the devil is performed at the first opportunity and is continued on subsequent days. Both rites are connected with the story of Abraham. This is the **ʕīd al?aḍḥa** which ends the pilgrimage.

Selection Thirty-One

assuɛūdiyya tigṭaɛ rūs[1] sittaɛshar kwēti bi sabab almutafaǰǰirāt fi lbēt alḥarām

assulṭāt assuɛūdiyya ɛalanan gaṭaɛat rūs sittaɛshar muwāṭin kwēti fi makka lmukarrama. fi wagt alḥaǰ yōm ɛashara yulyu faǰǰaru hadōla lmuǰrimīn ganābil fi lmasǰid alḥarām. kān fī aktar min malyōn ḥaǰ fi lmasǰid. hādi mū awwal marra biyṣīr fī iɛtidā?āt ɛala bēt allāh alḥarām. sanat alf wu tisɛ miyya wu sabɛa wu tamanīn ṣār fī ishtibākāt ɛanīfa bēn ?ulūf min alḥuǰǰāǰ al?īrāniyyīn almugātilīn wu bēn sulṭāt al?amn assuɛūdiyya. wu bi nnatīǰa māt aktar min arbaɛ miyyat ḥaǰ muɛẓamhum[2] īrāniyyīn. fa bi ṭṭabɛ assuɛūdiyya gaṭaɛat ɛilāgātha ddiblumāsiyya maɛ īrān ɛugb[3] hādi lmas?ala. baɛdēn assuɛūdiyya ḥaddadat ɛadad alḥuǰǰāǰ al?īrāniyyīn assanawi. hāda shshay mā ɛaǰab[4] īrān, fa gāṭaɛat alḥaǰ li muddat sanatēn.

fi sabtambar wāḥid wu ɛishrīn naffazat assulṭāt assuɛūdiyya garār al?iɛdām ɛala hadōla lkuwētiyyīn. alḥukūma ssuɛūdiyya tiɛtagid annu īrān hi illi khaṭṭaṭat hāda lɛamal al?irhābi alli naffazūh alkuwētiyyīn ashshīɛiyyīn. attilifizyōn assuɛūdi ɛaraḍ sharīṭ vidiyō ɛan iɛtirāf wāḥad min almaɛdūmīn. gāl innu hu wu aṣḥābu akhadu lmutafaǰǰirāt min assafāra līrāniyya fi lkwēt. hāda rriǰǰāl maɛrūf ɛannu innu mudarris fi madrasa ibtidā?iyya wu hu fi nafs alwagt gāyid kutlat almuslimīn ashshīɛa lmutaṭarrifīn fi lkwēt. li lḥīn mā simiɛna innu likwēt sawwat ay taṣrīḥ mubāshar min nāḥiyat hāda l?iɛdām. al?amīr ashshēkh ǰābir al?aḥmad ṣabāḥ kān fi baghdād fi hāda lwagt. kull almuslimīn ashshīɛa fi lkwēt zaɛlānīn ǰiddan li?annu lḥukūma khallat hadōla lḥuǰǰāǰ yinḥabsu fi ssuɛūdiyya wu yitḥākamu ḥasab ashsharīɛa ssuɛūdiyya[5].

laǰnat alɛafw addōliyya alli biddāfiɛ[6] ɛan ḥugūg al?insān bayyanat ihtimāmha bi mawḍūɛ iɛtigāl hadōla lmuwāṭinīn, wu ɛan imkāniyyat taɛarruḍhum li anwāɛ mukhtalfa min attaɛzīb. almalik fahd atkallam maɛ amīr likwēt w gallu innu mustaḥīl yitsāhalu maɛ ay wāḥad biyḥāwil yiḥarriḍ alḥuǰǰāǰ ɛala lɛiṣyān wu ttadmīr dākhil alḥaramēn.

wikālat al?anbā? alfaransiyya ṣarraḥat annu fī ǰamāɛa biysammu ḥālhum ǰīl alghaḍab alɛarabi aɛtarafu bi annhum humma alli ḥaṭṭu lmutafaǰǰirāt fi makka wu fi ǰidda. wazīr addākhiliyya ssuɛūdi ṣarraḥ bi annu ǰamāɛa kwētiyyīn sawwu khuṭṭat attafǰīr fi lkwēt wu ddarrabu[7] ɛala istiɛmāl alganābil. zay ma gāl wāḥad min almuǰrimīn innu humma kānu yibghu yiḥuṭṭu arruɛb wu lkhōf fi gulūb alḥuǰǰāǰ wu ḥabbu yibarhinu annu lmamlaka mū gādra tiḥmi bēt allāh alḥarām.

Vocabulary

gaṭaɛ/yigṭaɛ rās *v.tr.*	to behead
mutafaǰǰirāt	explosives; bombing
albēt alḥarām	the Holy Mosque in Mecca
ɛalanan *adv.*	publicly, openly
faǰǰar/yifaǰǰir *v.tr.*	to bomb; to explode
gunbala *n.pl.* ganābil	bomb
iɛtidāʔ *n.pl.* -āt	assault, attack
ishtibāk *n.pl.* -āt	clashes
bi ṭṭabɛ	naturally, certainly, of course
ḥaddad/yiḥaddid *v.tr.*	to limit
gāṭaɛ/yigāṭiɛ *v.tr.*	to boycot
garār alʔiɛdām	death sentence
iɛtirāf *n.*	confession
maɛdūm *pass.part.*	executed; beheaded
mubāshar *adj.*	immediate; direct
atḥākam/yitḥākam *v.pass.*	to be prosecuted; to be brought to trial
laǰnat alɛafw addōliyya	Amnesty International
dāfaɛ/yidāfiɛ + ɛan *v.intr.*	to defend
ḥugūg alʔinsān	human rights
iɛtigāl *n.*	detention
taɛarruḍ *n.*	subjection
taɛzīb *n.*	torture
ḥarraḍ/yiḥarriḍ *v.tr.*	to stir up, agitate; to provoke
ɛiṣyān *n.*	revolt, rebellion
tadmīr *n.*	subversion; destruction
ǰīl alghaḍab alɛarabi	the Generation of Arab Anger
ruɛb *n.*	terror, fear

Notes

1. **rūs**, s. **rās:** *heads.* Cf. MSA **ra?s**, pl. **ru?ūs** (pausal forms). A large number of Hijazi Arabic nouns form their plurals by vowel changes rather than by suffixation. Note the deletion of the glottal stop in the singular form and the compensatory lengthening of the vowel.

2. **muʕẓamhum:** *most of them, the majority of them.* Cf. MSA **muʕðamuhum.** Changing the sound **ð** ---> **ẓ** is very common in Hijazi Arabic. However, one should expect some speakers to use the MSA pronunciation.

3. **ʕugb:** *after.* In this context **ʕugb** functions as a preposition.

4. **mā ʕaʃab Irān:** *It did not please Iran, Iran did not like it.*

5. **ashsharīʕa ssuʕūdiyya:** *the Saudi law.* There are no public trials under Saudi Arabia's judicial system, a system which adhears to Islamic law. In this case the High Judicial Council had endorsed the death sentences and these are carried out in effect by royal decree.

6. **bit/ddāfiʕ:** *it defends.* This is an assimilated form of **tidāfiʕ.** As was mentioned before, the consonant **t** triggered this assimilation.

7. **ddarrabu:** *they were trained.* Cf. MSA **tadarrabū.** See #6 for more information.

Selection Thirty-Two

gatl masʔūl[1] suɛūdi fi bērūt

muḥammad ɛali almarzūgi hu muwaḍḍaf mutɛāgid[2] bi ssafāra ssuɛūdiyya fi lubnān. min waḍīfatu innu yidfaɛ ʔuǰūr annās alli byihtammu bi ṣiyānat assafāra. almamlaka saḥabat kull muwaḍḍafīn assafāra ddiblumāsiyyīn min lubnān mā ɛadāh huwwa. assayyid almarzūgi sākin fi bērūt algharbiyya.

alyōm kān assayyid almarzūgi ɛammāl[3] yidkhul assayyāra ḥaggatu lamma talāt riǰāl musallaḥīn haǰamu ɛalē wu ṭakhkhū bi rrashshāshāt ḥaggōnhum. ashshurṭa gālat annu māt gawām/dughri[4] wu lākin assawwāg assūri ḥaggu anṣāb bi ǰurūḥ basīṭa. ǰamāɛat alǰihād alʔislami alli humma muwālīn li īrān ṣarraḥu annu humma gatalū. humma gālu annu gatl almarzūgi māhu illa akhd tār[5] min assuɛūdiyya li annahum gaṭaɛu rūs sittaɛshar shīɛi bi tuhmat alʔirhāb alli sawwū fi makka lmukarrama.

ǰamāɛat alǰiḥād alʔislāmi baɛatu taṣrīḥ li wikālāt alʔakhbār w gālu fīh annu almarzūgi kān ɛamīl li lmabāḥit assuɛūdiyya. humma haddadu bi annu mumkin yigtulu afrād min alɛēla lmālka minshān yākhdu tārhum min alḥukūma liʔannha ɛadamat sittaɛshar kwēti shīɛi, alli ɛashara mimhum min aṣl īrāni. almamlaka gaṭaɛat rūs hadōla lʔikhwān ashshīɛa liʔannu faǰǰaru ganābil fi mōsim alḥaǰ fi makka lmukarrama. wu fi hāda lhuǰūm sammu alɛēla lmālka "khuddām ashēṭān." ǰamāɛat alǰihād alʔislāmi haddadūhum bi annu ḥayigtulūhum fi ay makān biylāgūhum. ḥatta wa law kānu fi guṣūrhum almuḥaṣṣana.

wizārat alkhāriǰiyya ssuɛūdiyya dānat alʔaɛmāl alʔiǰrāmiyya alli biysawwūha alʔirhābiyyīn alǰubana ḍud abnāʔ almamlaka fi lkhāriǰ. alwizāra ḥarraḍat assulṭāt allubnāniyya ɛala muḥākamat alʔashkhāṣ almasʔūlīn ɛan hādi lʔaɛmāl alhamaǰiyya. wu lāzim tikūn muɛāgabathum ṣārma ǰiddan li aǰil ǰarīmathum ashshanīɛa bi gatl muwāṭin suɛūdi barīʔ.

Vocabulary

mutɛāgid *act.part.pl.* -īn	contract employee
waḍ/ẓīfa *n.pl.* waẓāyif	job, task
mā ɛadāh	except him

ṭakhkh/yiṭukh *v.tr.*	to shoot s.o.
rashshāsh *n.pl.* -āt	machine gun
dughri	immediately, right away
gawām	immediately, right away
anṣāb/yinṣāb *v.pass.*	to be hit; to be stricken; to be injured
ǰurḥ *n.pl.* ǰurūḥ	wound, cut
akhd tār	taking revenge, retaliation
alǰiḥād alʔislāmi	Islamic Jihad
baɛat/yibɛat *v.tr.*	to send
ɛamīl *n.pl.* ɛumala	agent
almabāḥit assuɛūdiyya	Saudi intelligence
haddad/yihaddid *v.tr.*	to threaten
fard *n.pl.* afrād	individual, person
alɛēla lmālka	the royal family
min aṣl īrāni	of Iranian origin
mōsim *n.pl.* mawāsim	season
khuddām ashshēṭān	servants of Satan
gaṣr *n.pl.* guṣūr	palace
muḥaṣṣan *pass.part.*	entrenched; fortified
dān/yidīn *v.tr.*	to condemn; to judge
aɛmāl iǰrāmiyya	criminal acts
ǰabān *adj.pl.* ǰubana	coward
ḥarraḍ/yiḥarriḍ *v.tr.*	to incite, provoke
hamaǰi *adj.*	barbaric, savage, uncivilized
muɛāgaba *n.*	punishment, punishing
ṣārma *adj.*	severe, harsh, stern
shanīɛa *adj.*	horrible, brutal; ugly, disgusting, disgraceful

Notes

1. **masʔūl:** *official.* This pass. part. of the verb **saʔal** is also used as an adjective in Hijazi Arabic as well as in MSA to mean *responsible, accountable.*

2. **muwaḍḍaf mutɛāgid:** *contract employee.* Cf. MSA **muwaððafun mutaɛāqidun.** The first word is the pass. part. of the verb **waððafa**, *to employ,* and the second word is the act. part. of the verb **taɛāqada**, *to contract.*

3. **ɛammāl:** As it was mentioned before, **ɛammāl** is a particle used before the imperfect form of a verb to indicate an ongoing action. MSA does not have a verb form for the progressive tense.

4. **dughri:** *immediately; straight ahead.* This is not an Arabic word. Its cognate is the Turkish word **doğru**, which means *straight, direct.*

5. **tār:** *revenge, retaliation.* Cf. MSA **θaʔr.** Note the common change of **θ** ---> **t**, the deletion of the glottal stop, and the compensatory lengthening of the vowel **a**.

Selection Thirty-Three

kulliyyat almalik fēṣal alǰawwiyya ḥatkharriǰ dafɛa ǰadīda min aṭṭayyārīn

yōm arrubūɛ[1] algādim ḥatiḥtafil kulliyyat almalik fēṣal alǰawwiyya bi takhrīǰ dafɛa min aḍḍubbāṭ aṭṭayyārīn wu lfaniyyīn. ḥayirɛa lḥafla ṣāḥib assumuw almalaki alʔamīr ɛabd arraḥmān bin ɛabd alɛazīz[2] nāʔib wazīr addifāɛ wu ṭṭayarān. ṣāḥib assumuw ḥaysallim ashshahādāt wu rrutab alɛaskariyya wu lǰawāyiz li ṭṭullāb almutkharriǰīn. qāʔid[3] alkulliyya gāl innu hādi ddafɛa fīha ɛadad min almutkharriǰīn min dōlat alʔimārāt alɛarabiyya lmuttaḥida wu min albaḥrēn wu qaṭar wu lǰumhūriyya lɛarabiyya lyamaniyya. hadōl aḍḍubbāṭ taɛallamu wu zākaru[4] maɛ akhwānhum aṭṭalaba ssuɛūdiyyīn. kulliyyat almalik fēṣal alǰawwiyya bitkharriǰ dafɛatēn kull sana. fi lkulliyya ɛindahum niẓām innu baɛd takhrīǰ kull dafɛa, fī masʔūlīn min alkulliyya yisawwu tagyīm shāmil li mustawa kull dōra ɛalashān yiḥassinu mustawa ddafɛāt allāḥga. alɛamīd ṣarraḥ innu hādi ddafɛa bizzāt ḥaggagat mustawa ɛāli ǰiddan fi ttadrībāt alǰawwiyya wu lɛaskariyya wu lʔakkādīmiyya. min ḍimn albarnāmiǰ innu aṭṭalaba lmutkharriǰīn lāzim yiltaḥgu baɛd attakharuǰ bi dōrāt tadrībiyya mutgaddma, w baɛdēn yitwazzaɛu ɛala maǰālāt aṭṭayarān almugātil, wu ṭṭayarān lɛāmūdi w ṭayarān annagl.

atkallam alɛamīd ɛan niḍām addirāsa wu ttadrīb fi lkulliyya. gāl innu barnāmiǰ addirāsa wu ttadrīb ɛindahum hu ḍumn albarnāmiǰ alɛām almukhaṭṭaṭ li kull alkulliyyāt alɛaskariyya. muddat addirāsa fīha talāt sanawāt. alkulliyya bitḥāwil tgūm bi muhimmat tadrīb kull aṭṭalaba illi yitgaddamu laha dākhil niṭāg alkulliyya. kamān alkulliyya tigaddim li ṭṭalaba lmitfawwigīn ǰawāʔiz tashǰīɛiyya. masalan taɛṭi ǰāʔiza li lʔawwal fi lɛulūm alǰawwiyya, wu ǰāʔiza li lʔawwal fi lɛulūm alʔakkādīmiyya, wu ǰāʔiza li lʔawwal fi lɛulūm alɛaskariyya. fī ǰawāyiz tashǰīɛiyya tānya mitl ǰāʔizat alʔawwal fi nnashāṭ attagāfi wu fi nnashāṭ arriyāḍi. ziyāda ɛala ɛulūm aṭṭayarān wu lɛulūm alɛaskariyya tigaddim alkulliyya li ṭṭālib mawād fi ttagāfa lʔislāmiyya wu lɛulūm lʔinsāniyya wu ttadrībāt arriyāḍiyya wu lɛaskariyya ttānya.

Vocabulary

aḥtafal/yiḥtafil *v.intr.*	to celebrate
takhrīǰ *n.*	graduating, graduation
dafɛa *n.pl.* -āt	group; payment
ṭayyār *n.pl.* -īn	pilot

raɛa/yirɛa lḥafla *v.tr.*	to host a party
rutba *n.pl.* rutab	(military) rank; grade, level
ǰāʔi/yza *n.pl.* ǰawāʔiz	award
zākar/yizākir *v.tr.*	to study
tagyīm s͟hāmil	comprehensive evaluation
ḥassan/yiḥassin *v.tr.*	to improve
lāḥga *adj.*	following
ɛamīd *n.*	brigadier; dean (of a college)
ḥaggag/yiḥaggig *v.tr.*	to achieve, accomplish
ɛāli *adj.*	high
ḍumn	within, inside of, among
tadrīb *n.*	training
mutgaddim *adj.*	advanced
atwazzaɛ/yitwazzaɛ + ɛala *v.pass.*	to be distributed; to be assigned
ṭayarān mugātil	combat aviation
ṭayaran ɛāmūdi	helicopter aviation
ṭayarān nagl	commercial aviation, cargo aviation
niṭāg *n.*	confines, boundary; range, extent, scope, domain
mitfawwig *act.part.pl.* -īn	outstanding, successful; high achiever
tas͟hǰīɛiyya *adj.*	encouraging, incentive
nas͟hāṭ tagāfi	educational activity, cultural activity
nas͟hāṭ riyāḍi	athletic activity
ɛulūm insāniyya	the humanities

Notes

1. **arrubūɛ:** *Wednesday.* Cf. MSA **alʔarbiɛāʔ**. The word **rubūɛ**, pl. of **rabɛ**, in MSA means *home, quarters; region, territory,* but it never has the above meaning.

2. **ɛabd arraḥmān bin ɛabdalɛazīz:** It is an MSA rule to delete the **alif** from the word **ibn**, *son* and add a **kasra i** after the consonant **b** when it falls between two proper nouns. Hijazi Arabic often applies this rule. Note that the father's name takes the place of the family name.

3. **qāʔid:** *commander.* Normally this word is pronounced **gāyid**, but this is a military rank which most Saudis pronounce as it is in MSA.

4. **zākaru:** *they studied.* Cf. MSA **ðākaru.** This MSA verb form means *to call s.th. to s.o.'s mind, have a talk with,* e.g., **ðākarahu fī lʔamri**, *he talked with him about the matter.* Note that this colloquial usage has become accepted in MSA in some Arabic countries, e.g., Egypt.

Selection Thirty-Four

sālfa min sawālif ǰaddi

lamman kunna ɛawāyil ṣughār, kān ǰaddi raḥamahu llāh[1] yiǰmaɛna kull lēla wu yigɛud yisōlifna ɛan ayyām shabābu. daḥḥīn abghākum tiǰlisu ɛalashān tismaɛu sālfa min sawālif ǰaddi.

marra kunt rāǰiɛ min assūg. antu khābrīn annu lḥarīm ɛindana mā yirūḥu yitgaḍḍu la ḥālhum[2]. fa ana kunt ǰāy taɛbān marra liʔanni kunt ḥāmil almagāḍi ḥaggati. wa ana dakhil albēt samiɛt ɛwāli yiṣarrikhu bi ṣōṭ ɛāli ǰiddan. ḥaṭṭēt alḥawāyiǰ ḥaggati guddām albāb wu rakaḍt ila lǰinēna ɛashān ashūf ēsh illi ṣār. shuft ibni aḥmmad yiṣrakh wu ygūl, "fī tuɛbān/ḥannash kabīr! ɛaǰǰil ugtulu."

ana kunt misbil[3] yaɛni mū ḥāmil ay shay. dakhalt albēt wu ǰibt alkhanǰar ḥaggi wu ḥamalt ɛaṣāya kabīra wu raǰaɛt li lǰinēna. bi hāda lwagt kān alḥanash ṣār garīb min alǰadur ḥag alǰinēna. ṭallaɛt fīh[4] kida abgha aḍrubu bi lɛaṣāya, wa illa wagaf ɛala ḥēlu[5] kaʔannu yibgha yigātilni. ḍarabtu ɛala rāsu, wu lākinnu harab wu khash bi lǰadur. ana zaɛalt lamma dakhal fi lǰadur[6] liʔannani khishīt yinfaǰɛu lʔawlād marra tānya. bagēt mintaẓir ɛashān ashūf iza ḥayiṭlaɛ min alǰadur.

baɛd shwayya maddēt naẓari ɛala lǰamb attāni min alǰadur wu illa hu yimud rāsu wu lisānu yamīn wu yasār zay kida, kaʔannu yiḍḥak ɛalay. ana saḥbt alkhanǰar ḥaggi wu gharraztu fi rāsu bi guwwa. ṣarāḥa galbi kān yidug bisurɛa lannani kunt khāyif mā aṣību. lamman ɛaraft anni tamakkant minnu ṣirt ufruklu rāsu bi guwwa ɛala ḥaǰar kabīr. baɛd shwayya dalla lisānu. wagtaha ɛaraft annu māt. saḥabt alkhanǰar ḥaggi minnu[7] wu gashaɛt kam ḥaǰar min alǰadur wu saḥabtu wu ǰarrētu fi lʔarḍ. ḥaṭṭētu ɛala ǰamb addarb wu nādēt li lɛiyāl minshān yiǰu yitfarraǰu ɛalē. ṣāru lʔawlād yigayyisū, yishūfu kam ṭūlu kida. katīr min annās kharaɛu lamman shāfū wu ḍallu mudda ṭawīla khāyfīn yimurru min hādīk assikka.

Vocabulary

sālfa *n.pl.* sawālif	story, past event
sōlaf/yisōlif *v.tr.*	to chat
khābir *act.part.* -īn	aware, knowing
laḥālhum	by themselves
ṣarrakh/yiṣarrikh *v.intr.*	to scream

ǰinēna *n.pl.* ǰanāyin	garden; front yard, back yard
tuɛbān *n.pl.* taɛābīn	snake
ḥanash *n.pl.* aḥnāsh	snake
ɛaǰǰal/yiɛaǰǰil *v.intr.*	to hurry, speed, hasten, expedite
misbil *adj.*	unarmed
khanǰar *n.pl.* khanāǰir	dagger
ɛaṣāya *n.pl.* -āt, ɛuṣiy	stick; staff; cane; baton
ǰadur *n.pl.* ǰudrān	wall
khasha/yikhsha *v.intr.*	to fear, be afraid
naẓar *n.*	eyesight
mad/yimi/ud naẓaru *v.tr.*	to gaze, look; to glance at
yamīn	right side; right hand
yasār	left side, left hand
ḍaḥak/yiḍḥak + ɛala *v.intr.*	to laugh at ; make a fool of, make fun of
gharraz/yigharriz *v.tr.*	to prick; to stab; to insert
farak/yifruk *v.tr.*	to rub
dalla/yidalli *v.tr.*	to let fall down, drop
gashaɛ/yigshaɛ *v.tr.*	to lift; to remove
ǰarr/yiǰurr *v.tr.*	to drag; to pull
kharaɛ/yikhraɛ *v.tr.*	to be startled, be scared

Notes

1. **raḥamahu llāh:** *May God have mercy on him.* This expression is borrowed from MSA. It is very common in most Arabic dialects. Most people find it offensive if such an expression is not said after mentioning a deceased person. The expressions **almarḥūm**, **raḥmatu llāh ɛalē**, and **allāh yirḥamu** are equally common.

2. **laḥālhum:** *by themselves.* MSA does not use this construction. It uses rather **bi anfusihinna** in this case.

3. **misbil:** *without a dagger, unarmed.* The MSA meaning of this word is *something hung down/dropped down.* Note the figurative meaning of the Hijazi Arabic usage. One's **tōb** drops straight down unless the dagger is on the waist.

4. **ṭallaɛt fīh:** *I looked at it.* The verb **ṭalaɛa**, *to ascend, rise, come up* is the MSA source of this form. The MSA form **ṭallaɛa**, *to take something up,* always takes a direct object. It never collocates with the preposition fi as in Hijazi Arabic. **naḏartu ilayhi** is the corresponding expression in MSA.

5. **wagaf ɛala ḥēlu:** *It stood up high.* This expression is borrowed from MSA **waqafa ɛala ḥaylihi.**

6. **ǰadur:** *wall.* Cf. MSA **ǰadr** (pausal form). Note the epenthesis (inserting an extra sound) before the final sound. This phenomenon is quite common in Arabic dialects.

7. **minnu:** *from him.* Cf. MSA **minhu**. Note the gemination of **n** caused by the deletion of the **h**.

Selection Thirty-Five

iftitāḥ maḥaṭṭa li taḥliyat almūya[1] fi lbarak

zay ma kullukum tiɛrifu annu assuɛūdiyya muɛḍamha ṣaḥra, arāḍi gāḥla mā fīha anhur wu lā yanābiɛ katīra. ṣaḥīḥ annu fī wāḥāt wu lākin mū bi katra. li hāda ssabab kānu lbaduw yitnaggalu min makān li makān ɛashān ylāgu mūya. halḥīn taghayyarat alʔaḥwāl wu ṣār ɛindana mūya kāfya. fī maḥaṭṭāt li taḥliyat almūya fi muɛḍam almanāṭig fi lmamlaka, wu lissāthum[2] byiftaḥu maḥaṭṭāt ǰadīda.

ams aftataḥ ṣāḥib assumuw almalaki, alʔamīr māǰid bin ɛabdu lɛazīz, amīr mamṭagat makka lmukarrama almarḥala lʔūla min mashrūɛ maḥaṭṭaṭ taḥliyat almūya lmālḥa fi manṭagat albarak. tibni hādi lmaḥaṭṭa lmuʔassasa lɛāmma li taḥliyat almūya ɛala aḥdas ṭirāz fanni. aṭṭāga lʔintāǰiyya ḥaggat hāda lmashrūɛ sitta alf ǰalun[3] min almūya lḥulwa[4] yōmiyyan.

almashrūɛ fīh gismēn. kull gism fīh minǰar raʔīsi minshān yigaṭṭir almūya, wu ghallāya li intāǰ albukhār allāzim li taskhīn almūya. wu lgism attāni fīh muwallidāt alkahraba ɛashān timashshi lmaḍakhkhāt. wu kamān fī gism li lmukhtabar ɛashān yiḥallilu fīh almawād alkīmāwiyya.

ǰamb hāda lmashrūɛ fī maḥaṭṭat ḍakh minshān tawṣīl almūya li khazzān kabīr wu baɛdēn tawzīɛa[5] ɛala lbuyūt bi wāṣṭat shabaka khāṣṣa min albēbāt[6]. fī mabna khuṣūṣi li lʔidāra wu ǰambu fī masǰid, wu mustawdaɛāt, wu mawāgif li ssayyārāt, wu maṭɛam, wu markaz iǰtimāɛi fīh kull attashīlāt li nnashaṭāṭ arriyāḍiyya wu ttagāfiyya. wu banu muǰammaɛ sakani yitkawwan min sitt filal[7] muǰahhaza bi kull alkhadamāt allāzma.

ṣāḥib assumuw almalaki lʔamīr māǰid bin ɛabdu lɛazīz gāl kilma bi hādi lmunāsaba. hu madaḥ bi khiṭābu lǰuhūd alkabīra illi tubzal bi giyādat ǰalālat almalik fahd almuɛaẓẓam minshān taʔmīn almūya li kull almanāṭig wu lgura.

maɛāli wazīr azzirāɛa wu raʔīs maǰlis almuʔassasa, waḍḍaḥ addōr alkabīr illi tilɛabu ddōla bi giyādat ǰalālat almalik almufadda, w addōr illi tilɛabu wizārat azzirāɛa wa lmiyāh, wu lmuʔassasa lɛāmma li taḥliyat almūya lmālḥa minshān taʔmīn almūya ḥag ashshurb illi tuɛtabar min aham ɛanāṣir alḥayāt.

ahl manṭagat albarak sawwu ḥafla kabīra ashtarak fīha kull almuwāṭnīn. kull annās kānu farḥānīn bi ziyārat sumuw alʔamīr māǰid li lmanṭaga. hu ǰalas maɛ annās w aṭṭalaɛ ɛala iḥtiyāǰāthum wu mutaṭallibāt almanṭiga wu lgura ḥawalēnha. amīr almanṭaga raḥḥab bi kull almadɛwwīn wu gāl, "inshālla ḥatkūn ziyārat sumuw alʔamīr māǰid bi izn allāh khēr wu baraka ɛala lmanṭaga."

Vocabulary

taḥliya *n.*	desalination; sweetening
gāḥla *adj.*	arid, dry
yanbūɛ *n.pl.* yanābīɛ	spring, well, source
wāḥa *n.pl.* -āt	oasis
marḥala *n.pl.* marāḥil	phase, stage
mālḥa *adj.*	salty
almuʔassasa lɛāmma li taḥliyat almūya	the Saline Water Conversion Corporation
aḥdas *adj.*	most modern
ṭirāz *n.*	type, model, sort; fashion, style
ṭāga intāǰiyya	productive capacity, power of generating
mūya ḥulwa	fresh water
minǰar *n.pl.* manāǰir	apparatus for water distilation
gaṭṭar/yigaṭṭir *v.tr.*	to distill
ghallāya *n.pl.* -āt	an apparatus for boiling water, boiler
bukhār n.coll.	vapor
muwallid *n.pl.* -āt	generator
maḍakhkha *n.pl.* -āt	pump
mukhtabar *n.pl.* -āt	laboratory
ḥallal/yiḥallil *v.tr.*	to analyze
ḍakh *v.n.*	pumping
khazzān *n.pl.* -āt	reservoir
shabaka *n.pl.* -āt	net; network
bēb *n.pl.* -āt	pipe
mustawdaɛ *n.pl.* -āt	warehouse, storehouse
muǰammaɛ sakani	housing complex
kilma *n.*	speech; word
madaḥ/yimdaḥ *v.tr.*	to praise s.o.
waḍḍaḥ/yiwaḍḍiḥ *v.tr.*	to clarify, make clear, explain
aṭṭalaɛ/yiṭṭaliɛ + ɛala *v.intr.*	to be informed of, learn about
raḥḥab/yiraḥḥib + bi *v.intr.*	to welcome

Notes

1. **taḥliyat (almūya):** *desalination of water lit., sweetening of water.* This term has come into MSA and the Hijazi dialect as a consequence of advanced technology. The word **mūya** does not occur in MSA. **māʔ**, pl. **miyāh, amwāh** is the corresponding word.

2. **lissāthum:** *they still.* This word is used before the impf. form of the verb to designate an ongoing action. The word **lissaɛ** is the source of this expression. Note the substitution of **ɛ** for **t** and the lengthening of **a** before the pronominal suffix.

3. **Jala/un:** *gallon.* This is an English loanword.

4. **mūya ḥulwa:** *fresh water.* This is a pure Hijazi Arabic expression. MSA uses **māʔun ɛaðbun**, pl. **miyahun ɛaðbatun.**

5. **tawzīɛa:** *its distribution.* Often the pronominal suffix for the third person singular feminine **-ha** is replaced by a short **a** when suffixed to nouns, e.g., **bēta**, *her house* instead of **bētha.** This is a common phenomenon in Hijazi Arabic.

6. **bēbāt:** *pipes.* Hijazi Arabic borrowed this English word and assigned to it a regular plural.

7. **filal:** *villas.* This is another English loanword which occurs here with a broken plural.

Selection Thirty-Six

almuʔtamar attāni li buḥūt alwigāya min alǰarāyim

alyōm aftataḥu lmuʔtamar addōli[1] ttāni ḥag alwigāya min alǰarāyim, fi lmarkaz arraʔīsi li ddirāsāt alʔamniyya fi rriyāḍ. almasʔūlīn fi marākiz albuḥūt alɛarabiyya badaʔu[2] lʔiǰtimāɛ attaḥḍīri ttāni ḥaggahum. wāḥad daktōr gāl kilma, akkad fīha ɛan ahammiyyat attaɛāwun bēn mudara marākiz albuḥūt fi dduwal alɛarabiyya. hāda ddaktōr ɛabbar ɛan āmālu lamma gāl, "inshālla hada lʔiǰtimāɛ hayidɛam alli badāh[2] alʔiǰtimāɛ alʔawwal in kān min tansīg aw min alʔistifāda min imkāniyyāt marākiz albuḥūt alɛarabiyya li maṣlaḥat hadaf wāḥad alli kullana nisɛālu[3], khidmat almuǰtamaɛ alɛarabi." wu gāl kamān innu ɛamaliyyāt attaḥḍīr mustamirra, wu innu kull adduwal alɛarabiyya lāzim yitbādalu khibrāthum fi hāda lmaǰāl.

raʔīs almarkaz bayyan ahammiyyat hāda lmuʔtamar. hu akkad annu lbaḥt alɛilmi lu ahammiyya kabīra, ɛala asās annu lmawāḍīɛ almaṭrūḥa ɛala hada lmuʔtamar ḥatkūn bi mafhūmiyya ɛarabiyya mushtaraka. hādi lmawāḍīɛ nafsaha ḥaynāgishūha[4] fi almuʔtamar assābiɛ li lʔumam almuttaḥida minshān manɛ alǰarāyim wu muɛāmalat almudnibīn. hāda lmuʔtamar raḥyinɛagid[5] fi madīnat milānu fi hāda ṣṣēf.

alwufūd almushtarkīn fi hada lmuʔtamar tishmil mumattilīn ɛan wizārāt addākhiliyya wu lɛadl, wu shshuʔūn alʔiǰtimāɛiyya fi dduwal alɛarabiyya bi lʔiḍāfa li lmunaḍḍamāt wu lhēʔāt addawliyya, wu kamān aǰa wufūd min marākiz albuḥūt alɛarabiyya wu ddawdliyya.

alḥagīga, anni agdir agūl innu blādna kānat khālya min alǰarāyim. kunna nisayyib kull shay bidūn ma ngaffil ɛalē. mā kunna nkhāf innu ḥad yisrig shay. wu lākin daḥḥīn kitru lʔaghrāb ɛindana, wu kitrat assirgāt wu lǰarāyim. allāh yākhud bi yad ḥukūmatna rrashīda ɛashān tiḥmīna wu tiḥmi awlādana min kull shar.

Vocabulary

baḥt *n.pl.* buḥūt	research, study
wigāya *n.*	prevention
ǰarīma *n.pl.* ǰarāyim	crime, murder
dirāsa *n.pl.* -āt, amniyya	security studies

taḥḍīri *adj.*	preparatory
kilma *n.*	speech; word
akkad/yiʔakkid *v.tr.*	to assure, verify, affirm
taʿāwun *n.*	cooperation
ʿabbar/yiʿabbir + ʿan *v.intr.*	to express
amal *n.pl.* āmāl	hope
daʿam/yidʿam *v.tr.*	to support
tansīg *v.n.*	arranging, arrangement; preparation
istifāda *n.pl.* -āt	profiting, benefiting, making use of
imkāniyya *n.pl.* -āt	potential, ability, capacity; possibility
saʿa/yisʿa + li *v.intr.*	to seek, strive, pursue
maṭrūḥa *pass.part.*	presented, broached or raised (of a question/problem)
mafhūmiyya *n.pl.* -āt	understanding; mentality
bi lʔiḍāfa	in addition to, besides; furthermore
hēʔa *n.pl.* -āt	organization; association; appearance
k͟hālya *adj.*	empty; free (from)
sarag/yisrig *v.tr.*	to steal
sirga *n.pl.* -āt	theft
yāk͟hud bi yad	to stand by s.o.
ras͟hīda *adj.*	rightly guided; enlightened; mature
ḥama/yiḥmi *v.tr.*	to protect, keep

Notes

1. **dōli:** *international.* Cf. MSA **dawli**. Very often the MSA **aw** is changed to **ō** in Hijazi Arabic but the MSA pronunciation is also used.

2. **badāh:** *He started it.* Hijazi Arabic uses the MSA form **badaʔ** (pausal form). However, if the verb has an object pronominal suffix, then the glottal stop is deleted and the final vowel is lengthened, as is the case here.

3. **nisʿālu:** *We strive for it.* A preposition with a pronominal suffix is never added to the verb in MSA, although it is quite common in most Arabic dialects. Note the lengthening of the vowel a before the preposition plus pronominal suffix.

4. **yināgis͟hūha:** *They discuss it.* Cf. MSA **yunāqis͟hūnaha** with the changing of the preformative vowel **u** ---> **i**, the **q** ---> **g**, and the deletion of the suffix **-na**, and the shortening of the final vowel. These changes are very common in Hijazi Arabic.

5. **raḥyinʿagid:** *It will be held.* The prefix **raḥ-** is used with the imperfect of the verb to form the future. Hijazi Arabic borrowed this construction from Egyptian Arabic.

Selection Thirty-Seven

iɛlān munāfasa

almuʔassasa lɛāmma li ttaʔmīnāt alʔiǰtimāɛiyya tirīd tanafīz mashrūɛ mabna raʔīsi laha fi lmanṭaga lwusṭa[1] fi rriyāḍ ḥasab hadōla shshurūṭ:

1. alʔarḍ alli ḥayinbana ɛalēha hāda lmashrūɛ mawǰūda ɛala shāriɛ garīb min almustashfa lɛaskari. almabna ḥaykūn sitt adwār[2], wu dōrēn gabw, wu fīh alkhadamāt almikānīkiyya wu lkahrabāʔiyya wu niẓām takyīf markazi, wu lāzim yikūnfī maṣāɛid wu mawāgif ḥaggat assayyārāt, wu taswiyat alʔarḍ ḥawalēn[3] almabna. masāḥat alʔarḍ ḥaggat hāda lmashrūɛ ḥawāli itnēn wu talatīn alf mitr murabbaɛ.

2. bima annu[4] lmashrūɛ ḥayishmil aɛmāl miɛmāriyya wu mikānīkiyya wu kahrabāʔiyya alli btiṭṭallab[5] mustawa ɛāli min attanfīz, almuʔassasa ḥaṭṭat hadōla shshurūṭ ɛala shsharikāt alli titgaddam li dukhūl hādi lmunāfasa:

   A. lāzim tigaddim bayān bi aɛmālha ssābga khilāl attalāt sinīn almāḍya bi sharṭ innu tkūn naffazat mashārīɛ li mabāni ḥaggōn makātib shabīha bi lmashrūɛ ḥaggana. lāzim tigaddim mustanadāt muṣaddaga minshān tisabbit tanfīz hadōl alʔaɛmāl bi ṣūra mumtāza.

   B. lāzim tigaddim bayān ɛan waḍɛaha lmāli ḥāliyyan bi sharṭ innu yishmil almīzāniyya ssanawiyya ḥaggat ashsharika li ssinīn attalāta lmāḍya. lāzim tizkur ḥajm aɛmālha ssanawi wu rāsmālha[6] wu asāmi lbunūk alli btitɛāmal maɛha.

   C. lāzim tigaddim wasīga ɛan ǰihāzha lʔidāri wu lfanni, w bayān ɛan almaɛaddāt wu lʔaǰhiza alli btimlukha.

   D. lāzim tigaddim naskha ɛan assiǰil attiǰāri wu lʔintisābi li lghurfa ttiǰāriyya, wu shihāda min maṣlaḥat azzakā wu ddakhl, wu shihāda min attʔamīnāt alʔiǰtimāɛiyya minshān tibayyin tasdīd mustaḥiggātha.

3. bi nnisba li shsharikāt assuɛūdiyya lāzim yigaddimu ziyāda ɛala lʔashya illi zakarnāha, shihādat taṣnīf min wizārat alʔashghāl alɛāmma wu lʔiskān min addaraja lʔawwala aw attānya fi maǰāl almabāni. amma shsharikāt alʔaǰnabiyya lāzim tigaddim shahādat taṣnīf lā tgill ɛan addaraja rrābɛa fi maǰāl almabāni.

4. mā ḥatinbāɛ wasāyig almunāfasa illa li shsharikāt almuʔahhala ḥasab ashshurūṭ almazkūra min gabl.

5. mumkin alḥuṣūl ɛala ṭalabāt attaʔhīl min almuʔassasa lɛāmma li ttaʔmīnāt alʔiǰtimāɛiyya bi rriyāḍ, shāriɛ almaṭār, idārat almashārīɛ.

6. lāzim titɛabba kull aṭṭalabāt almazkūra wu titgaddam maɛ kull almustanadāt almaṭlūba li lmuʔassasa gabl assāɛa itnaɛsh aḍḍuhr yōm alʔitnēn.

7. ashsharikāt almuʔahhala mumkin tiḥṣal ɛala wasāyig almunāfasa li hāda lmashrūɛ min almuʔassasa bi mablagh khamsa wu talatīn alf riyāl.

8. ākhir mōɛad li bēɛ alwasāyig hu assāɛa itnaɛsh aḍḍuhr yōm attalūt.

9. titgaddam alɛurūḍ fī mughallafāt makhtūma li lmuʔassasa mū min baɛd ḍuhr yōm arrubūɛ. ḥayinrafaḍ kull ɛarḍ ḥayiǰi baɛd attārīkh almuḥaddad li tagdīm alɛurūḍ.

Vocabulary

iɛlān *n.pl.* -āt	announcement, advertisement
munāfasa *n.pl.* -āt	competition; contest, match; (here) contract, bids, bidding
gabw *n.*	basement; vault
takyīf markazi	central air-conditioning
maṣɛad *n.pl.* maṣāɛid	elevator
taswiyat alʔarḍ	(here) landscaping
miɛmāri *adj.*	architectural
bayān *n.pl.* -āt	statement
shabīha *adj.*	similar
mustanad *n.pl.* -āt	document
muṣaddaga *adj.*	notarized
sabbat/yisabbit *v.tr.*	to verify, prove
waḍɛha almāli	its financial statement
mīzāniyya *n.pl.* -āt	budget
ḥaǰm *n.pl.* aḥǰām	volume
rāsmāl *n.*	(financial) capital
maɛaddāt *n.*	equipment, machinery
naskha *n.pl.* nusakh	copy
siǰil tiǰāri	commercial register, business credentials
ghurfa tiǰāriyya	chamber of commerce
maṣalḥat azzakā wu ddakhl	religious income tax office
tasdīd almustaḥiggāt	no money owed, payment of claims
taṣnīf *n.*	classification
wasīga *n.pl.* wasāyig	document
muʔahhal *adj.*	qualified

mu<u>gh</u>allaf *n.pl.* -āt	envelope
ɛarḍ *n.pl.* ɛurūḍ	offer, proposal
anrafaḍ/yinrafaḍ *v.pass.*	to be rejected, refused

Notes

1. **wuṣṭa:** *central, middle.* This MSA word is not used very often in Hijazi Arabic, but its masculine form **waṣaṭ** is very common. Note the change of **s** ---> **ṣ** via regressive assimilation.

2. **dōr**, pl. **adwār**: *floor, story; role; turn.* Hijazi Arabic uses the MSA word **dawru** in all of its different meanings. Note the common Hijazi Arabic change of **aw** ---> **ō** and the loss of the final vowel.

3. **ḥawalēn:** *around.* Cf. MSA **ḥawla.** Adding the **-ēn** suffix and putting the final vowel **a** before l is a Hijazi Arabic characteristic.

4. **bima annu:** *since, inasmuch as.* This construction is borrowed from MSA.

5. **btiṭṭallab:** *requires.* Cf. MSA **tataṭallabu** (fully vocalized). The prefix **b-** is prefixed to the imperfect verb to denote a habitual action. Note the change of the preformative vowel **a** ---> i, and the deletion of the second vowel which contributed to the change of **t** ---> **ṭ** via regressive assimilation.

6. **rāsmālha:** *its capital.* Cf. MSA **ra?sa māliha.** The deletion of the glottal stop along with the compensatory lengthening of the vowel **a** is a common phenomenon in Hijazi Arabic.

Selection Thirty-Eight

mushkilat al?alghām fi lbaḥr al?aḥmar

bīgūlu[1] lana nnās alkubār annu fi l?awwalāt[2] kānu lgabāyil byithārabu[3] maɛ baɛḍhum. lamma tṣīr almaɛārik bēnhum kān yiṭīḥ magātīl. aḥyān kān fi nās yiṣīr fīhum taṣwīb[4], zay kusūr wa ma ashbah zālik. lamma kān yiṣīr ishtibāk bēn gabīlatēn, tiǰi gabīla, zay ma ngūl, yifukku shshar[5], yaɛni yisawwu firāɛ bēn algabīlatēn.

ɛagib ma tgaddamat albilād, wu traggat annās, mā ɛād ɛindana hādi lmashākil. lākin alḥaḍāra wu ttagaddum ǰābu lana mashākil min nōɛ tāni. fa masalan khallīna halḥīn nitkallam ɛan mushkilat al?alghām fi lbaḥr al?aḥmar. fī nās kutār maḥsūdīn minnana, li?ann allāh subḥānhu wa taɛāla aɛṭāna khērāt katīra. fa bitshūfahum yibghu yisabbibu lana mashākil. ḥasab ma bnismaɛ fi l?akhbār byiẓhar annu hadōl annās humma aɛdā?ana, wu mā bīrīdu khērana abadan. wāḥda min hādi l?iɛtidā?āt hi zarɛ al?aghām fi lbaḥr al?aḥmar, ɛashān yishillu ḥarakat almilāḥa wu yiḍaɛɛifu al?igtiṣād assuɛūdi, li?annu ḥatgill mas?alat al?istirād wu ttawrīd fi almanṭaga. zay ams masalan, safīnat shaḥn bōlandiyya aṣṭadamat bi lughm ɛind madkhal albaḥr al?aḥmar. hādi ssafīna ḍaḥiyya ǰadīda li ɛamaliyyāt al?alghām almitnaggla fi lbaḥr al?aḥmar wu khalīǰ assuwēs. hādi ssafīna tiblugh ḥumulatha khamsa alf wu sabɛ miyyat ṭan, wu kānat tibaḥḥir fi mīna ǰidda lamma anfaǰar fīha allughm.

alwilāyāt almuttaḥida wu faransa wu bariṭānya bada?u ɛamaliyāt almasḥ albaḥriyya. humma byitwaggaɛu wuṣūl kāsiḥāt al?alghām wu ṭayyārāt halikōbtar kāsḥa li l?alghām wu khubara min hadōla lbilād ila lmanṭaga baɛd shi yōmēn. min almuḥtamal innu lyūnān tibɛat kāsiḥāt al?alghām ḥaggōnha li lmanṭaga ɛashān tshārik fi ḥal hadi lmushkila. aẓun annu amrīka ṭalabat min alḥukūma lyūnāniyya minshān tisāhim fi hādi lɛamaliyyāt. kull hādi l?istiɛdādāt min adduwal algharbiyya bitbayyin innu ḥurriyyat almilāḥa muhimma ǰiddan fi hadīk almanṭaga.

Vocabulary

lughm *n.pl.* alghām	mine, explosive device
awwalāt	the past
thārab/yithārab + maɛ *v.intr.*	to fight with (s.o.)
maɛraka *n.pl.* maɛārik	battle

gatīl *n.pl.* magātīl	casualty
taṣwīb *n.*	injury
kusr *n.pl.* kusūr	fracture (of a bone), break
ishtibāk *n.pl.* -āt	clash, fight
zay ma ngūl	as we might say
firāɛ *n.*	reconciliation
nōɛ *n.pl.* anwāɛ	kind; sort, type
maḥsūd *adj.pl.* -īn	envious
sabbab/yisabbib *v.tr.*	to cause
khabar *n.pl.* akhbār	news
ẓahar/yiẓhar annu	it seems
ɛaduw *n.*	enemy
iɛtidāʔ *n.pl.* -āt	aggression
shal/yishil *v.tr.*	to paralyze
istirād *n.*	import
tawrīd *n.*	export
safīnat shaḥn	cargo ship
aṣṭadamat/tiṣṭadim + bi *v.intr.*	to collide with; to strike
ḍaḥiyya *n.pl.* ḍaḥāya	victim; blood sacrifice
mitnaggla *adj.*	mobile; portable
balagh/yiblugh *v.tr.*	to amount to
ḥumūla *n.pl.* -āt	load capacity
baḥḥar/yibaḥḥir *v.intr.*	to sail
anfaǰar/yinfaǰir *v.tr.*	to explode
masḥ *n.*	wiping, wiping off; *here* [mine] sweeping
atwaggaɛ/yitwaggaɛ *v.tr.*	to expect
kāsiḥāt alʔalghām	mine sweepers
khabīr *n.pl.* khubara	expert
sāham/yisāhim + fi *v.intr.*	to participate in, take part in; to share
istiɛdād *n.pl.* -āt	willingness
ḥurriyyat almilāḥa	freedom of navigation/sailing

Notes

1. **bīgūlu:** *they say/tell.* Note the deletion of the tense marker **y** and the compensatory lengthening of the preformative vowel.

2. **awwalāt:** *(in the) past.* Cf. MSA **awāʔil** s. **awwal.** This regular feminine plural form is typical of Hijazi Arabic.

3. **byitḩārabu:** *they fight.* This verb form expressing the reciprocal voice is normally formed by inserting a **t** between the tense-person marker and the stem of a perfect verb which has the pattern $C_1\bar{a}C_2aC_3$, e.g., **ḩārab, atḩārab**, impf. **yitḩārab**.

4. **taşwīb:** *injury.* This is an MSA word meaning *aiming, pointing; correction.* Note that Hijazi Arabic may borrow words from MSA but may alter their meanings.

5. **yifukku <u>shsh</u>ar:** *They break up the fight.* This expression is quite common in Hijazi Arabic as well as other Arabic dialects. Very often the peace maker pays for whatever the dispute is all about.

Selection Thirty-Nine

musāɛadāt assuɛūdiyya li dduwal annāmya

assuɛūdiyya muɛtabara daḥḥīn min akbar[1] almutbarriɛīn arraʔīsiyyīn li lmusāɛadāt addōliyya li dduwal annāmya. ḥukūmatna ssakhiyya btaɛti ḥawāli arbaɛa aw khamsa bi lmiyya min muntaǰātha ddākhiliyya li musāɛadāt attanmiya. ashshay almusharrif hu annu ḥukūmatna bitshārik alʔākharīn bi lkhērāt illi allāh anɛam fīha ɛalēna[2].

muʔassasat almusāɛadāt assuɛūdiyya ḥaggat attanmiya taʔassasat sanat alf wu tisɛ miyya wu arbaɛa wu sabɛīn. fi hadāk alwagt[3] kān raṣīd almuʔassasa balyōnēn wu nuṣ[4] dulār. binshūf annu hāda rraṣīd ṣār yizīd shwayya shwayya/ bishwesh[5]. fi sanat wāḥid wu tamānīn ṣār sabɛa balyōn dulār. min khilāl hādi lmuʔassasa btitwazzaɛ kull almusāɛadāt assuɛūdiyya. mū lāzim ninsa annu ttabarruɛāt assuɛūdiyya hi ǰuzʔ raʔīsi min almusāɛadāt addōliyya. ṭāl ɛumrak bitshūf annu bilādna ɛammāl bitsāhim aktar wu aktar maɛ muʔassasāt tānya zay albank addawly wu lmuʔassasa lʔamrīkiyya li ttanmiya ddōliyya wu lmuʔassasa lkuwētiyya wu ghērhum fi tamwīl mashārīɛ katīra.

ṣar maǰmūɛ almusāɛadāt assuɛūdiyya li ḥatta sanat sabɛa wu tamānīn sitta balyōn dūlār. hāda lmablagh twazzaɛ ɛala mitēn wu sitta wu sabɛīn mashrūɛ fi wāḥid wu sittīn dōla. min siyāsat almuʔassasa ssuɛūdiyya innu taɛti alʔafḍaliyya li dduwal alli fīha ddakhl alfardi galīl marra. muɛẓam almusāɛadāt assuɛūdiyya bitrūḥ li afrīqya. khāṣṣa liʔann katīr min adduwal alʔafrīqiyya aǰālhum kawāris katīra zay alǰafāf wu lmaǰāɛāt wu lfayaḍānāt wu ghēru.

almusāɛdāt bititwazzaɛ ɛala mashārīɛ mukhtalfa. gism kabīr minha byinṣaraf ɛala mashārīɛ handasiyya mitl shag aṭṭurgāt wu ssikak alḥadīdiyya wu lmawāniʔ albaḥriyya wu lmaṭārat wu lkahraba wu lmuwāṣalāt. wu gism byinṣaraf ɛala masharīɛ iǰtimāɛiyya zay alʔiskān wu taʔmīn almūya wu zzirāɛa wu ttaɛlīm wu masharīɛ tānya.

ɛādatan almusāɛadāt btitwazzaɛ bi ṭurug mikhtalfa. fī musāɛadāt btindafaɛ mubāsharatan li lḥukūmāt attānya min khilāl wizārāt almāliyya wu lkhāriǰiyya. alḥukūma ssuɛūdiyya bitgaddim musāɛadāt tānya bi wāṣṭat wikālāt tābɛa li lʔumam almuttaḥida wu li lɛālam alʔislāmi. kamān fī musāɛadāt li lḥālāt aṭṭārʔa. masalan tibɛat alḥukūma musāɛadāt ghizāʔiyya zay ma tgūl gamḥ wu tamr, wu tibɛat kamān maɛaddāt li dduwal illi byiǰīha kawāris ṭabīɛiyya zay fayaḍānāt wu ma ashbah zālik. ḥukūmatna arsalat biɛsāt ṭubbiyya muǰahhaza bi kull almaɛaddāt wu lḥāǰāt allāzam minshān yisāɛidu ikhwānana alyamaniyyīn, mankūbīn alhazza lʔarḍiyya. fa anna biftakhir bi bilādi wu bi ḥukūmati wu inshālla allāh ḥayzīd khērātu ɛalēna.

Vocabulary

dōla nāmya	developing country
muɛtabara *adj.*	considered
mutabarriɛ *act.part.pl.* -īn	contributor, donor; volunteer
sakhi *adj.*	generous
muʔassasat almusāɛadāt assuɛūdiyya ḥaggat attanmiya	the Saudi Fund for Development
musharrif *adj.*	honorable, noble
anɛam/yinɛim *v.intr.*	to bestow, give
raṣīd *n.*	fund; capital; balance
min khilāl	through
atwazzaɛ/yitwazzaɛ *v.pass.*	to be distributed
tabarruɛ *n.pl.* -āt	contribution, donation
sāham/yisāhim *v.intr.*	to participate, take part
almuʔassasa lʔamrīkiyya li ttanmiya ddōliyya	USAID
tamwīl *v.n.*	financing
mablagh *n.pl.* mabāligh	amount, sum
afḍaliyya *n.pl.* -āt	priority
dakhl *n.*	income
kārisa *n.pl.* kawāris	disaster, calamity
ǰafāf *n.*	drought
maǰāɛa *n.pl.* -āt	famine
fayaḍān *n.pl.* -āt	flood
handasi *adj.*	engineering
mubāsharatan *adv.*	directly
wikāla *n.pl.* -āt	agency
ḥāla ṭārʔa	emergency
ghizāʔi *adj.*	nutritional, (relating to) food
gamḥ *n.coll.*	wheat
tamr *n.coll.*	date

biɛsa *n.pl.* -āt	mission, delegation; group of people, team
muǰahhaza *adj.*	equipped
mankūb *adj.pl.* -īn	afflicted with disaster; ill-fated; victim
hazza arḍiyya	earthquake
afta<u>kh</u>ar/yifta<u>kh</u>ir + bi *v.intr.*	to take pride in

Notes

1. **min akbar:** *one of the biggest.* Although this is an MSA construction, it is very common in Hijazi Arabic.

2. **anɛam fīha ɛalēna:** *(God) has bestowed on us.* Cf. MSA **anɛama biha ɛalayna.** It is worth noting here that in addition to vocalic changes and deletion, the Hijazi verb collocates with the preposition fī, while the MSA verb collocates with the preposition **bi.**

3. **hadāk alwagt:** *that time.* The MSA **ðāka** is the cognate of this demonstrative substantive. The prefix **ha-** is a Hijazi Arabic innovation.

4. **nuṣṣ:** *half.* Cf. MSA **niṣf** (pausal form). Note the deletion of f and the gemination of ṣ. All one-word fractions in Hijazi Arabic have the pattern CuC_2C_3, e.g. **tult,** *one third;* **rubɛ,** *one fourth.*

5. **bi<u>sh</u>wē<u>sh</u>:** *slowly.* This type of adverbial expression normally consists of the preposition **bi** and a noun or a noun phrase, e.g., **biguwwa,** *forcefully;* **bisurɛa,** *quickly.*

Selection Forty

amtāl wu ʕibārāt ʕāmma
Common Proverbs and Expressions

- alʔinsān bittafkīr wu allāh bi ttadbīr.
  Man proposes and God disposes.

- taḥt assawāhi dawāhi.
  Still waters run deep. (Lit., under still waters there are smart fellows.)

- bēt aḍḍīg yisāʕ alf ṣadīg.
  A small hut holds a thousand friends.

- ḥabl alkizb gaṣīr.
  Lies have short wings. (Lit., the rope of lies is short.)

- ḍulmin bi ssawiyya ʕadlin bi rraʕiyya.
  Equal injustice to all people is better than justice for some and injustice for others.

- wild alkalb kalb mitlu.
  Like father like son. (used in a pejorative sense, lit., the son of a dog is a dog like him.)

- ḥāmīha ḥarāmīha.
  The guard turned out to be the thief.

- khudu srārhum min zghārhum.
  Learn their secrets from their youngsters.

- dirham wigāya khēr min ginṭār ʕilāǰ.
  An ounce of prevention is worth a pound of cure. (Lit., an ounce of protection is better than a ton of medicine.)

- rās alkaslān maʕmal ashshēṭān.
  An idle brain is the devil's workshop.

- zād ʕala ṭṭīn balla.
  He added fuel to the fire. (Lit., he added more water to the mud.)

- assukūt akhu rriḍa.
  Silence gives consent. (Lit., silence is the brother of consent.)

- aṣṣudfa khēr min mīɛād.
  [Meeting by] coincidence is better than a set date.

- aṣṣabr muftāḥ alfaraǰ.
  Patience is the key to relief. (e.g., from sorrow, pain, etc.)

- khashmak minnak lō kān aɛwaǰ.
  Do not be ashamed of family. (Lit., your nose is part of you even if it is crooked.)

- illi ɛaḍḍu ttuɛbān yingaz min alḥabl.
  He who has been bitten by a snake is afraid of a rope.

- ɛala gadd lḥāfak mid riǰlak.
  Don't bite off more than you can chew. (Lit., stretch your foot as far as your comforter goes.)

- alʔaɛwar bēn alɛumyān malik.
  Among the blind the one-eyed [man] is king.

- alɛaṣa min alǰanna.
  Don't spare the rod. (Lit., the staff is from paradise.)

- mū kull bēḍa shaḥma wa lā kull sōda faḥma.
  Don't judge a book by its cover. (Lit., not every white woman is a piece of fat and not every black woman is a piece of charcoal.)

- illi fi lgidir biṭṭalliɛu lkhāshūga.
  Whatever is in the pot, the ladle brings it out.

- wēsh ɛala ddīb min ḍrāṭ alɛanz.
  How can a fart of a goat harm a wolf.

- gidir wu lāga ghaṭāh.
  Birds of a feather flock together. (Lit., a pot that found its lid.)

- alɛaǰala min ashshēṭān.
  Haste makes waste. (Lit., haste is from the devil.)

- alganāɛa ghina.
  Contentment is better than riches. (Lit., contentment is riches.)

- gūl alḥag wa lō ɛala gaṭɛ rāsak.
  Tell the truth even if it hurts. (Lit., tell the truth even though you may be beheaded.)

- katīr alḥaraka wu galīl albaraka.
  Much movement does not make much profit.

- alklāb tinbaḥ wu lgāfla māshya.
  I couldn't care less. (Lit., the dogs bark while the caravan moves on.)

- man sāwāk bi nafsu mā ḍalamak.
  He who treats you like he treats himself is not unfair to you.

- mā ḥak ǰildak zay ḍufrak.
  Nothing can scratch your back better than your own nail.

- waʕd alḥur dēn.
  Do not make promises you cannot keep. (Lit., the noble person that promises runs into debt.)

- waʕd bila wafa ʕadāwa bila sabab.
  A promise unfulfilled is enmity uncalled for.

- min faḍlat algalb byitkallam allisān.
  Whatever the heart thinks the tongue speaks.

- lā yiḥin ʕala lʕūd illa gishru.
  Nothing is kind to the wood but its own bark.

- muftāḥ albaṭn lugma.
  The key to the stomach is a mouthful.

- algharqān yitʕallag bi ḥbāl alhawa.
  A drowning person would clutch at a straw. (Lit., a drowning person would cling to robes of air.)

- alʕēn mā tiʕla ʕala lḥāǰib.
  The eye does not rise above the eyebrow. (used as an expression of respect for superiors or the elderly.)

- hāda ʕuzr agbaḥ min zanb.
  The excuse is worse than the offense itself.

- alḥala yidfaʕ albala.
  Desserts prevent all sicknesses.

- lā tʔaǰǰil ʕamal alyōm li lghad.
  Never put off till tomorrow what you can do today.

- inna li llāh wa inna ilayhi rāǰiʕūn.
  Surely we are Allah's, and to Him we shall surely return.

- aɛūzu bi llāh mina shshēṭān. arraǰīm.
  I take refuge in God from the evil of the devil.

- alkamāl li llāh waḥdu.
  Perfection belongs to God alone.

- lā ḥawla wa lā guwwata illa bi llāh.
  There is no power but in God.

- wa mā ɛala rrasūli illa lbalāgha.
  It is for the messenger only to deliver his message.

- ɛind libṭūn ḍāɛat liɛgūl.
  When the stomach is concerned, wisdom withdraws.

- rizg alyōm akhadnāh wu rizg bukra ɛala llāh.
  We have gotten our livelihood for today and God will take care of tomorrow.

- aṣṣadīg wagt aḍḍīg.
  A friend in need is a friend indeed.

- lamma yiṭīḥ albaɛīr btiktar sallākhīnu.
  When it rains, it pours. (Lit., when a camel falls down, the butchers/skinners are numerous.)

- lō fīh khēr mā gaṭṭu ṭṭēr.
  It is a worthless thing. (Lit., if it were good, the vulture would not have dropped it.)

Translations of the Selections

Selection One

Information about the Kingdom of Saudi Arabia

Saudi Arabia occupies the largest part of the Arabian peninsula. The area of the Kingdom is about 870,000 square miles. Its mineral resources include: gold, silver, brass/copper, lead, iron, and some other minerals. The population of Saudi Arabia is about nine million inhabitants.

Islam is the religion of the Kingdom, and the Prophet Muhammad (God bless him and grant him salvation) was born there. It [also] has the two holy shrines, the holy city of Mecca and the Radiant Al-Medina. The Saudis believe in Moses, in our Father Ibrahim and in our Lord Jesus (peace be upon Him). The government does not allow non-Muslims to pray in churches or in temples. The building of churches is not permitted in all of Saudi Arabia.

Muslims have the Islamic calendar which is based on (lit., depends on) the lunar month which is twenty-nine and a half days long. This calendar started when the Prophet emigrated from Mecca to Medina in the seventh century A.D. All Muslims have to fast during the month of Ramadan. This means that they must abstain from eating, drinking and smoking throughout the day. Saudi law obligates all people, Muslims and non-Muslims, not to eat, drink or smoke in public places during the Fast of Ramadan. The Muslim months are: Muharram, Safar, Rabee' Al-Awwal, Rabee' Al-Tani, Jumad Al-Awwal, Jumad Al-Tani, Rajab, Sha'ban, Ramadan, Shawwal, Zu-Lqida, and Zu Lhijjah. There are five pillars of the Muslim religion. They are: the declaration that there is no god but Allah and Muhammad is His prophet, prayer five times a day, almsgiving [amounting to] $2^1/_2\%$, fasting during the month of Ramadan, and the pilgrimage to Mecca (lit., of the house).

Selection Two

The History of Saudi Arabia and Its Government

Since ancient times Saudi Arabia has played a vital/important role in history in the areas of trade, religion and culture. The kingdom extends from the Red Sea in the west to the Arabian Gulf in the east. Saudi Arabia's terrain is varied, but generally it is barren and most of it is desert. The Empty Quarter is the largest sand area in the world. However, we must not forget that in Saudi Arabia there are valleys, plains, rocky terrain and mountains, especially in the Asir area. There are also relatively small agriculturally cultivated areas. It is said that these areas, such as Al-Qatif Oasis, are among the most fertile and productive in the Middle East.

The population of Saudi Arabia is Semitic. They are all of an Arab background. About ten percent of them are bedouins. The Saudis did not intermarry with other peoples/races. As a matter of fact, Saudi Arabia was never under any [colonial] domination. This fact has contributed to (lit., helped) the unity of the country and to social stability. The Saudi Arab is a proud individual in his religious and moral values and in his heritage.

Arabia has a very rich history. Starting from the seventh century A.D., the Arabs spread the message of Islam from Mecca and Medina. They also spread their Arabic language as well as their culture. The religion spread rapidly to North Africa and to Central Asia. But the modern history of Saudi Arabia starts from 1902, when Abdul Aziz recaptured the home of his tribe in Riyadh. After thirty years of fighting, Abdul Aziz reunited all the hostile factions, and he proclaimed himself the King of Saudi Arabia.

Most of the oil storage tanks were opened after WWII. Abdul Aziz began using all the oil revenues to expedite modernization and progress in his country. This progress continued under the leadership of his successors, King Faysal, King Khalid and King Fahd. Saudi Arabia has an absolute monarchy. It is ruled by the Saud family, the offspring of Abdul Aziz. The leaders of the family appoint the king. The current Saudi constitution is the Islamic Shari'a/law, the holy Qur'an.

Selection Three

Some Cities of Saudi Arabia

1. Holy Mecca is the capital of all Muslims. Mecca was established when God created the well of Zamzam in order to save Hagar and her son Ismail from dying of thirst. Everyone knows that the Arabs are descendents of Ismail. Ibrahim and his son worked very hard to build the Ka'aba, which was a place for worship even before Islam. The Muslim religion states that every Muslim in the world should visit Mecca during the pilgrimage at least once in a lifetime. Now Mecca has changed greatly from the past. It has large buildings, wide streets, and many hotels especially for pilgrims.

2. Radiant Medina is an important city for Muslims because it has the famous mosque of the Prophet and his grave as well as his library. It [also] has the Islamic University. Every pilgrim has to visit the Prophet's grave in Medina. In the past, Medina was a small [village], but now it has grown to be a big city, and its population has increased (lit., the people are numerous in it). You see that they have rebuilt Medina since that time, and you may not recognize it. It has modern markets and many buildings.

3. Riyadh is a modern city which is growing rapidly. King Abdul Aziz, who is usually known as the Son of Saud, had made Riyadh the capital of Saudi Arabia. Riyadh has an old history. It is considered to be the first capital of the Yamama region. Up until the fifties there were no paved roads leading to Riyadh. It was a desert in which there were palaces of clay. People came to Riyadh because it had vast oases, palm trees and vegetables, and it had

sufficient water. The word Riyadh means gardens or paradises. Its climate is very dry, and it has very little rainfall. Riyadh was the capital of the Saud Clan, but the Sauds were cast out of it. In 1902 King Abdul Aziz surrounded it and recaptured it from Ibn Rashed.

4. Jidda is called the Bride of the Red Sea. It surrendered to Abdul Aziz and his men in 1925. However, its history did not start until 1933 when the Minister of Economics signed an agreement with Standard Oil of California. [The company] paid thirty-five thousand British gold pounds. Since that time Jidda has changed, and its population increased from 25,000 to about a million in 1980. It has one of the most modern airports. The National Airport of King Abdul Aziz has an area of more than 40.5 square miles. This airport provides services for a million and a half Muslim pilgrims annually, and for six million travelers.

5. Jubayl and Yunbu' are developing tremendously. Both of them are industrial cities in which there are huge projects.

Selection Four

The Difference Between Life in the Kingdom and Life in America

The United States differs completely from the Kingdom. First of all it [is different with respect to] modernization. Here they are more modernized/developed than we are, but this does not mean that we do not have modernization. We have buildings and streets. Everything one may imagine is found in Saudi Arabia, but not to the extent that it is in America or in the European countries.

Concerning the weather, it is completely different, [they have] cold and snow. We do not have snow except in the northern region. Sometimes we have snow, but not always. For example, last year in Ha'il it snowed on the heights. The weather is very cold because Ha'il is in the north close to Jordan. Sometimes when we have winds, northelies as we call them, the weather is cold. The Kingdom of Saudi Arabia is a desert. Its weather is dry when cold, and dry when hot except in coastal areas which of course are humid because of the sea.

With respect to traditions, there is a very great difference (between the two). In our country, women do not go shopping by themselves. They do not go to the suq and buy their personal things. In Saudi Arabia the man is responsible for everything. He is the one who brings [home] the household items and the groceries. If the woman goes out, she has to be dressed in (complete) Saudi fashion which is the veil (the black thing on the face) and the aba which must be black. There are many kinds of abas. When a woman goes out she should be wearing a long dress. This means she should be covered from head to toe (lit., from the head and the neck to the feet). The veil should be worn in two layers so that the face will not be shown.

Selection Five

The Women's Chamber

A woman sits in the women's chamber. It is not possible for her to sit with the men. There are places for feasts; one quarter designed especially for women and one for men. Even the entrance for women is separate. There is no common entrance for both women and men. For example, one entrance should be on the north [side] and the other on the south, east or west side. It is not possible for the two entrances to be next to each other. There are [some] houses built with one entrance. Even though there might be men and women in the same house, the host (of the feast) himself would always arrange to have the women's entrance on one side and the men's entrance on the other. If a person has one entrance or has one apartment, he sometimes finds it necessary to use his neighbor's house to separate the women from the men. These are traditions, so it is not possible to have a common entrance.

In Saudi Arabia women shake hands with each other but not with men. A woman won't face/meet you even though you are her relative. We have some traditions that often will not permit the paternal cousin (m.) to look at his paternal aunt's daughter. Why? Because he can marry her legally. [Likewise] a maternal uncle's son cannot look at his paternal aunt's daughter. The only ones who have the right to look at a woman are her brother, maternal and paternal uncles, and her nephews. Only the persons who do not have the right to marry her can see her face unveiled. But as for the person who can marry her, we call him marriageable. Mahram (unmarriageable) refers to someone who does not have the right to marry a woman, and mush mahram means a person who can ask for a woman's hand in marriage. However, in our town we do not follow these traditions. Sometimes when I go on vacation to see my family, all of us sit and eat together. No one would be absent from the table, unless he had an appointment or he was busy and could not come home for lunch or supper. We all sit at one table and eat together, women and men. Why? Just because I am married and my brother is married, and this means that it is possible for him to look at my wife unveiled, but according to the religion it is unlawful.

Selection Six

A Car Accident

Once my wife and I were going to spend a weekend with my parents. What happened was that we got stuck on the road because there was an accident. We stopped for a while. I got out of the car to see what kind of an accident it was. I found out that one of the drivers was speeding. At the same time another driver was trying to change lanes, but he did not have a chance to do that, so the other car was in front of him and [their] cars collided. The road was blocked because of the two cars and of a third one which was coming from the opposite direction. We had to stop until the police came. In Saudi Arabia we have highway patrols on duty twenty-four hours a day.

One of the drivers of the cars involved in the accident was unconscious. Of course in a situation like this, first aid is needed. One person in the crowd tried to help him. First of all, he stopped the bleeding until the ambulance came. In Saudi Arabia we have at every fifty kilometers an infirmary, a complete station, a complete rest area with a restaurant, a mosque, a gas station, and [a shop for] car maintenance. It also has lounges for women, and houses to be rented by the room on an hourly bases. The travelers come and rest in them. Such a station was not less than thirty kilometers away from the scene of the accident. Therefore, it was very difficult to send an unconscious person all that distance.

We waited until the police came and investigated the accident. The ambulance came and took the unconscious man away while the police were [still] investigating the accident. Later it became evident that the driver who had changed lanes and was [now] unconscious, was at fault. First of all they took his license to write him a ticket. They gave him a ticket, and the tow truck came, towed the cars away, cleared the road and brought it back to normal.

Certainly, the driver who was at fault was obligated to pay the other driver (for the damages) to repair his wrecked car. As for car insurance, it is available, but not everyone has it. In Saudi Arabia it is not mandatory to have car insurance (it is something optional). You may insure your life or anything else, but from a religious point of view, life insurance is unlawful. It is against the religion in Saudi Arabia. If one has car insurance, then the insurance company pays everything.

If someone dies in an accident and the violation is not intended, then the driver [at fault] is obligated to pay a penalty, which is called "blood money". But if the violation is intended, then the driver will receive the religious penalty, which is death. The religion says, "A tooth for a tooth and an eye for an eye." Anything [wrong] a person does, he should get the punishment for it. In Saudi Arabia if a burglar steals anything, they cut off his hand.

Selection Seven

The Penalty for Drunkenness in the Kingdom

Drunkenness does not exist in the Kingdom to any great extent. Certainly, in our country the government is very strong. If any drunken man is caught, he must be punished. It is impossible for him to be set free. Basically, this is a religious matter. Saudi Arabia is a Muslim country; of course it prohibits all things [like] this. If a person drinks, this means that he has drifted away from the religion. Our system and laws are in accordance with the religion. For example, cutting off the hand of a burglar is something written in the Qur'an. It is written in our religion that the murderer should be killed and the adulterer should be stoned. We live according to the religion. We do not make up these things by ourselves. These are laws written in the Qur'an and in the Islamic Shari'a/Law through the guidance of the Prophet (God bless him and grant him salvation). We have the word of God (to whom be ascribed all perfection and majesty). Definitely, we live according to God's word. The drunkard is judged in accordance with the penalty for drinking which is six months in jail and lashing every day after prayer. He should be beaten with a reed, God knows how many times, maybe sixty lashes.

Lashing is in accordance with the Islamic method. The person who performs the lashing must not raise up his hand and then strike forcefully. He should put something under his arm to control himself. The soldiers wear berets, so the lasher takes off the beret and puts it under his arm and then strikes with the condition that he does not raise his hand enough to allow the beret to fall (fly). If he lifts his hand and the beret falls, this means that he is violating the law. This method is not as painful as striking with [full] force. So something is put under the arm to show mercy for the offender so that he may repent and come back to his Lord.

Selection Eight

The Donation Fund and Paying Blood Money

As we have said [before], if a person intentionally kills someone else, the Shari'a states that he must be killed. However, if the killing is not intentional then the government orders the murderer to pay blood money. He must also pay a fine to the government. If the family of the victim says, "We forgive him, and we do not want any blood money," then the government will say that this is their prerogative. Nevertheless, the government should get its due, for example, throwing the murderer in jail and forcing him to pay a fine.

In Saudi Arabia we have many tribes. Every tribe has a fund [from individual] contributions. For instance, you are a member of a tribe, you pay fifty riyals a month. Each tribe has no less than twenty to thirty thousand members. So you pay fifty [riyals] and another one pays fifty, and the money piles up every year. The fund pays out [whenever] anyone gets in trouble. This may help the individual a great deal whenever he has a crisis.

In most cases the family of the victim does not ask for blood money because your loss is either your father, your brother, your mother or your child, and money will not replace them. This is a basic principle in Saudi Arabia. However, there are some families who may say, "We would benefit from this money. We would give it to the children if it were their father who was the victim." Of course they would benefit [from the money], especially if all the children of the victim were small and if the oldest of them were fourteen or fifteen years old and if he were still in school. The blood money is given to the children to build a house for themselves or at least to buy them one to live in. The purpose of taking the blood money is not to use it for leisure or for going on trips. It should be used appropriately.

Selection Nine

The History of Aramco in Saudi Arabia

The story of Saudi Arabia is not complete if we do not talk about the oil story. The history of Aramco started in 1933, when the Saudi government signed the basic concession agreement with Standard Oil Company of California (SOCAL). Later this company assigned the concession to California Arabian Standard Oil Company (CASCO). In 1936 the Texas Company became a half owner of CASCO, which had changed its name to Aramco in 1944. It revised the original concession agreement several times. In 1948, two of the big American companies bought some of the Aramco stock. SOCAL owned 30%, Exxon and Texaco 30% each, and Mobil 10%. In 1980, the government of Saudi Arabia acquired all the Aramco concession rights, crude oil, facilities and production.

When oil was found in 1932, America started sending specialists, materials, and drilling equipment to Dhahran, the town which the company had built on the Dammam field. At the beginning several wells were drilled, but less oil was found than expected. In March, 1938, a very deep well was drilled and oil was found in large quantities.

The Kingdom stopped all oil production operations when the war broke out in Europe. And in 1943 the company announced that it was going to build a refinery at Ras Tanura. The demand for oil increased after the war, and the company began increasing its production at a great rate to secure for itself a share in the international market.

Aramco is considered the largest producer in the world of crude oil and natural gas liquids. That was why the Kingdom ranked first among oil-producing countries in the Middle East, and the third largest in the world after the United States and the Soviet Union. We should mention that Saudi Arabia is the largest exporter of natural gas liquids in the world.

Aramco has other very important projects for developing the Eastern Province, one of which is the electric power network. The government has asked Aramco to establish and manage an electric company in the Eastern Province. Until now, this company has been asking Aramco for administrative assistance. The company provides electricity for the towns and villages in the Eastern Province. [It also provides power] for gas projects and for all other industries in the region.

Selection Ten

A Study of the Rising Cost of Dowries

The Department of Social Studies in the College of Arts at King Saud University, under the guidance of the Ministry of Justice, undertook a study of the phenomenon of the rising cost of dowries in Saudi society. A team from the Sociology Department which was delegated to study this problem arrived at Qurayyat last Wednesday. The team consisted of an assistant professor in the Social Studies Department at the College, Dr. Muhammad Hani Issa, the intern of the department, Salih Abraham Al-Khudayri, and five students.

His Excellency, the Inspector of the Western Boundaries, met the team. The prince of the Qurayyat region, Sultan Bin Abdul Aziz As-Sudayri, welcomed them and put at their disposal all [available] facilities.

The team went on field trips to the villages of the region. They also took a tour of the various neighborhoods in the city to gather information from citizens of different social classes. Dr. Hani thanked the regional prince for his cooperation with the team. He also thanked the citizens of Qurayyat for their (fine) cooperation. He said that the purpose of this study was to illustrate the reality of the rising cost of dowries throughout the Kingdom, and to present a comprehensive study to the Ministry of Justice. Moreover, having the students work at gathering information and interviewing citizens will make their work easier when serving their Muslim society after they graduate (if God permits).

Selection Eleven

The Threat of Foreign Nannies Concerns the Ministers of Labor in the Gulf

The Ministers of Social Affairs of the six countries, members of the Gulf Cooperation Council, requested a comprehensive study on the subject of Arab Gulf families and their increasing use of women from India and South East Asia to take care of their children. This matter is troubling the ministers. The Ministers of the Gulf Cooperation Council met in Masqat to discuss the threat of the foreign nannies. The ministers stated that children who are raised by foreign nannies do not know how to speak Arabic well. Furthermore, they learn customs which do not conform to the national traditions.

There are no comprehensive statistics in the Gulf [concerning this matter]. However, in Bahrain, there were 13,000 nannies in '82. This is a rate of one per every two or three families, keeping in mind that Bahrain is the least rich among the Gulf countries. Its population is 360,000 inhabitants including immigrants and the unmarried.

Yesterday the Bahraini newspaper 'Akhbar Al-Khalij' denounced this trend which [began to] spread ten years ago. The [original] intention of the people then was to keep nannies to cook, clean house and raise the children. Later, this practice became a basic element in the structure of the society.

All the Gulf newspapers constantly report on accidents that happen to children because of the lack of experience of those girls and women who were originally from rural areas in Asia, and especially from Sri Lanka. In most cases the government sentenced them to imprisonment or expelled them from the country because of their shameful behavior with other immigrants of the same nationality. [Such behavior] is not a good example for families.

In '81, a Gulf newspaper called for a halt to granting work permits to those foreign ladies who would have a bad influence on the children. The Bahraini authorities announced on Monday that it was putting a stop to [granting] work permits. Currently there is a campaign against illegal residence in the country by workers who have fled from their sponsoring employers.

The Ministry of Planning of the United Arab Emirates found out from a study that there are between 2.5 and 3 million persons who were expelled from their countries and who are working in the Gulf area. This amounts to 90% of the labor force in the Emirates and 40% in Saudi Arabia and Bahrain.

At the end of their meeting in Masqat yesterday, the Ministers of Labor and Social Affairs of the Arab Gulf countries emphasized the importance of the study on the effect of foreign nannies on the Arab family in the Gulf region.

The Ministers authorized the Follow-up Office [to conduct] a comprehensive study on this subject based on the studies to be conducted by each country. The Office should present all the results of these studies during the next meeting of the Ministers of Labor and the Social Affairs Council.

Selection Twelve

The Problem of the Lack of Vocational Guidance

Folks, I think that the education offered by a society to its people is to be considered a great economic treasure, and that the society will reap its fruits after [a period of] constructive guidance, training and education. In fact, the need for academic education as well as vocational education is very crucial.

Society needs the [working] hands (lit., wrist) of its people in order to be built properly. We have to raise vigilant generations who are willing to learn trades and careers in industry such as, automotive mechanics, automotive electricity, carpentry, smithery, construction [work], brick laying, plumbing, and other trades, all of which are impossible for us to do without in our normal life.

It is better that we start planting in the minds of school children at an early age the idea of teaching trades and having respect for them. It is preferable to have vocational workshops in the schools to teach the basic principles of some industrial careers. This idea should be started in the upper elementary grades and continued throughout high school. These subjects must be graded just like other subjects. This would make the students interested in such skills.

The school's vocational program would help the administration and the students as well to sort out their inclinations, desires and aptitudes/abilities. Later [the administration] would guide the student according to his ability. At the end of the program, there would be a number of students who would choose a trade and love to work in it. These students should be enrolled in career centers [since] they would have the proper vocational guidance at once. [Having] this program begun at an early age would produce great results in the future.

Many people look at trades and careers in industry as having little value. They think that anyone who goes in that direction is a failure in the academic field. This is not true because learning a trade is an important matter in the progress and growth of the society. We should acquire these trades which we are in need of at all times. These students are the youth of the future who will lead the society to a better [life].

Besides educating and teaching, it is also the school's duty to prepare students who are self-confident in the use of their expertise and skills. It should also discover their aptitudes and gifts and guide them in the right [direction], especially the students who have the ability for technical work, such as drawing and other skills. This would enable the citizen to feel that the school has a great role in building the society both economically and industrially.

Therefore, we are in need of careers in industry as well as other vocations. The goal of this program is [to strive] for the benefit of all members of the society and the well-being of everyone.

Selection Thirteen

Riyadh Broadcasting [Network] Prepares a Program for Teaching the Arabic Language

The Kingdom (may you have a long life) is concerned about the well-being of every Saudi citizen. So we see social and educational progress in every region of Saudi Arabia. As you have read in the previous lessons, the Kingdom has improved incredibly the life style of the Saudi citizen. This progress is not just for the Saudis, but also for all the foreigners living in our country.

As you may know, most of the labor force in Saudi Arabia are foreigners and they do not speak Arabic. Therefore, we see that the Kingdom is concerned about teaching the Arabic language to those workers.

Currently, Riyadh's broadcasting network, with the cooperation of the Arabic Language Institute at the Islamic University of Muhammad Ben Saud, is preparing lessons for teaching the Arabic language by means of TV broadcasts. These lessons were written especially for teaching Arabic to non-Arabs. The Arabic Language Institute is preparing this program because it is a part of its major project, which is the spreading the the Arabic language, the language of our true religion, throughout the world. The program includes elementary books and other Arabic books which are written entirely within the framework of Islamic culture. There are [also] other books written in the language of daily life.

On the other hand, the Institute has developed a number of dictionaries in order to make learning the language easier for those who are non-speakers, and are interested in learning it. For instance, there is an A.B.C Arabic dictionary, with colored pictures to indicate the meanings [of words], which appeared in the series published by the Institute for teaching the Arabic language to non-natives (lit., not to its sons). The Institute is to publish another dictionary [using] the same previous words arranged according to subject matter. For example, everything about food will be under one heading. These dictionaries are to be designed on the basis of analytical studies of [previous] experiments and the available expertise in this field, whether in the Arabic language or in other languages.

Selection Fourteen

Preparing a Workshop in Adult Education to Wipe Out Illiteracy in the Dar'iyyah Region

His Excellency the Minister of Education has approved the preparation of a training workshop on the subject of adult education in order to wipe out illiteracy. [This preparation is to be done] at the Center for Training and

Applied Scientific Research in Dar'iyyah. The General Administration of the Adult Education Department in Riyadh Province is organizing this workshop. The specific conditions for joining this workshop are:

1. The participant must be a teacher at the elementary level.
2. He must have three years experience (lit., spent three years) in teaching.
3. His professional evaluation for the last two years must not be less than good
4. He must not have attended other workshops such as this.

On the other hand, the Director of Education has notified all schools to expedite the sending of the names of all those who are interested in participating in this workshop. They must finish filling out all the necessary information concerning this matter because the last date (lit., appointment) for accepting the nominees' applications is 11-6-1404 A. H.

Selection Fifteen

My Grandmother, May God Have Mercy on Her

Once I wanted to keep up with those [associates] who leave their work; particularly those who just go and leave God's people behind waiting until they come back. So I went to my supervisor and asked him to give me a five-day vacation. My excuse was that my grandmother was taken away to the One who has in His hand dominion over the heavens and the earth. He was understanding of my situation, God bless him (for me). He granted me twenty days so that I could take care of the old lady's business. He said to me, "May God reward you greatly my son. All of us are going to walk this road. Do not forget to give alms. I hope you will be a good fellow." But as the time went by, I forgot the story about my late grandmother. Once again I went back to my supervisor just like an innocent child. I asked him for a five-day vacation. My excuse was that my grandmother was taken to her maker, may He be praised and exalted! Suddenly he lifted his head up from the papers which were in front of him and said to me with surprise, "Praise be to God who revives the dead bones. But my son, I remember that your grandmother died ten months ago. Did she rise up from the grave? Anyway, take a five-day rest and don't ever do this again."

Selection Sixteen

The Bengali Servant Who Kidnapped the Son of the Family That Had Been Generous to Him

Part One

When a person is stripped of his humanity, even the animals are ashamed of his actions. Last Friday, the Ayn police in the United Arab Emirates arrested a Bengali criminal who had kidnapped an Omani baby named Sa'eed Jum'a Shami who was less than two years old. They found the baby's body buried near the New Hajar area. That is how they exposed a crime that deeply shocked the citizens of the entire Gulf area. [The disclosure of this crime] ended the torture of the parents of the kidnapped baby.

The details of the crime are as follows. The incident began on April 25, '82. A friend of the family brought a Bengali person to work as a cook for Mr. Jum'a Shami. This family accepted [the Bengali], sheltered him, clothed him and paid him a good salary. The family's trust in him grew stronger when they saw him praying at the designated prayer times.

The cook requested a salary increase, taking advantage of the goodness of the family. During the holy month of Ramadan, the family noticed that he was praying and fasting, so they increased his salary by 200 dirhams. However, the cook's greed had blinded him and made him forget all human values. He insisted on another increase [again]. He threatened the family with resignation if they did not comply with his request.

When Mr. Jum'a did not respond to his request, the cook gathered his belongings and asked to leave. The baby's father felt sorry for him and gave him all his rightful pay with some increase. Three or four weeks later the cook came back to the family and asked them to give him a job on their farm as a gardner. The father's heart was full of compassion for him and he decided to give him back his first job as a cook. He continued to deceive the family and showed them how well-mannered he could be. The family decided not to turn down any of his requests because their baby had become very attached to the cook.

Selection Sixteen . . . *continued*

The Bengali Servant Who Kidnapped the Son of the Family That Had Been Generous to Him

Part Two

Three days before the Day of Immolation/Greater Bairam, the cook came and asked Mr. Jum'a to let him spend the holiday with his friends in Dhuby. He said to them, "If I do not come back, consider that I have quit my job." He asked for his salary. Mr. Jum'a gave him the money plus a hundred dirham more, a bonus for the holiday. The next day in the afternoon the cook took the baby out as usual, and then he disappeared.

He did not come home at sunset. The family became very worried and afraid, especially the baby's mother who started looking for them in every place the cook might have gone to. When they failed to find them, the baby's father went to the police station and notified them about the incident. Since then, all [kinds] of search operations for the kidnapper began.

Four months went by. The mother went on a hunger strike (lit., abstained from eating) until her son would come back. She had a nervous breakdown as a result of this shock. The father ended up with two tragedies, his wife on the one hand and his missing baby on the other. The husband did not leave out a single specialist doctor but that he took his wife to him for treatment. But she used to refuse and scream night and day, "My son Sa'eed! O my son! I want my son!"

After that long period of time, the father became frantic and he [even] offered a big monetary reward to anyone who would lead him to his son. Many months went by without any lead (lit., news) [to finding his son]. He lost sleep (lit., the sleep flew away from his eyes). However, he never lost hope, and he continued to look for his son everywhere. But [the search] was in vain. The police interrogated many of the suspect's friends and those who saw him after he had disappeared. The police sent teams of undercover/secret police to all parts of the Emirates. They watched the mail boxes and the places which the kidnapper might often go to.

On Friday, January seventh, the police arrested the kidnapper and began the investigation. The criminal tried to trick them by playing a new role, but he did not succeed at all. When he was confronted with all the evidence, he collapsed and confessed. He took the police to the place where he had buried the baby. They found the baby's body buried in a hole 80 centimeters deep, and it was covered with sand.

The frightening thing about this mind-boggling tragedy is that the criminal admitted his strong love for the baby. That was the reason why he kidnapped the baby and kept him in order to raise him. The baby stayed with him for twenty-five days. Later, he got sick and started coughing. The criminal was afraid to take him to the hospital or to any clinic, for then his crime would be discovered. Twenty-six days after he became sick, the baby died. The criminal took him and buried him in a place about five kilometers away from his residence. Later he fled to another area where he stayed with his friend until he was arrested.

Selection Seventeen

The Ministry of Commerce Takes Strict Measures Against a Fictitious Wholesale Company

The Ministry of Commerce has taken strict measures against a fictitious Saudi wholesale (lit., distribution) company which is a joint-stock corporation [in the process of] being established. This company had sent invitations to some citizens through the mail boxes. The fictitious company has indicated that its headquarters is in Jiddah, its capital is a hundred million riyals, and that the share value is ten thousand riyals. The company [has also indicated] that the capital will be used for imports and wholesale distribution of all [sorts] of goods. Furthermore, with the help of Mr. So-and-So, the owner of such and such a company in Jiddah, this corporation was to open wholesale branches in all the cities of the Kingdom.

After the necessary investigation in regard to this matter, the owner of this corporation stated that the idea of establishing this company occurred [to him] two years ago. He [then] asked one of the officials of his establishment to study the subject and to write up the basic requirements (lit., elements) for starting this project. However, when the official presented the documentation of his study, which involved invitations to citizens, the owner of the corporation consulted with his assistants and they decided to give up the idea of establishing the company. Later they destroyed all the aforementioned documents. He [went on] to say that everything the local newspapers had published about this company was mere allegations by someone [who was] against him. He confessed to officials from the Ministry of Commerce that his establishment had not received any amount [of money] from any citizen for buying shares in this company.

Based on all these investigations, the Ministry of Commerce issued the following statement concerning the fictitious company [called] "the Saudi Wholesale Company."

The Ministry would like to make it clear that this company is not chartered to be established in the Kingdom. No one of the persons concerned has submitted an application for a permit or has even given its name for registration. This [whole thing] is considered to be the marketing of banknotes for the benefit of a company that does not exist and is not chartered. This is against corporation law and the regulations which govern these matters. The Ministry wants to make it clear that the law does not allow any corporation or individual to establish any company, nor to accept shareholding [funds] until after the Ministry's approval.

The Ministry is warning all citizens of the danger/risks of investing their money in companies, whether Saudi or foreign, which are not chartered to operate in the Kingdom.

Selection Eighteen

Speeding and Reckless [Driving]

What is wrong, driver? You are racing with the speed of an arrow. Are you in a hurry or afraid that your livelihood will fly away? Your livelihood will stay in place even if you go after it on foot. It is not for anyone other than you, no matter how slowly you walk. Obey the rules, take care of yourself and the others. The police intend good by their regulations. See what has happened to others, wake up, don't fall asleep. Do not expect to have any warning from what you are doing. I am afraid it will be too late after you have made a mistake. Neither a guide nor a counselor will help you then. O God! Who has followed His day by darkness. Many have died just because of one. You cannot control the circumstances once death has come. This is the creator's law which one cannot escape. Even if your property is destroyed and gone, this is of little importance if you remain unharmed. He who is reckless may harm others, even if he escapes injury himself. Even though he escaped injury before, this does not mean he will do so later. Your motorcar is under your control. It never disobeys the foot even if it throws you out. It never feels what is going on. There is no more to it than to be taken to the station junkyard. But you, poor one, on to your eternity you go. Now I have finished saying what I have in mind. Farewell, I hope what I have said will do some good.

Selection Nineteen

How a PhD in Literature Became an Obstetrician

My friend Dr. Ahmad, is a professor of history at a Canadian university. He went to visit one [member] of his family in a remote town in an Arab country. Many of the family members, relatives and neighbors came to congratulate him on his safe [journey]. All of them said to him "Welcome, welcome doctor." The people of the village thought that he was a physician, a doctor for human beings and that he specialized in obstetrics. Now the doctor is going to tell us about an incident that happened to him in that village.

One night, after I had gone to sleep, I heard very strong knocking on the door of [my] room. I woke up annoyed and frightened. I said, "I hope there is nothing wrong, friends. What is the matter?" A lot of people along with the family [I was staying with] were begging me and saying, "We beg you doctor! Please hurry!"

- I hope everything is all right! I hope there is nothing wrong!
- The woman in the house...
- Which woman?
- My wife!
- What do I have to do with your wife?
- She is giving birth.
- I shouted, "She is giving birth? What do I have to do with it?"
- The midwife is not available, and she is having a lot of difficulty in her labor...I beg you!
- I then said, "Please, please understand me!"
- Hurry! Hurry!! We are not going to understand!
- I am a doctor of history!

- [A doctor] of history, geography... it does not matter!

And before I finished my objection, they carried me to a nearby house from which the screaming was coming. I saw around me men and women shouting and saying, "Save her! Doctor, save her before she dies."

I pretended that I was feeling her pulse, and checking her temperature with my hand. Then I said in a loud voice, "Is there a car here?" They said, "Mr. So-and-So has one. His house is about a fifteen-minute walk." "All right, follow me!"

They followed me to the house of the owner of the car. They woke him up. We drove very fast (lit., it flew us) to where the lady was. They rushed her (lit., carried her and raced the wind) to the city while she was almost on the brink of death. While in the hospital, I followed them saying, "Don't worry, I myself will supervise the delivery (operation)."

Everything went fine and the voice of the newborn filled the place (lit., roared) to inform us of its arrival. At this point, all the people were quiet and they just thanked the real obstetrician who had saved the woman's life. Then they began cursing me and said, "Leave history alone... we have lived long enough to see that there are doctors for history and geography."

Selection Twenty

A Funny Social Satire

I have a friend named Matlaq whom you all know. Every time my friend drives (lit., rides) his car, it occurs to me to call a tow truck to come and to tow him away. Once Matlaq came to me. He was very afraid. When I saw him, I said to myself, "May [God] protect me from his evil. God knows what the problem is. Today is my day." When he arrived, I said to him, "Just name it! What do you want?" He said, "I want a cow." I said to him, "What did you say? You want a cow? You are pushing me [into getting] a cow?" He said to me, "Yes, I want a cow. I want you to find me a cow to lick my head like the bald man whose picture with a cow the agencies published two days ago. This is the treatment for baldness. I (your brother) am about to be bald (lit., am having a baldness project), and I would like to arrange for a treatment before it becomes a problem." I was confused. I tried to make my friend understand that I did not know if there was a cow market. I did not know who had a cow and who might sell it to us, or might lend it to us so that it would have the honor of licking my friend Matlaq's bald head (lit., baldness), [a head] which, when one sees, one thinks that it is a slippery slope in Ta'if. So in order to gain his approval, I tried to convince him of my lack of knowledge about breeds of cows. I began looking for a cow just as you look for the truth during a sale. I suggested to my friend that we bring him a goat of the kind that in a certain neighborhood enters your house if you open your door. And if finding a goat is hard, we may look for an ox of the kind that does not know what traffic lights are [for].

My friend Matlaq was not convinced by either suggestion (lit., neither by this nor by that). His only concern was the business of his baldness. So I said to him, "What do you think about our looking for a cat so that it would make your bald head shine until the hair grows on it, just as traffic signs spring up on sidewalks where there is no need for most of them." But my friend did not accept all these suggestions. He said that if he carried out all these suggestions, then his bald head would be a target for the experiments of those who gossip and those who do not (lit., the long and short tongues of God's creatures). Then he would have a psychological complex. Wherever he was going or coming he would always be imagining that there was a tongue over his head. Although he refused all my suggestions, I did not despair as you despair in trying to know the secret of the high cost of dowries in our country. It seems that the brain of my friend is stubborn and he does not want anything other than a cow's tongue. So I suggested that if he finds a cow and I am not there, that first of all he should wipe his head with butter that is not adulterated just like the butter sold in the market (lit., as is usual at the shops of those who sell it).

Selection Twenty-One

The Islamic Watch and Its Virtues

This is an Interview with the Inventor of the Islamic Watch, a doctor of engineering, Ibrahim Salih.

Q. *How did the idea of this invention come about, and how did you start implementing it?*

A. First, I am a Muslim, and I am honored by serving Islam. I have had several previous inventions. The times for prayer and the direction towards the "qibla" have been a problem for Muslims in Europe. [Because of this] the idea of the watch occurred to my mind, and I started constructing it in 1977. This idea was realized after seven hard years of research and experiments. But thank God that the patent on this unique invention was obtained (completed) in Switzerland, England, Japan, Hong Kong, Singapore and in many of the industrial nations.

Q *What are the benefits and the characteristics of this invention?*

A. This watch (may you live long) is easy to use. The common person can use it without [the need of] any reference [to another source]. The wristwatch is programmed [to last] a hundred years. Its memory contains [the names of] 114 nations arranged alphabetically. Once you press on one button, it gives you on its screen the names of the countries. Then you choose the country you want. It also gives you automatically the Hegira and the solar dates, the prayer time and the right direction towards the Holy Ka'aba. Furthermore, it gives the geographical location of [that particular] place. At the same time it shows you the local time, day, month, and year in both the solar and lunar calenders. This watch (may God guide you) has other benefits for people such as pilots, sailors, and astronauts. It has important information for the military and for businessmen while they are traveling.

Q. *Tell us about some of the problems and difficulties you have encountered while designing and making this watch?*

A. First, in 1981 I made a battery-operated office clock with the [same] specifications for office use. After my experiment was successful [I was then encouraged] to begin the project of designing a wristwatch. The making [of this watch] was much more difficult than the office clock from the point of view of designing a 1.5 volt battery-operated computer which practically did not need any significant [amount of] energy, and yet had to contain all of these complicated mathematical and astronomical computations. The problem was in reducing the size [of the computer]. Thank God I succeeded in designing the computer, and the making of the watch was completed two years later.

Q. *Are you afraid that competing companies will imitate this invention?*

A. There have been several attempts at imitation. But probably it will take them two to three years to get the secrets of this advanced technology. In spite of everything, we are taking [the necessary] measures to guarantee the protection of this Muslim invention.

Q. *What is your ambition in life?*

A. I pray that God will always lead us to the good. I [also] wish that the Nation of Islam will be united and be of one mind (lit., one heart) and join hands (lit., be one hand) in spreading the true religion.

Selection Twenty-Two

Important Instructions for Gulf Vacationers

The Department of Information of the Secretariat General of the Gulf Cooperation Council has prepared instructions for Gulf people vacationing in Europe and in other countries. Every person who wishes to take a summer vacation should know the laws of the countries he wishes to travel to. Lately, the Secretariat General has published instructions for the Gulf resident [to use] while he travels outside the [Council] member countries, especially in European countries. We hope that by publishing these instructions, we will enable the citizen [of the Gulf] to benefit from them. [We also hope] that he will follow them so that he may spend a summer vacation free from the problems and worries which otherwise he may be exposed to (God forbid). That is why we expect the honorable Gulf citizen to take into consideration the following matters:

- Going from the airport, do not ride in any car except in regular taxicabs which are distinguished by their colors and shapes.
- Every [vacationing] citizen must declare the jewelry and the money he has, or else this may be confiscated because there are many differences between European custom regulations and those of the Gulf.
- Obtain visas to enter foreign countries from the country one comes from.
- Upon arrival [in any country], the traveler must check with [his] Consulate for the registration of his trip and his address.
- One must not carry a large amount of money or gold, and one must not keep it where he is staying.
- Deposit the passport, the airplane ticket, and jewelry in a bank or in a safety deposit box at the hotel where one is staying. It is preferable to make a copy of the passport.
- Withdrawing money as is needed. If there is a need for withdrawing a large sum of money, you must ask the bank to provide the money at the place you want it.
- Do not open the main gates of the building to a stranger.
- It is preferable not to take children to shopping centers.
- Keep the shopping bag with the receipt because it is the only proof of payment of the price of the goods.
- It is necessary to pay for an item (the goods) in its specific department, and it should not be carried to other departments because that could be considered shoplifting.
- Do not examine the goods outside the store unless you ask for the salesman's permission. The salesman himself should take it outside.
- The bags of purchased goods from other stores should not be left unattended.
- Do not accept any services offered by strangers.
- While trying on clothes or shoes, do not leave handbags on floors or chairs to expose them to theft.
- It is preferable to open an account in Arab banks in France. It is [also] preferable to use [credit] cards and travelers checks.
- Do not wear extravagant jewelry which may expose a person [wearing it] to danger.
- Read the menu before ordering. Make sure to check the prices when you pay, and add the tip to the bill.
- Ask the hotel staff to sign every bill on behalf of the vacationer and his family members. Check the bills carefully before leaving.
- Since traffic regulations are different in some countries, we emphasize paying close attention to the children and the elderly crossing the streets to prevent painful accidents.

Selection Twenty-Three

My Annoying Friend

I have a friend who is impossible to please. His judgement of people is based on standards which no critic has used before. Neither a fool nor a wise person would even think of them. Every time he sees me coming, he starts his attack on journalism and on journalists, on authors and on educated people. I tried to convince him that I am not an important person nor a chief journalist, and that I am not a consultant either. Nevertheless, all this reasoning was not of any help.

Once I tried to gain his friendship and his sympathy, so I chose four books. All the critics said that they were important and valuable. I gave these books to my friend as a small gift and as a token of truce so that I might have rest from his fiery tongue (lit., and be safe from his rockets and fires). Then my responsibility to journalism and to journalists would come to an end.

My friend took the books. In a sarcastic way, he tossed them from one hand (lit., palm) to the other. I thought he was checking their weight. He did not pay attention to their titles, and he did not even bother to look at their table of contents. But he pursed his lips and frowned (lit., arched his eyebrow) and said, "I will give you my opinion tomorrow."

I was convinced that whatever the subject matter of these books was, one would need several days to read them. But I bought today at the price of tomorrow. I spared myself today, and I let tomorrow take care of itself (lit., let tomorrow be whatever it may be).

Tomorrow came. My friend came carrying the four books. He accused me of lack of taste, and [said] that my knowledge/education was superficial. He started anew (the record) about journalism and journalists. He referred to the silliness of those who wrote the books, (whoever they were).

Now, I confess that I doubt my previous judgement of the personality of this man. I was confused [about him], I wondered, "Is he a conceited educated person, or an ignorant person pretending to be learned?" In order to give myself and others a break, I decided to invite him to a writing [contest]. A few days later he came back carrying his pitiful (lit., orphaned) article. He made copies of it because he was afraid that it might get lost, or that I might neglect it, God forbid. It was [bad] enough that the title of the article was "Who is More Courageous, Abu Zayd or Antara." That was why I decided to be more courageous than both of them, and I wrote my complete story about him. Maybe the reading of this story will be of help as a source of inspiration for a learned person who is pretending to be ignorant or an ignorant pretending to be learned. May God help him who is plagued by a friend like mine.

Selection Twenty-Four

The Strangest Drug Stories in the Kingdom

A Saudi newspaper has published some strange stories about the drug problem in the Kingdom. One story was about a driver who killed thirty pilgrims. A second story was about a person who caused the burning of a bride and groom and their relatives on the wedding night. A third story was about a man who raped his daughter, and who was [later] given the death sentence. The fourth story was about a man who put drugs in wine glasses and killed his friends and partners at a party.

All of these stories are not fables out of [some] folk tales, nor are they some of grandmother's stories that she tells her grandson to lull him to sleep. These are true pictures of the tragedies which resulted from spreading the use of drugs among some groups of people in our society, a society which has lived for a period of time free of this deadly poison.

Major General Muhammad is going to answer all the questions about the drug problem in the Kingdom. He has given us a chance to interview a number of prisoners on drug charges [incurred] under a variety of circumstances. Some of them were smugglers, some were pushers and some were users and middlemen. We are going to present this case to the public. We hope that by these efforts we will inform the public about the dangerous results and the harm caused by being involved in drugs.

Your Excellency, Major General, how could drugs possibly spread like that in spite of the strong emphasis on closing the Kingdom's seaports, land[routes], and airports against (lit., in the faces of) the smugglers?

First, I am very proud of all the efforts of the customs officers and of the border defense forces to strictly stop smuggling operations. However, drug [smuggling] is an organized crime, and those who are engaged in it play numerous roles which are changing constantly. As the proverb says "Necessity is the mother of invention," so we see the smuggling gangs using all sorts of techniques and methods which enable them to smuggle (lit., enter) this poison into the kingdom.

Now, let me talk about the [different] kinds of people who are involved in drugs and about their severe punishments.

1. The supplier is the one who uses his intelligence and money to finance the smuggling operation. He uses all sorts of attractive devices in order to achieve his material goals. The supplier is considered the "head of the snake."
2. The smuggler is the person who is in charge of transporting and smuggling the drugs into the region. This one is considered the "bridge of evil." The penalty for these two [the supplier and the

smuggler] is fifteen years in prison and a 10,000 riyal fine, along with the punishment of lashing.

3. The smuggler's partner is the person who helps smugglers and cooperates with them in smuggling operations. The penalty for this person is seven years in prison and a discharge from the service if he is a [government] employee.
4. The giver is the enemy friend who seduces his friends in order to induce them to use the deadly poison. He gives them drugs without charge. This one is considered the "evil companion," and he is considered more dangerous than the pusher. The penalty for the giver is five years in prison and a 10,000 riyal fine along with the punishment of lashing.
5. The pusher plays the role of the dealer and the distributor of this poison. He is considered the evil (lit., destructive) financier. He is given the same penalty as that of the giver.
6. The user is the only target of the smuggling operations and often he is a sick or a deluded person. The user will be jailed for two years along with a punishment of lashing decided upon by the judge.

Let me say that His Royal Highness, the Deputy Minister of the Interior, has ordered an exposé of smugglers and pushers by having their pictures published in the local newspapers and by imposing the punishment of a lashing to be executed openly in public places so that they will be a lesson to everyone who may think of this criminal act.

Selection Twenty-Five

An Interview With a Drug Dealer

-What is your name?

-Salih.

-What is your nationality?

-Yemeni.

-What are the reasons for your arrest?

-He spoke in a voice choked with expressions of sadness. There is no power and no strength save in God. They had arrested me because I was selling amphetamine pills. In fact, I did something wrong. I hurt [other] people and myself. Talking about it now is useless, but let me tell you that I regret what I have done. I am coming back to God to ask for His goodness and mercy.

-Did you know that these pills were forbidden and that there were strict penalties for its marketing?

-Yes, I was aware of that, but the devil and my evil friends deceived me, and made me forget the harsh penalty.

-What made you sell the pills?

-Nothing at all except monetary gain.

-How much did you buy the pill for and how much did you sell it for?

-I used to buy a box for 100 riyals, and sell it for 150 riyals.

-Therefore, your profit was 50 riyals per box.

-Yes, but believe me, unlawful gain disappears before one benefits from it. Before one knows it, these gains go and along with them goes my salary which I get from the company I work at. When lawful gain is mixed with the unlawful, both are spent on bad things.

-When did you start selling these pills, and did you use them?

-I sold them for a month before they arrested me, but I did not use them because they are harmful to the health and the mind.

-Since you know that they are harmful to the health and mind, why did you sell them?

-I have told you that the devil deceived me, and that I regret what I have done.

-Who are the people you used to sell the drugs to?

-Most of my clients were drivers of large trucks and tractors.

-How did the idea of selling drugs occur you?

-I had met a person who was working in this losing business, and I was attracted by his words.

-Did you tell the Drug Enforcement Administration about your friend?

-Yes I did, and they are still looking for him.

-Did you tell them about your clients also?

-Yes, I have told the Administration about them.

-Would you like to say anything else?

-Yes, I would like to say that I deeply regret [what I have done], and I have turned to God. I advise my Muslim brothers, especially my Yemeni brothers who have left their country and (immigrated and) come to the Kingdom to earn an honest livelihood, to stay away from selling these pills, and from any unlawful gain. Because if they do this, their end will be just like mine and then regret will be useless.

Selection Twenty-Six

An Interview with a Studio Owner Who Uses Drugs

-May I have your name please?

-My first name is Abdulla. I do not think there is a need to know my full name.

-What is the reason for your arrest, (brother)?

-I was involved in using amphetamines.

-How did you fall into this trap?

-At the beginning one of my evil friends (and how numerous they are) tricked me into using amphetamines.

-Were you addicted to amphetamines?

-Yes.

-Since when?

-A month before my arrest.

-What kind of a job did you have which made it necessary for you to use amphetamines?

-I have a photography studio. I often had to stay up late.

-Since you were an addict, you must have suffered from some symptoms because you have stopped taking the drug. Is that true?

-At first I felt very severe pain and tightness. I was depressed and nervous for the first two days of my arrest. However, my health started to improve after I had started the treatment.

-Did the drug affect your dealing with [other] people?

-Yes, when I took the pills, I became very nervous, I mean edgy. Anything used to upset me. I felt that I had to fight anyone who provoked me.

-Did you ever have a car accident because of the drug?

-No, thank God. I used to avoid driving a car whenever I took the pills.

-How do you feel now after being arrested and put in this place?

-I feel that I have sinned against myself, my family and my children. I became aware of the dirty pit which my evil friends (may God not grant them success) have led me into. Now I am turning in repentence to God to whom be ascribed perfection and majesty, asking for His pardon and forgiveness.

-How much did you spend on the drug?

-I used to spend around 300 riyals daily.

-Were you aware of the penalty for using drugs?

-I knew that there was some penalty, but I did not know that it was like this.

-How do you like the care you are receiving in this prison?

-The care is good and life here is good [also]. The most important thing of all is what we are learning from a religious awakening and from having group prayer. We benefit from the sermons and from reading good books which are available in the prison library.

Selection Twenty-Seven

General Modernization Boom in the Kingdom

You are asking me about progress in the Kingdom. Frankly, I do not know where to start. The Kingdom (may God prolong your life) is now living in a period of general progress and great achievements in every area of growth and development. You see that the Kingdom has progressed greatly in record time, not more than ten years. In fact, I can say that we have made accomplishments and [carried out] projects which other countries could not achieve in a hundred years. The Kingdom has advanced greatly. Without any doubt, these past ten years were a challenge to our strong government. But thank God that, under the leadership of our King, the Kingdom was able to accomplish the goals of this general period of growth. So you find huge accomplishments in every field: industrial, agricultural, educational, medical, social and in the infrastructure.

We must not forget that the Kingdom has made a great effort in improving the well-being (personality) of the Saudi citizen before anything else. We can say that those efforts go hand in hand with efforts for growth and development. The Kingdom has prepared an educated generation. So we see that the government has established thousands of schools, hundreds of institutes, and seven large universities with tens of colleges.

At the time being, there are more than two million male and female students in elementary schools, junior high schools, high schools and universities. There are schools in the villages and in all the rural areas. With respect to hospitals, there are modern hospitals and other services which the government provides for the Saudi citizen for his happiness, comfort and leisure. We see that the Saudi youths have earned high degrees in education whether in the Kingdom or through special programs abroad. Currently they have great responsibilities in schools, factories and farms.

We feel very proud when King Faysal University in the Eastern Province celebrates the graduation of a number of our youth who have specialized in medicine. They have proved by their credentials and abilities that they are not any less than those who have graduated from the universities of the developed countries.

Selection Twenty-Eight

Marriage

Part One

My mother came and said to me, "I have found you a bride, and as a matter of fact, I like her." She brought up the subject to me. Frankly speaking, I did not have any objection because I felt that I could take on this responsibility. I said to my parents, "Go ahead and ask for her hand, discuss this subject and tell me what happens." Our custom is that the [man's] parents go and ask the girl's parents for her hand. They tell her parents about their son, that he works at such and such a place, and the nature of his job. [They tell them] everything about him. Later, they say, "We would like to betroth your daughter to our son." Of course, the answer will be either that they approve or they refuse.

Anyway, my mother came back to me and told me that they had agreed. Naturally she told me who the girl was, her family, and whose daughter [she is]. She described her to me very precisely. I wanted to see the girl very badly, and this is very difficult in our culture. In one way or another I did see her, but it was very important that she did not know about it. Most people in Saudi Arabia are still very conservative, and they do not like the husband to see the girl before the marriage. I saw her, and I really liked her. I gave my mother my word that I approved of the girl. At this time the mother's role is over (lit., she lifts her hand from the subject), and the father takes over.

My mother informed [the girl's family] that if God is willing, my father would go and ask for the girl's hand. My father went and talked with the girl's father, and both of them agreed. Of course they read the opening chapter of the Qur'an, which is considered in our culture to be the initial approval of marriage. After this, you are given some time to make yourself ready. You have to bring the rings at the time of the engagement party, a ring for the bride and a ring for the groom. It is customary that the rings be of (white) platinum, not yellow gold, because that is against our religion. The man's ring in particular should be (white) platinum. The girl's ring does not matter. There are other things that you should bring. You prepare a cart for a collection of perfumes, and at the time you bring cosmetics (for the face), nail polish and incense, many kinds of incense, frankincense, gum, cardamum, and rock candy. [You bring] things like these. You fix a cart decorated with all these things and you go and present them [to the bride].

There is a certain period of time between the time they ask for the girl's hand and the engagement party. When it is time for the engagement, the parents get in touch with the bride's family and they say to them, "We have set a date for the engagement," for instance, next week. The grooms family will invite [others] and there will be a celebration. The groom will go to put the ring on the bride's hand. The ring should be on the right hand during the engagement. There is also a period of time between the engagement and the wedding, so that the bride and groom can get acquainted with each other. For example, during this period the man may find out that the girl's manners are not good, or her way of dealing with others is not ideal. Maybe she is not as educated as he wants her to be. Likewise, she may find out that he is very different. Maybe she would not want him (lit., you). Maybe he is short or fat. During this period, they get to know each other. At any rate, she may see all of his good traits or his bad habits, but there will be no criticism. He tries to change a few things in her, and at the same time, she changes a few things in him.

Marriage

Part Two

During the engagement, she tries to find out every little thing about him as a husband. She must know his favorite food, clothes, [for example] how he likes to dress, whether he likes to go out a lot or not at all. Do his friends visit him often, or does he visit them a lot. Does he like children? How does he react when he is angry? There must be something that makes a person angry, and she likes to know how he reacts so that she can avoid such things. In our culture, the wife usually is very careful not to let her husband get angry. Therefore, during this period each one studies the other. If the girl suits him, he sets the wedding date, and if she does not [he divorces her]. Up until now they do not have any physical relationship with each other. There is nothing between them, they just sit and talk, and respect each other; nothing more than just a normal conversation. They do not have any intimate contact with each other, although she is legally his wife. At the engagement party the clergyman comes and officiates at the wedding according to the law of God and His Prophet. The minute the groom comes in and sees her on the day of the engagement, she legally becomes his wife.

When the clergyman arrives, the fathers of the bride and groom come [also] and sit down. The clergyman asks about the trustees of the bride and groom. Of course, according to our traditions, the fathers are the trustees. The clergyman asks the bride's father if he agrees to marry off his daughter. He tells him, "Yes I have agreed." The clergyman asks, "How much is the dowry?" [The bride's father] will give him an amount, ten thousand, twenty thousand, according to the dowry they have agreed upon. Sometimes [the bride's father] adds some stipulations. For example, [the groom] should not take his daughter abroad, nor should he travel and leave her behind. Probably the father does not want her living far away from his area. After [the bride's father] has finished, the clergyman asks the groom's father if he has the dowry. Sometimes handing over the dowry takes place in front of the clergyman. Often times the clergyman likes to hear [consent] from the bride's mouth, so he says to her, "Do you agree to take this man as your husband?" This is because sometimes some girls are forced to marry their paternal cousins. In our country people still hold on to [old] customs. For example, I have a son and my brother has a daughter, and we have to force our children to marry each other. In the past they used to call this taslīm, handing over.

We set the place and the time for the wedding. The place should definitely be large because there will be many guests. We invite five or six hundred people, men and women. We must fix whole lambs for the men. We bring in lambs and we slaughter them. As for the women, we fix them a buffet.

On the wedding day, the groom's family goes to get the bride. The groom will be waiting in the wedding hall in order to welcome the guests who have come to congratulate him. When the bride comes, the tambourine players come along with her. She walks with the groom from the entrance of the women's chamber. They walk very slowly. I mean they barely move their feet (lit., one foot after the other). They move very slowly. People sing until the bride and groom get to their place. When they sit down, there will be another type of singing, because there is a special song with tambourine playing for the march. Then [the bride and groom] go and sit in the koosha. The koosha is the place where the women sit. There will be singers and musicians. They sit for half an hour or an hour. The women utter shrill, long drawn-out and trilling sounds, and they sing. Later, the groom takes his bride to his house. Finally, I would like to say that these customs vary from one place to the other, and from one family to the other.

Selection Twenty-Nine

Religion and State

The issue of separation of religion and state is something that does not exist in our country. This is a Western notion which could never be applied in Muslim countries. In our country, religion is the basis of everything. We consider that the Muslim religion has been a way of daily life for every Muslim since the days of the Prophet Muhammad (God bless him and grant him salvation) until this day. Therefore, the way we dress, our food, our occupations, our laws, and our politics, all are linked to religion. The Saudi King considers himself the custodian of the two holy shrines. He is a political and a religious leader at the same time. The constitution of the country is the Shari'a, the Holy Qur'an.

Saudi Arabia considers it an honor and a duty to take care of everything that concerns religious issues. Concerning the hajj for example, we see that the government has built huge buildings in the City of Pilgrims, Jiddah. The pilgrims stay there until everything is ready before they start their trip to Holy Mecca. The rulers of the region ask every pilgrim to pay a small fee, just to cover his expenses. In the past, the hajj was the largest source of income for Saudi Arabia, but nowadays [the cost of the hajj] is no more than a small fee. The Kingdom has enough money from its oil to pay for most of the hajj expenses and for the maintenance of the two holy shrines. The government spends its own money in the service of Islam and the Muslims, and in spreading the Qur'an throughout the world.

The Saudi government makes a great effort whether in opening up new roads or in providing transportation for millions of pilgrims. Saudi Arabia buys the most modern equipment to insure the comfort of the pilgrims and to make their noble endeavor easier. The government provides huge numbers of employees, be it doctors, nurses, technicians, policemen and drivers, who work night and day during the hajj. So without these efforts it would be impossible for the hajj [facilities] to accomodate millions of pilgrims. Saudi Arabia considers that it is its duty to provide all these facilities for the Muslim world in order to comply with this ordinance which God (praise be to Him) has made one of the Pillars of Islam.

In Saudi Arabia (may God prolong your life) religion is the basis of everything in the society. For instance, the government forces you to fast during the month of Ramadan if you do not have a health problem or if you are not traveling, the only reasons which the Qur'an allows. So, you cannot eat, drink and smoke in front of people who are fasting or in public places. The religious police may arrest you. Let me give you another example. Our religion forbids liquor, therefore, drinking is against the law. Saudi Arabia is a Muslim country. It is impossible to separate religion and state. Mecca is the city for Muslims from all over the world. It has the Ka'aba. The Prophet Muhammad was born there, and it was there that the first revelation came down to him, and it was there that the credo of Islam was lifted up. "There is no God but Allah and Muhammad is His messenger." This is our declaration and our credo and our flag. Therefore, we are living according to the law of God and His messenger.

Selection Thirty

The Pilgrimage [to Mecca]

"Here I am in answer to thy call, O God. Here I am, Thou hast no partner. Here I am, all praise and grace and dominion are Thine. Here I am, Thou hast no partner." You will hear millions of pilgrims from all over the world repeating this call as they are entering Holy Mecca.

The pilgrimage to Mecca is one of the Five Pillars of Islam. In the past, pilgrims used to endure a lot of hardships and difficulties to make the pilgrimage. Many of them died on their way to Mecca because of the trip inland, the heat and the thirst. The situation has changed nowadays. Transportation is easy and available, whether by air, sea, or land. You see hundreds of thousands of pilgrims at Jiddah Airport and at its seaport also, all of them awaiting the buses to take them to Mecca. Usually, Jiddah is very crowded during the first days of the month of Zu-Lhijja. About a hundred thousand buses and cars are traveling at the same time in the same direction. The Qur'an does not allow non-Muslims to enter Mecca. There is a police station for passport verification right before Mecca's city limits. Every pilgrim must prove that he is a Muslim in order to obtain a pilgrimage visa. At present there is a special road that non-Muslims must exit on, fourteen miles before the Mecca city limits.

The Saudi government takes care of the pilgrims as soon as they arrive in Saudi Arabia. There is a government agency to guide the pilgrims through all the rites of the pilgrimage. They provide transportation and tents so as to make sure that every pilgrim is performing all the necessary rites for the hajj. All pilgrims enter Mecca wearing the same dress, two seamless pieces of white cloth. This garb is called al-ihram. This is something that shows that all of them are equal, and that they are in a state of purity as they come to God. When a person is in a state of ihram, he has to abstain from many things, such as sex, quarreling, wearing tailored clothes, cutting/shaving the hair, cutting the nails and other things.

Before entering Mecca everyone must perform the ritual of ablution because this is obligatory before prayer. Ablution at Mecca is something very important because the water is drawn from the Well of Zamzam. As soon as the pilgrims arrive in Mecca, they must go immediately to the Holy Mosque. The Ka'aba is in the middle of the mosque. The Ka'aba is covered with the Kiswa, a black cloth embroidered in gold and silver with verses from the Qur'an. The believer must enter the Ka'aba humbly and reverently while repeating this prayer, "God forgive me my sins and open the gates of thy mercy for me."

The hajj rites inside the Mosque begin with going around the Ka'aba seven times passing behind the Stone of Ismael/the Black Stone, and then running between Safa and Marwa seven times. The run must begin in Safa and end in Marwa. After the run, on the 8th of Zu-Lhijja, the pilgrims must to go to Arafa, which is about ten miles from Mecca. They stay there until the next morning. The rite of standing on the plain of Arafa and asking for God's mercy and forgiveness should be performed on the 9th day, early in the morning. Then they must go to Muzdalifa after the evening prayer. While there, each pilgrim must gather 49 stones. The pilgrims go to Mina on the following day. The Day of Immolation is a feast day on the 10th of Zu-Lhijja. While at Mina, they stone Satan. Every day they must cast a specific number of stones. Every pilgrim must offer a sacrifice. He eats half of it and gives the other half to the poor.

At the end, each pilgrim must come back to Mecca in order to circle the [Ka'aba] seven times and also to perform the run seven times, after which the hajj rites are completed. May your pilgrimage be acceptable, your efforts be rewarded, and your sins be forgiven.

Selection Thirty-One

Saudi Arabia Beheads 16 Kuwaitis for Bombings in Mecca

The Saudi authorities publicly beheaded 16 Kuwaitis in Holy Mecca. On July 10th, during the hajj, these criminals had set off bombs in the Grand Mosque. There were more than a million pilgrims inside the Mosque. This is not the first assault on God's Holy Mosque. In 1987 there were violent clashes between thousands of militant Iranian pilgrims and the Saudi Security authorities in which more than 400 pilgrims, most of them Iranians, died. Naturally, Saudi Arabia broke diplomatic relations with Iran after this incident. Later, Saudi Arabia put a limitation on the number of Iranians making the pilgrimage annually. Iran was not pleased with this [action]; therefore, it boycotted the pilgrimage for two years.

On September 21st the Saudi authorities carried out the death sentence on those Kuwaitis. The Saudi government believes that Iran had planned this terrorist act which was committed by Kuwaiti Shiites. Saudi television aired a video-taped confession of one of the men [who was later beheaded]. He said that he and his friends took the explosives from the Iranian Embassy in Kuwait. This man was known as an elementary school teacher. At the same time he was also the leader of a radical Muslim Shiite cell in Kuwait. Until now, we have not heard that Kuwait has made a direct statement concerning these executions. Prince Sheik Jabir Ahmad Sabah was in Baghdad at that time. All Shiite Muslims in Kuwait were very angry because the government had let those pilgrims be detained and prosecuted under Saudi religious law.

Amnesty International, which defends human rights, has expressed concern about the detention of those citizens and about the possibility of [their] being subjected to different sorts of torture. King Fahd spoke with the Kuwaiti Prince and told him that it was impossible to be lenient with anyone who tries to stir up sedition and subversion among the pilgrims in the two holy places.

The French Press Agency reported that there is a group calling themselves the Generation of Arab Anger that claimed that they planted the explosives in Mecca and in Jiddah. The Saudi Interior Minister stated that a group of Kuwaitis had planned the bombing in Kuwait, and that they were [also] trained to use bombs. As one of the criminals said, they wanted to spread terror and fear in the hearts of the pilgrims. They [also] wanted to show that the Kingdom is not able to protect God's Holy Place.

Selection Thirty-Two

Killing of a Saudi Official in Beirut

Muhammad Ali Al-Marzuqi was a contract employee of the Saudi Embassy in Lebanon. His job was to pay the salaries of those who take care of the maintenance of the Embassy. The Kingdom had pulled out all the Embassy diplomats from Lebanon except for him. Mr. Marzuqi lives in West Beirut.

Today Mr. Marzuqi was getting into his car when three gunmen attacked him and shot him with their machine guns. The police said that he died instantly, but his Syrian driver suffered minor wounds. The Islamic Jihad, who are loyal to Iran, claimed that they killed him. They said that the slaying of Marzuqi was in retaliation for Saudi Arabia's beheading of 16 Shiites convicted for the terrorism they perpetrated in Holy Mecca.

The Islamic Jihad sent a statement to the press agency in which they said that Marzuqi was an agent for Saudi intelligence. They threatened to kill members of the royal family to avenge the government's beheading of the 16 Shiite Kuwaitis, 10 of whom were of Iranian origin. The government beheaded these Shiite brothers because they set off bombs in Holy Mecca during the hajj season. During that attack they called the royal family "the servants of Satan." The Islamic Jihad threatened to kill them wherever they would find them, even in their well-constructed palaces.

The Saudi Foreign Ministry condemned the criminal acts by these cowardly terrorists against Saudi people abroad. The Ministry urged the Lebanese authorities to punish those responsible for these barbaric acts. Their punishment should be very severe for the brutal crime of killing an innocent Saudi citizen.

Selection Thirty-Three

King Faisal Air Academy Graduating a New Group of Pilots

Next Wednesday King Faisal Air Academy will celebrate the graduation of a group of pilot officers and technicians. His Royal Highness, Prince Abdul Rahman Bin Abdul Aziz, Deputy Minister of Defense and Aviation, will host the commencement. His Royal Highness will confer the diplomas, the military ranks and the awards on the graduates. The commanding officer of the academy said that this group includes a number of graduates from the United Arab Emirates, Bahrain, Qatar and the Arab Republic of Yemen. These officers have studied with their Saudi brothers (students). King Faisal Air Academy graduates two groups each year. The Academy has a procedure whereby after the graduation of each group, officials of the Academy will conduct a comprehensive evaluation of the level of the graduates (lit., of each group) in order to improve the level of the up-coming groups. The Dean stated that this group in particular had achieved a very high level in flight, military and academic training. As a part of the program, the students must join advanced training workshops after their graduation. Later, they will be assigned to combat, helicopter and cargo aviation.

The Dean talked about the system of studies and training at the Academy. He said that their studies and training program falls within the general program planned for all the military academies. It has a three year program. The Academy undertakes the task of training every student enrolled within the confines of the Academy. The Academy also grants incentive awards to outstanding students. For instance, the academy gives first-place honors in aerial studies, first-place honors in academic studies and first-place honors in military studies. There are also other incentive awards, such as the outstanding cultural award and the outstanding athletic award. Over and above the aviation and military studies, the Academy offers students courses in Islamic culture, the humanities and athletic and military training.

Selection Thirty-Four

One of My Grandfather's Tales

When we were little children, my grandfather (may God have mercy on him), used to gather us together every night and tell us a story about his youth. Now I want you to sit down and listen to one of my grandfather's tales.

Once I was coming back from the suq. You know that women in our country do not shop by themselves, so I was coming back [home]. I was very tired because I was carrying all my groceries. While entering my house, I heard children screaming very loudly. I put my groceries in front of the door and ran to the yard to see what had happened. I saw my son Ahmad screaming and saying, "There is a big snake! Hurry up and kill it!"

I was unarmed, I mean I was not carrying anything. I went into the house and got my dagger. I picked up a large stick and went back to the yard. By this time the snake was near the wall of the garden. I looked at it and I wanted to hit it with the stick. Suddenly it stood up high, as if it wanted to attack me. I hit it on the head, but it escaped and crept into the wall. When it went into the wall I became angry because I was afraid that it might scare the children again. I waited to see if it was going to come out of the wall.

After a while, I looked at the other side of the wall, and there it was turning its head and darting out its tongue as if it were laughing at me. I pulled out my dagger and stuck it forcefully into the snake's head. Frankly, my heart was pounding fast because I was afraid of missing. When I knew I had a good grip on it, I started rubbing its head forcefully against a large stone. After a little while, it let its tongue drop. I knew then that it had died. I pulled my dagger out of the snake and removed a few stones from the wall. Then I pulled it out and dragged it along the ground. I put it on the side of the road, and called the children to come and look at it. The children started measuring it to see how long it was. Many people were scared when they saw it, and for a long time, they were afraid to take that road.

Selection Thirty-Five

Opening a Desalination Plant in Barak

As you all may know, most of Saudi Arabia is desert, arid land that does not have a lot of rivers or springs. It is true that there are some oases, but not many. For this reason, the Bedouins used to move from one place to the other to find water. Nowadays, situations have changed, and we have enough water. There are desalination plants in most provinces in the Kingdom, and new plants are still being opened.

Yesterday, His Royal Highness Prince Majid Ben Abdul Aziz, Prince of Mecca Province, opened the first stage of a projected water desalination plant in the Barak area. The Saline Water Conversion Corporation is building this plant in the most modern technical fashion. The plant has a capacity to generate 600,000 gallons of fresh water daily.

The project has two sections. Each section has a main condenser for distilling water and a boiler to produce the necessary vapor for heating the water. The second section has electric generators for running the pumps. There is also a section for the laboratory where chemical substances are analyzed.

There is a pumping station near this project to take the water to a huge reservoir and then distribute it to the homes by means of a special network of pipes. There is a special building for the administration, and next to it there are a mosque, warehouses, parking lots, a restaurant and a center equipped with all facilities for athletic and cultural activities. A housing complex consisting of six villas equipped with all the necessary appliances was also built.

His Royal Highness Prince Majid Bin Abdul Aziz delivered a speech on this occasion. In his speech, he praised the many efforts made under the leadership of His Majesty, the sublime King Fahd, to provide water for to all the provinces and villages.

His Excellency, Minister of Agriculture, and Chairman of the board of this corporation, explained the major role that the government plays under the leadership of His Majesty, the beloved King, as well as the role played by the Ministry of Agriculture and Water, and by the Saline Water Conversion Corporation in providing drinking water, which is considered one of the most important elements of life.

The people of Barak Province had a huge party in which all the citizens participated. All the people were pleased with His Royal Highness Prince Majid's visit to the area. He sat among them and learned about their needs and the needs of the area and the surrounding villages. The Prince of the Province welcomed all the guests, and said, "We hope that His Royal Highness Prince Majid's visit will be, God willing, a blessing to the region."

Selection Thirty-Six

The Second Conference on Crime Prevention Studies

Today the Second International Crime Prevention Conference was opened at the headquarters for security studies in Riyadh. Officials at the Arabic Research Center have already started their second preparatory meeting. One doctor delivered a speech in which he emphasized the importance of cooperation among the directors of the research centers in the

Arab countries. This doctor expressed his hopes when he said, "We hope that this meeting will support what the first meeting began, whether it is in the preparation of or in making use of the potential of the Arabic research center in the interest of the one goal, which we are all striving for, serving Arab society." He also said that preparatory operations are continuing and that the Arab countries ought to exchange their expertise in this field.

The president of the Center emphasized the importance of this conference. He emphasized that scientific research has great importance. The subjects to be discussed at the conference will be presented from a common Arab point of view. These same subjects will be discussed at the United Nations Seventh Conference on crime prevention and dealing with offenders. This conference will be held this summer in the city of Milan.

The participating delegates at this conference include representatives of the ministries of interior, justice, and social affairs of the Arab countries. In addition to international organizations and associations, delegates from Arab and international research centers have also attended.

I can say in fact that our country used to be free of crime. We used to leave everything unlocked. We were not afraid of anyone stealing anything. But now foreigners are numerous and theft and crime have increased. May God stand by our enlightened government in order to protect us and protect our children from every evil.

Selection Thirty-Seven

An Advertisement for Contract Bids

The General Social Insurance Organization wants to carry out a project for the construction of a building [to serve as] its headquarters office in the central area of Riyadh in accordance with the following stipulations:

1. The land on which this project will be built is located on a street close to the Military Hospital. The building will consist of six stories and two stories underground, and there will be mechanical and electrical services and central air conditioning. There must [also] be elevators, parking lots and landscaping around the building. The lot size for this project is about 32,000 square meters.

2. Since the project is going to include architectural, mechanical and electrical works which require a high level of [skill in] execution, the organization has placed the following conditions on the companies entering the bidding:

   A. The [company] must submit a statement of previous works [completed] during the last three years provided that they have undertaken projects for office buildings similar to our project.

All documents must be notarized to verify that those works were carried out in an excellent manner.

B. It must submit a current financial statement which includes the annual budget of the company for the last three years. It must state its annual work volume and its capital as well as the names of the banks it deals with.

C. It must submit a statement of its administrative and technical system and the machinery and equipment it owns.

D. It must submit a copy of its commercial register, its chamber of commerce membership, and a "no money owed" statement from the Religious Income Tax Office and from Social Insurance.

3. But as for the Saudi companies, along with the aforementioned statements, they must submit a classification statement from the Ministry of Public Works and Housing indicating class one or class two in the field of construction. The foreign companies must submit no less than a class-four statement in the same field.

4. The bid documents will be sold only to qualified companies and in accordance with the previously mentioned conditions.

5. The qualification application forms can be obtained from the General Social Insurance Organization in Riyadh, Al-Matar Street, Projects Department.

6. All the necessary applications should be filled out and submitted, with all the required documents, to the Organization no later than twelve o'clock noon on Monday.

7. The qualified companies may obtain the bid documents for this project from the Organization for the amount of 35,000 riyals.

8. The last date for purchasing the document is twelve o'clock noon on Tuesday.

9. The offers are to be submitted to the Organization in stamped envelopes no later than Wednesday at noon. Any offer submitted after the date designated for accepting applications will be rejected.

Selection Thirty-Eight

The Problem of Mines in the Red Sea

The old people tell us that in the past the tribes used to fight each other. There were casualties when there were battles between them. Sometimes there were people who received injuries, such as broken bones and the like. When there was any clash between two tribes, [a third] tribe would interfere, as we might say, to break up the fight, and to bring about a reconciliation between the two tribes.

We stopped having these problems after the country had progressed and the people became educated. However, modernization and progress have brought us problems of a different kind. For instance, let us now talk about the problem of mines in the Red Sea. There are many people who are envious of us because God (to whom be ascribed all perfection and majesty) has given us an abundance of blessings. So, you see that they want to cause us trouble. According to what we hear on the news, it seems that these people are our enemies, and that they do not want us to be successful at all. They are trying to commit aggression against us. One of these [acts of] aggression is planting mines in the Red Sea in order to paralyze navigation activities and to weaken the Saudi economy, because this will reduce important export activities in the area. Like yesterday for example, a Polish cargo ship bumped into a mine at the entrance of the Red Sea. This ship is a recent victim of the mobile mine operations in the Red Sea and the Gulf of Suez. The load capacity of this ship is 5,700 tons. It was sailing into the Port of Jiddah when the mine exploded.

The United States, France, and Britain have begun naval mine sweeping operations. They are expecting the arrival in the area of mine sweepers and mine sweeping helicopters as well as experts from their [respective] countries in the next two days. It is possible that Greece will send its mine sweepers to the area to take part in resolving this problem. I think that the United States has asked the Greek government to take part in these operations. All this willingness of the Western countries [to act] shows that freedom of navigation in this area is very important.

Selection Thirty-Nine

Saudi Aid to Developing Countries

Saudi Arabia is now considered one of the largest of the major contributors of international aid to developing countries. Our generous government gives up to four or five percent of its domestic product for development assistance. The noble thing is that our government shares with others the blessing which God has bestowed on us.

The Saudi Fund for Development was established in 1974. The fund's capital was $2.5 billion at that time. We see that this capital was increasing little by little. In 1981 it had increased to $7 billion. All Saudi aid is distributed through this fund. We must not forget that the Saudi contributions are a major portion of international aid. (May you live long.) You see that our country is participating more and more with other organizations, such as the World Bank, USAID, the Kuwait Fund, and others in financing many projects.

The total Saudi aid up to 1987 amounted to $6 billion. This amount was distributed to 276 projects in sixty-one countries. It is the policy of the Saudi Fund to give priority to the countries whose per capita income is very low. Most of the Saudi aid goes to Africa, particularly since many of the African nations were hit (lit., came to them) by numerous disasters such as drought, famine, floods and others.

The aid is distributed to different projects. A large portion of it is spent on engineering projects such as, paved roads, railways, sea ports, airports, electricity and communication. Another portion is spent on social projects such as housing, water supply, agriculture, education and other projects.

Usually the aid is distributed through different channels. Some aid is paid directly to other governments through the Ministries of Finance and Foreign Affairs. The Saudi government gives out other aid through agencies of the United Nations and the Islamic world. There is also some aid for emergencies. For instance, the government has sent food such as (lit., as you might say) wheat and dates. Just as it also has sent equipment to countries which were struck by natural disasters such as floods and the like. Our government sent a medical team equipped with all the equipment and the necessities needed to assist our Yemeni brothers, the earthquake victims. I am proud of my country and its government. I hope that God will increase His blessings on us.

Glossary

a

abadan absolutely not

abs͟hir *v.imp.* just name it! go ahead!

abtala/yibtali + bi *v.intr.* to be afflicted, be plagued

abtaɛad/yibtaɛid + ɛan *v.intr.* to be far from; to avoid

abu rās aṣlaɛ bald-headed person

adab *n.pl.* ādāb literature

adīb *n.pl.* udaba scholar, one who is learned (in literature); author

adman/yudmin + ɛala *v.intr.* to be addicted

adnab/yidnib *v.intr.* to commit an offense, be at fault, do something wrong

aḍrab/yiḍrib + ɛan *v.intr.* to abstain from; to go on strike

aḍṭarr/yiḍṭarr *v.intr.* to have to do something, find it necessary to do something

afḍaliyya *n.pl.* -āt priority

aftak͟har/yiftak͟hir + bi *v.intr.* to be proud of, take pride in

ag͟hlab alḥālāt in most cases

ag͟hrab *adj.* stranger, strangest

aglag/yiglig *v.tr.* to worry, concern, upset, disturb, trouble

agtana/yigtani *v.tr.* to own, possess

ahhal/yiʔahhil nafsu *v.tr.* to prepare oneself; to be qualified; to enable

ahtamm/yihtamm *v.intr.* to be concerned, take care

aḥdas *adj.* most modern

aḥdas almaɛaddāt the most modern equipment

aḥtafal/yiḥtafil *v.intr.* to celebrate

aḥtal/yiḥtal *v.tr.* to occupy

aḥya/yiḥyi *v.tr.* to bring back to life, revive; to commemorate

aǰār bi ssāɛa rent on an hourly basis

aǰbar/yiǰbur *v.tr.* to force, compel, oblige

aǰǰal/yiʔǰǰil *v.tr.* to postpone, put off

aǰnabiyya *adj.,n.* foreign; foreigner

aǰr *n.* reward; wage, pay; fee, rate

ak͟had bi ɛēn lʔiɛtibār to consider

ak͟had iǰrāʔāt s͟hadīda took strong measures

ak͟hd tār taking revenge, retaliation

ak͟hlāg *n.* manners

ak͟htafa/yik͟htafi *v.intr.* to disappear, become invisible, be missing, vanish

ak͟htalaṭ/yik͟htaliṭ *v.intr.* to be mixed

ak͟htār/yik͟htār *v.tr.* to choose, select

akkad/yiʔakkid *v.tr.* to assure, verify, affirm

aktaras/yiktaris + li *v.intr.* to care for; to pay attention to

aktariyya *n.* majority, most of

aktas͟haf/yiktas͟hif *v.tr.* to discover

alam *n.pl.* ālām pain

albēt alḥarām the Holy Mosque in Mecca

alga/yilgi lgabḍ + ɛala *v.intr.* to arrest

algibla *n.* direction facing the ka'aba in Holy Mecca. Every Muslim has to face the 'qibla' while praying.

alhind *pro.n.* India

alḥaramēn *n.* the two holy places of Mecca and Medina

alif bāʔi in alphabetical order

alkiswa *n.* the covering of the Ka'aba

allāh aɛlam God knows

almabāḥit assuɛūdiyya Saudi intelligence

almasǰid alḥarām the Holy Mosque in Mecca

almuʔassasa lʔamrīkiyya li ttanmiya ddōliyya USAID

almuʔassasa lɛāmma li taḥliyat almūya the Saline Water Conversion Corporation

almukarrama *adj.* the honored, the revered; (with def.art.) epithet of Mecca

altazam/yiltazim *v.intr.* to be committed to

alɛēla lmālka the royal family

amal *n.pl.* āmāl hope

amākin rīfiyya rural places

amda/yimdi *v.tr.* to last; to go far, to keep on (doing s.th.)

amman/yiʔammin *v.tr.* to insure; to provide; to guarantee; to trust s.o.

amtad/yimtad + min...ila *v.intr.* to stretch, extend from...to

anfaḍaḥ/yinfaḍiḥ *v.pass.* to be disclosed, be revealed, become public; to be dishonored

anfaǰar/yinfaǰir *v.tr.* to explode

anfaɛal/yinfaɛil *v.intr.* to react; to be irritated, be upset, be angry angad/yingid *v.tr.* to deliver, save, rescue

anhār/yinhār *v.intr.* to collapse, break down

anḥāʔ almamlaka every part of the kingdom

anrafaḍ/yinrafaḍ *v.pass.* to be rejected, be refused

anṣāb/yinṣāb *v.pass.* to be hit; to be stricken; to be injured

anṭabaq/yinṭabiq + ʿala *v.pass.* to be applicable; to correspond

anʿam/yinʿim *v.intr.* to bestow, give

arrubʿ alkhāli the Empty Quarter

artakab/yirtakib *v.tr.* to commit a crime or offense, engage in criminal activity

artāḥ/yirtāḥ *v.intr* to rest

asar *n.pl.* asār trace; effect, influence

asāsi *adj.* basic, fundamental, elementary, essential; chief, main, principal

asāsiyya *adj.* basic

ashghal/yishghil *v.tr.* to occupy

ashǰaʿ *adj.comp.* more courageous

ashsharīʿa *n.* Islamic law, the Shari'a

ashsharīʿa lʔislāmiyya Islamic law, the Shari'a

ashtara/yishtari *v.tr.* to buy

asnāʔ during, while

assas/yiʔassis *v.tr.* to found, establish

assin bi ssin wa lʿēn bi lʿēn a tooth for a tooth and an eye for an eye

astaghna/yistaghni + ʿan *v.intr.* to be able to do without

astaǰwab/yistaǰwib *v.tr.* to interrogate, question, hear (a defendant or witness), examine

astarǰaʿ/yistarǰiʿ *v.tr.* to get back, recover, regain; recapture

astaslam/yistaslim + li *v.intr.* to surrender

astashhad/yastashhid + bi *v.intr.* to quote; to refer to; to die as a martyr, a hero

astawʿab/yiståwʿib *v.tr.* to contain; to have room; to comprehend

aṣarr/yiṣirr + ʿala *v.intr.* to insist, persist, be determined

aṣl *n.pl.* ʔuṣūl roots, background

aṣṭadamat/tiṣṭadim + bi *v.intr.* to collide with; to strike

atʔakkad/yitʔakkad + min *v.intr.* to be sure of, make sure of, verify

atʔammal/yitʔammal *v.intr.* to hope; to expect; to meditate

atḍāhar/yitḍāhar *v.intr.* to pretend

atgāḍa/yitgāḍa *v.tr.* to be paid

atḥākam/yitḥākam *v.pass.* to be prosecuted; to be brought to trial

atḥāwar/yitḥāwar + maʿ *v.intr.* to debate; to interview; to talk

atǰānas/yitǰānas *v.intr.* to intermarry

atǰannab/yitǰannab *v.tr.* to avoid

atǰarrad/yitǰarrad + min *v.intr.* to be stripped, deprived; to be disarmed; to be detached, be free of

atkawwam/yitkawwam *v.intr.* to be piled up

atkhayyal/yitkhayyal *v.tr.* to imagine

atlaf/yitlif *v.tr.* to destroy, damage, ruin, waste

atmashsha/yitmashsha *v.intr.* to have a good time; take a walk, stroll; to go on a trip

atraddad/yitraddad + ʿala or li *v.intr.* to frequent a place

atraǰǰa/yitraǰǰa *v.tr.* to beg for; to plea for s.th.

atṣawwar/yitṣawwar *v.tr.* to imagine; to expect; to photograph; to draw

atṣādam/yitṣādam *v.intr.* to collide, hit

attaḍaḥ/yittaḍiḥ *v.pass.* to be clear, obvious, evident

attafag/yittafig + maʿ *v.intr.* to agree with; to suit; (with the preposition ʿala) to agree on

attaham/yittahim *v.tr.* to accuse

atwaḍḍa/yitwaḍḍa *v.intr.* to perform the ritual ablution before prayer

atwaggaf/yitwaggaf + ʿala *v.intr.* to depend on, be based on

atwaggaf/yitwaggaf + ʿan *v.intr.* to abstain from

atwaggaʿ/yitwaggaʿ *v.tr.* to expect

atwazzaʿ/yitwazzaʿ + ʿala *v.pass.* to be distributed; to be assigned

atzayyan/yitzayyan + li *v.intr.* to be adorned, be made attractive; to seduce

atʿallag/yitʿallag *v.intr.* to cling; to hang on (to); to be fond (of)

aṭṭalaʿ/yiṭṭaliʿ + ʿala *v.intr.* to be informed of, learn about

awa/yiʔwi *v.tr.* to shelter, lodge, accomodate, house, give refuge

awrāg māliyya nagdiyya money, cash

awwalāt the past

aʕma *adj.pl.* ʕumyān, ʕumy blind

aʕma/yiʕmi *v.tr.* to blind, cause to lose one's sight

aʕmāl iǰrāmiyya criminal acts

aʕrāḍ *n.* symptoms

aʕtada/yiʕtadi + ʕala *v.intr.* to rape; to assault

aʕtagad/yiʕtagid + bi *v.intr.* to believe

aʕtamad/yiʕtamid + ʕala *v.intr.* to depend on

aʕtazz/yiʕtazz + bi *v.intr.* to be proud of, take pride in

aʕūzu bi llāh I take refuge in God

aʕwaǰ *adj.pl.* ʕōǰān, ʕūǰ crooked

aʕwar *adj.pl.* ʕōrān one-eyed

ā

ānisa *n.pl.* -āt unwed girl

āya *n.pl.* -āt Qor'anic verse; miracle

b

bagha/yibgha *v.tr.* to want

baḥas/yibḥas *v.tr.* to discuss; (with ʕan) to look for, for search

baḥḥar/yibaḥḥir *v.intr.* to sail

baḥḥār *n.pl.* baḥḥāra sailor, seaman, mariner

baḥriyya *adj.* sea

baḥt *n.pl.* buḥūt research, study

bakhkhūr *n.coll.* incense

bala *n.* sickness; affliction

balagh/yiblugh *v.tr.* to amount to

balāgh *n.pl.* -āt message; announcement; communique'

balla *n.* moistening, wetting

ballagh/yiballigh *v.tr.* to notify

ballash/yiballish *v.tr.* to start, begin

banghāli *adj.n.pl.* -yyīn Bengali, native of West Bengal (India) or Bangladesh

bannāʔ *adj.* productive, constructive

baraka *n.pl.* -āt blessing

barāʔa *n.* innocence

barḍu still

barhan/yibarhin *v.tr.* to prove

barīʔ *adj.* innocent

barriyya *adj.* land

bashar *n.coll.* human beings

baṭn *n.pl.* buṭūn stomach, abdomen

bayān *n.pl.* -āt information, news; official report, official statement

bazal/yibzil *v.tr.* make (an effort); to spend; to sacrifice

baʕat/yibʕat *v.tr.* to send

baʕīr *n.* camel

bār *adj.* righteous; good

bāri *act.part.* creator (referring to God)

bāt/yibīt *v.intr.* to spend the night

bāʕ/yibīʕ *v.tr.* to sell

bēb *n.pl.* -āt pipe

bi gaṣd intentionally, deliberately

bi giyādat under the leadership of

bi hāda lkhuṣūṣ concerning this matter

bi hudūʔ calmly

bi ihdāʔ by the guidance of

bi istimrār continuously, always

bi izni llāh if God is willing; if God permits

bi khuṣūṣ concerning, regarding, with respect to

bi lʔiḍāfa in addition to, besides; furthermore

bi lgadam on foot

bi lḥagīga frankly, in fact, indeed

bi lǰumla wholesale

bi lwāgiʕ indeed, as a matter of fact

bi muǰarrad as soon as, at the very moment when

bi nōʕ khāṣ especially

bi rrughm in spite of

bi sharṭ on the condition that

bi ṣifatu in its capacity as

bi taʕaǰǰub surprised, astonished

bi ṭṭabʕ naturally, certainly, of course

bi wāṣi/ṭat by means of, through, on the part of

bi wuddak would you like, do you desire

bidūn murāgaba unattended

biḍāʕ *n.coll.pl.* -āt goods, commodities

bila without

binā?an ʢala based on, on the basis of; according to; in accordance with, by virtue of

biʢsa *n.pl.* -āt mission, delegation; group of people, team; expedition

bīr *n.pl.* ābār well

bīr zamzam Zamzam Well

blātīn *n.coll.* platinum; white gold

buḥūs ʢilmiyya scientific research

bukhār n.coll. vapor

bukra *n.* tomorrow

buna *n.* building, construction

bustān *n.pl.* basātīn garden

buzūra *n.coll.* children

būfē *n.pl.* -yāt buffet

d

dabdūb *adj.* fat

dabīḥa *n.pl.* dabāyiḥ slaughtered animal; sacrifice

dafʢa *n.pl.* -āt group; payment

dahab *n.coll.* gold

dakhīlak if you please; I beg of you

dakhl *n.* income

dalla/yidalli *v.tr.* to let fall down, drop

dawra *n.pl.* -āt workshop

dawriyya ḥaggat alkhaṭ highway patrol

daʢam/yidʢam *v.tr.* to support

dā?iriyya *adj.* circular

dāfaʢ/yidāfiʢ + ʢan *v.intr.* to defend

dāmiǰ *n.* damages

dān/yidīn *v.tr.* to condemn; to judge

dēn *n.pl.* duyūn debt; liability; obligation

dibla *n.pl.* dibal wedding band

dirāsa mi/utkāmla comprehensive study

dirāsāt amniyya security studies

dirāsāt iǰtimāʢiyya social studies

diyya *n.pl.* -āt blood money, indemnity for bodily injury

dīb *n.pl.* dyāb wolf

dōla nāmya developing country

dōr *n.pl.* adwār role, part (played by s.o. or s.th.); turn; floor

dōr adwār mutaʢaddida numerous roles

dughri immediately, right away

duwal l?aʢḍā? member countries

ḍ

ḍaḥak/yiḍḥak + ʢala *v.intr.* to laugh at ; make a fool of, make fun of

ḍaḥiyya *n.pl.* -āt, daḥāya blood sacrifice; victim

ḍakh *v.n.* pumping

ḍakhma *adj.* huge, gigantic

ḍalam/yiḍli/um *v.tr.* to be unjust, unfair; to oppress

ḍarr/yiḍurr *v.tr.* to harm

ḍarūri *adj.* necessary

ḍāʢ/yiḍīʢ *v.intr.* to get lost; to disappear

ḍīg *n.* lack; poverty; tightness

ḍrāṭ *n.* fart

ḍufr *n.pl.* aḍāfir fingernail; toenail

ḍulm *n.* unfairness, injustice; oppression, tyranny

ḍumn within, inside of, among

f

faḍla *n.pl.* -āt leftover, remnant; surplus

fagad/yifgid *v.tr.* to lose; to miss; to be bereaved

faḥma *n.pl.* -āt, faḥm charcoal

faǰǰar/yifaǰǰir *v.tr.* to bomb; to explode

faǰ?a suddenly

fakhūr *adj.* proud

falaki *n.pl.* -īn astronomer; astronaut

faraḍ/yifriḍ + ʢala *v.intr.* to impose; to order; to make incumbent

farag/yifrug *v.intr.* to exit, part

farak/yifruk *v.tr.* to rub

faraǰ *n.* relief

fard *n.pl.* afrād individual, person

farḍ *n.* order, command

farg *n.pl.* furūg difference

farīḍa *n.pl.* farāy/?iḍ religious duty; ordinance of God

farīg *n.* team, group

farz *n.* sorting out, classifying

faṣl min alkhidma discharge from the service

fatḥ ḥisāb opening a (bank) account

fatra giyāsiyya record time, record-breaking time

fattāka *adj.* devastating

fatūra *n.pl.* fawātīr invoice, bill

fayaḍān *n.pl.* -āt flood

fāshil *act.part.* failure

fāyda *n.pl.* fawāyid benefit, gain, profit; interest (on money)

fi lmiyya percent

fi maḥallu appropriately

fiḍḍa *n.coll.* silver

fikra *n.* idea, thought

firāɛ *n.* reconciliation

fulān alfulāni Mr. So-and-So

furṣa *n.pl.* furaṣ chance, opportunity

g

gabaḍ/yigbaḍ + ɛala *v.intr.* to arrest, catch, capture

gabīḥ *adj.comp.* agbaḥ worse; uglier

gabr *n.pl.* gubūr grave, tomb

gabw *n.* basement; vault

gaddar/yigaddir + ẓ/ḍurūfi *v.tr.* to be understanding of one's situation

gadīfa *n.pl.* gadāyif missile, projectile, rocket

gadīm azzamān ancient times, former times

gaḍa/yigḍi *v.tr.* to spend (time)

gaḍḍa/yigaḍḍi *v.intr.* to go shopping

gaḍḍa/yigaḍḍi *v.tr.* to spend (time)

gaḥ/yiguḥ *v.intr.* to cough

galgān *act.part.pl.* -īn worried, anxious, sleepless, agitated

gall/yigill *v.intr.* to be less

gallab/yigallib *v.tr.* to turn, turn over

gallābiyya *n.pl.* -āt bulldozer, tractor

gamḥ *n.coll.* wheat

ganāɛa *n.* contentment

garār alʔiɛdām death sentence

garrar/yigarrir *v.tr.* to decide

garya *n.pl.* gura village

garya nāʔya remote village

gashaɛ/yigshaɛ *v.tr.* to lift; to remove

gaṣd *n.* purpose, goal

gaṣīr *adj.* short

gaṣr *n.pl.* guṣūr palace

gatīl *n.pl.* magātīl casualty

gatɛ rās beheading

gat/yiqut *v.tr.* to throw away; to drop

gaṭaɛ/yigṭaɛ lʔamal *v.tr.* to give up hope

gaṭaɛ/yigṭaɛ rās *v.tr.* to behead

gaṭaɛ/yigṭaɛ yaddu cut off his hand, amputate his hand

gaṭṭar/yigaṭṭir *v.tr.* to distill

gawām immediately, right away

gawwas/yigawwis *v.tr.* to bend, curve; to arch (the eyebrow)

gābal/yigābil *v.tr.* to meet, to face; to compare

gābila *n.pl.* -āt midwife

gāḍa/ yigāḍi *v.tr.* to judge, punish, sentence

gāfla *n.pl.* gawāfil caravan

gāḥla *adj.* dry, arid, barren

gām/yigūm *v.intr.* to undertake; to get up

gās/yigīs *v.tr.* to try on, fit on

gatīl *act.part.pl.* -īn, gatala killer

gāṭaɛ/yigāṭiɛ *v.tr.* to boycott

gāymat almuḥtawayāt table of contents

gāymat lʔakl menu

gidir *n.pl.* gudūr pot

ginṭār *n.pl.* ganāṭīr ton; (in the pl.) tremendous sums

gishr *n.pl.* gushūr bark; skin (of fruit)

gism *n.pl.* agsām department; part, portion

giṣāra *n.* brick laying

giṣṣa *n.pl.* giṣaṣ story, tale; problem

giyam *n.* values, norms; worth

giyam akhlāgiyya moral values

gīma *n.pl.* giyam value; price

gubbaɛa dāʔiriyya beret

gubūl *n.* acceptance

gunbala *n.pl.* ganābil bomb

gh

ghad *n.* tomorrow

ghaḍab/yighḍab *v.intr.* to be angry, be mad; to become upset

ghala *n.* inflation, high cost, rising cost

ghallāya *n.pl.* -āt an apparatus for boiling water, boiler

ghamīg *adj.* deep

gharaḍ *n.pl.* aghrāḍ articles of everyday use, household items, odd and ends, things

gharāma *n.pl.* -āt fine; compensation; penalty

ghargān *act. partl.pl.* -īn drowning person

gharr/yighurr *v.tr.* to deceive, trick, mislead, seduce; to dazzle

gharraz/yigharriz *v.tr.* to prick; to stab; to insert

ghaṭa *n.pl.* aghṭiya lid, cover

ghaṭraf/yighaṭrif *v.intr.* to utter shrill, long-drawn-out trilling sounds (as a manifestion of joy by Arab women)

ghāb/yighīb + ɛan *v.intr.* to be absent; to hide

ghāz ṭabīɛi natural gas

ghina *n.* riches, wealth

ghizāʔi *adj.* nutritional, (relating to) food

ghumg *n.* depth

ghurfa tiǰāriyya chamber of commerce

h

haddad/yihaddid *v.tr.* to threaten

hadiyya *n.pl.* hadāya gift

hamaǰi *adj.* barbaric, savage, uncivilized

hamal/yihmil *v.tr.* to ignore, neglect

handasi *adj.* engineering

hanna/yihanni *v.tr.* to congratulate

hawa *n.* air; love; romance

hawa shamāli northern wind

haykal *n.pl.* hayākil temple; skeleton, framework (of a structure), frame

hazz/yihizz mashāɛir *v.tr.* to shock

hazz/yihuzz *v.tr.* to shake

hazza arḍiyya earthquake

hāǰar/yihāǰir *v.intr.* to immigrate; to emigrate

hārib *act.part.pl.* -īn escapee

hāyil *adj.* huge, vast, gigantic

hēʔa *n.pl.* -āt organization; association; appearance

hēl *n.coll.* cardamom

hu bi nafsu he himself

huǰūm *n.* attack, raid

ḥ

ḥabba *n.pl.* ḥubūb pill, tablet; one piece (of fruit)

ḥabbat shaɛīr a seed of barley; (fig.) of no value

ḥabl *n.pl.* ḥibāl rope

ḥaddad/yiḥaddid *v.tr.* to limit

ḥadīd *n.coll.* iron

ḥadīsa *adj.* modern, up-to-date

ḥaḍāra *n.pl.* -āt modernization; development; civilization

ḥaḍāriyya *adj.* modernizing

ḥaḍḍar/yiḥaḍḍir *v.tr.* to prepare, make ready

ḥafīd *n.pl.* aḥfād grandson

ḥafr *v.n.* drilling, digging

ḥag *n.* truth

ḥaggag/yiḥaggig *v.tr.* to achieve, accomplish

ḥaggag/yiḥaggig + bi *v.intr.* to investigate

ḥaggōn *poss.pron.* their

ḥaǰariyya *adj.* rocky, stony

ḥaǰǰ *n.* pilgrimage

ḥaǰǰ *n.pl.* ḥuǰǰāǰ pilgrim

ḥaǰm *n.pl.* aḥǰām volume

ḥak/yiḥuk *v.tr.* to scratch

ḥaka/yiḥki *v.tr.* to tell (a story); speak

ḥakīm *n.pl.* ḥukama physician; wise

ḥal/yiḥil + li *v.intr.* to be lawful, permitted, allowed

ḥala *n.* dessert; sweetness; sweet pastry

ḥalāl *adj.* lawful, according to God's will

ḥallal/yiḥallil *v.tr.* to analyze

ḥama/yiḥmi *v.tr.* to protect, keep

ḥamla *n.pl.* -āt campaign, expedition

ḥan/yiḥin *v.intr.* to feel compassion; to have mercy

ḥanas̲h̲ *n.pl.* aḥnās̲h̲ snake

ḥanīf *adj.* true (in reference to the Islamic religion)

ḥann galbu ɛalē He had sympathy for him. His heart was full of compassion for him. He had pity on him.

ḥaraka *n.* movement, motion

ḥarām *adj.* unlawful, forbidden; sacred; sin; offense

ḥarāmi *n.pl.* ḥarāmiyya thief, robber

ḥarf *n.pl.* ḥurūf edge; letter of the alphabet

ḥarīm ɛala riǰāl women and men

ḥarīṣa *adj.* careful, cautious

ḥarraḍ/yiḥarriḍ *v.tr.* to stir up, agitate; to provoke, incite

ḥassan/yiḥassin *v.tr.* to improve

ḥawl *n.* power, might

ḥawwal/yiḥawwil *v.tr.* to assign s.th. to s.o.; to transform; to transfer

ḥay *n.pl.* aḥyāʔ neighborhood

ḥayawān *n.pl.* -āt animal, beast

ḥayya *n.pl.* -āt snake

ḥazm *n.* strictness; strength

ḥādis *n.pl.* ḥawādis event, happening; accident

ḥāǰib *n.pl.* ḥawāǰib eyebrow

ḥākim *n.pl.* ḥukkām governor, ruler

ḥāla ṭārʔa emergency

ḥāmi *act.part.pl.* -īn guard, protector, defender

ḥāṣar/yiḥāṣir *v.tr.* to surround, besiege

ḥidāda *n.* smithery, the trade of a smith

ḥikāya *n.pl.* -āt matter, story

ḥimāya *n.* protection

ḥirfa *n.pl.* ḥiraf vocation, career, trade

ḥisābāt riyāḍiyya mathematical computation

ḥiwār *n.* dialogue, text (of a play); talk, conversation; interview

ḥubūb musahhira amphetamine

ḥudūd *n.* borders, boundaries

ḥufra *n.pl.* ḥufar hole, pit

ḥugūg alʔinsān human rights

ḥuǰǰa *n.pl.* ḥuǰaǰ reasoning; excuse

ḥula *n.coll.* jewelry

ḥumūla *n.pl.* -āt load capacity

ḥur *adj.* noble; freeborn

ḥurriyyat almilāḥa freedom of navigation/sailing

ḥuṣṣa *n.pl.* ḥuṣaṣ share, portion

ḥuzn *n.* sadness

i

i/aftak̲h̲ar/yiftak̲h̲ir + bi *v.intr.* to take pride in

ibtidāʔi *adj.* elementary, basic

idāʔ *n.* fulfilling (a prayer, an obligation); accomplishment (of a task)

idāra ɛāmma general administration

idārat mukāfaḥat almuk̲h̲addirāt Drug Enforcement Administration

iḍāfa *n.* adding, annexation

iḍṭarr/yiḍṭarr *v.intr.* to find it necessary, have to

igāma *n.* residence, stay

igtaraḥ/yigtariḥ *v.tr.* to suggest

igtirāḥ *n.pl.* -āt suggestion

ihtam/yihtam + bi *v.intr.* to be concerned, take an interest; to go to the trouble

ihtimām *n.pl.* -āt concern, care

iḥṣāʔiyyāt *n.* statistics, census

iḥtawa/yiḥtawi + ɛala *v.intr.* to contain, include

iḥtirām *n.* respect

iǰāza *n.pl.* -āt vacation, leave; license, authorization

iǰāza ʔusbūɛiyya weekend

iǰmālan *adv.* on the whole, in general, generally speaking

iǰrāʔāt *n. in the pl. form* measures, steps, proceedings; precautions

iǰtimāɛi *adj.* social

ik̲h̲talaf/yik̲h̲talif + ɛan *v.intr.* to be different from

ik̲h̲tirāɛ *n.pl.* -āt invention

ik̲h̲tiṣāṣi *adj.* specialized

ik̲h̲tiyāri *adj.* optional, voluntary

iktiʔāb *n.* depression

imkāniyya *n.pl.* -āt potential, ability, capacity; possibility

infaɛal/yinfaɛil *v.intr.* to react; to be irritated, be upset, be angry infiṣāl *v.n.* separation; disengagement

inhiyār ɛaṣabi nervous breakdown

inǰāz *n.pl.* -āt achievement, accomplishment

insān *n.* human being; mankind

insāniyya *n.* humanity; humanness, politeness, civility

intāǰ *n.* production

intibāh *n.* paying attention, awareness

intigād *n.pl.* -āt criticism; objection; critique; satire

irs͟hād *n.pl.* -āt instruction; guidance; information; advice

irtafaɛ/yirtafiɛ *v.intr.* to go up

irtāḥ/yirtāḥ *v.intr.* to rest

isbāt *n.pl.* -āt proof, evidence; confirmation, documentation, verification

istafād/yistafīd + min *v.intr.* to benefit from s.o. or s.th.

istagbal/yistagbil *v.tr.* to receive (people), to welcome

istarǰaɛ/yistarǰiɛ *v.tr.* to get back, recover, regain; recapture

istifāda *n.pl.* -āt profiting, benefiting, making use of

istigrār *n.* stability

istik͟hdām *n.* using

istirād *n.* import, importing

istirāḥa *n.* rest area

istiɛdād *n.pl.* -āt readiness; willingness; ambition

istudyō *n.* studio

isɛāf *n.* first aid; ambulance

is͟htibāk *n.pl.* -āt clash, fight

is͟htirāk *n.pl.* -āt participating; subscribing (to a magazine)

ittaḍaḥ/yittaḍiḥ *v.pass.* to be clear, obvious, evident

ittifāgiyyat alʔimtiyāz concession agreement

ittiǰāh *n.* direction

iṭār *n.pl.* -āt framework; frame

izan therefore

izāɛa *n.pl.* -āt broadcasting; network

izdihār *n.* progress

iɛdām *n.* execution, death sentence

iɛlān *n.pl.* -āt announcement, advertisement

iɛtidāʔ *n.pl.* -āt aggression; assault, attack

iɛtigāl *n.* detention

iɛtirāḍ *n.pl.* -āt objection, opposition

iɛtirāf *n.* confession

īdāɛ *n.* depositing, consigning

ǰ

ǰabān *adj.pl.* ǰubana coward

ǰadda *n.pl.* -āt grandmother

ǰadur *n.pl.* ǰudrān wall

ǰafāf *n.* drought

ǰald *n.* lashing

ǰalda *n.pl.* -āt lash, lashing

ǰalīs *n.pl.* ǰulasa companion, friend

ǰallād *act.part.pl.* -īn person who performs the lashing

ǰammaɛ/yiǰammiɛ *v.tr.* to gather, collect

ǰana/yiǰni *v.tr.* to reap

ǰana/yiǰni + ɛala *v.intr.* to offend, sin (against); to harm; to hurt

ǰann ǰunūn + *poss.pro.* to become frantic, become angry, become furious

ǰanna *n.pl.* -āt paradise, garden

ǰanūb s͟harg āsya South East Asia

ǰara/yiǰri + li lg͟hēr *v.intr.* to happen to others

ǰarīma *n.pl.* ǰarāyim crime, murder

ǰarīma munaẓẓama organized crime

ǰarr/yiǰurr *v.tr.* to drag; to pull

ǰaw *n.* weather

ǰawla mīdāniyya field trip

ǰawwiyya *adj.* air

ǰayyid *adj.* good

ǰaza *n.* punishment, penalty

ǰaɛl I hope, may God

ǰāʔ/yiza *n.pl.* ǰawāʔiz award

ǰāʔiza māliyya monetary award

ǰāf *adj.* dry

ǰāhil *adj.* ignorant

ǰāra/yiǰāri *v.tr.* to be in conformity with/in accordance with, to keep up with

ǰāyiz *adj.* possible

ǰāzā/yiǰāzi *v.tr.* to reward, punish

ǰihād ʔislāmi Islamic Jihad

ǰild *n.* skin; leather

ǰimāɛ *n.* sexual intercourse

ǰinēna *n.pl.* ǰanāyin garden; front yard, back yard

ǰinsiyya *n.pl.* -āt nationality

ǰisr *n.pl.* ǰusūr bridge

ǰīl *n.pl.* aǰyāl generation

ǰīl alghaḍab alʕarabi the Generation of Arab Anger

ǰurḥ *n.pl.* ǰurūḥ wound, cut

ǰutta *n.pl.* ǰutat body, corpse, cadaver, carcass

k

kaff *n.pl.* kufūf palm; glove; hand

kafīl *n.pl.* kufala sponsor, legal guardian; responsible; guaranteeing

kahraba ssayyāra automotive electricity

kalām allāh God's word

kalb *n.pl.* kilāb dog

kallaf nafsu to take the trouble to do

kallaf/yikallif *v.tr.* to commission, authorize

kamāl *n.* perfection

kammiyya *n.pl.* -āt quantity

kanīsa *n.pl.* kanāyis, kanāʔis church

karīma *n.adj.* daughter; precious; generous

kasa/yiksi *v.tr.* to clothe, dress, garb

kasab/yiksab *v.tr.* to win, gain

kasb *n.* gain, earning; winning, profiting

kashaf/yikshif ʕalēha *v.intr.* to look at her unveiled; to examine her medically

kaslān *adj.pl.* -īn idle, lazy

kāmil *adj.* complete

kāmla *adj.* complete

kārisa *n.pl.* kawāris disaster, calamity

kāsiḥāt alʔalghām mine sweepers

kilma *n.* speech; word

kizb *n.* lies, lying

kulliyya *n.pl.* -āt academy; college

kusr *n.pl.* kusūr fracture (of a bone), break

kūsha *n.* the place where women sit during the wedding and where the bride and groom enter for the final wedding procession

kwayyis *adj.* good, fine

kh

khabar *n.pl.* akhbār news

khabīr *n.pl.* khubara expert

khalag/yikhlag *v.tr.* to create, make; to shape, form

khalīfa *n.pl.* khulafa successor; caliph

khalīǰ *n.* gulf

khamr *n.coll.pl.* khumūr wine, alcoholic beverage

khanag/yikhnug *v.tr.* to choke, suffocate

khanǰar *n.pl.* khanāǰir dagger

kharaǰ/yikhruǰ + ʕan addīn to deviate, drift away from the religion

kharaʕ/yikhraʕ *v.tr.* to be startled, be scared

kharūf *n.pl.* khirfān lamb

khasha/yikhsha *v.intr.* to fear, be afraid

khashm *n.* nose

khaṣīb *adj.comp.* akhṣab fertile, productive

khaṭ *n.pl.* khuṭūṭ lane; line

khaṭaf/yikhṭi/uf *v.tr.* to kidnap, highjack, abduct, snatch; to elope

khaṭar *n.pl.* akhṭār danger, threat

khaṭar ʕala bāl + *obj.pron.* it occurs to the mind; to think of s.th.

khazzān *n.pl.* -āt reservoir

khabbar/yikhbbir *v.tr.* to tell, inform

khābir *act.part.* -īn aware, knowing

khāli *adj.* empty; free (from)

khālya *adj.* empty; free (from)

khāshūga *n.pl.* -āt ladle; spoon

khāsra *adj.* losing

khēr *n.* good, goodness; blessing; wealth

khēzarān *n.* reed, bamboo, cane, rattan

khibra *n.* expertise

khidma *n.* tip; service

khilāl during, through

khiṣṣīṣan *adv.* especially

khuddām ashshēṭān servants of Satan

khushūʕ *n.* submission, humility

l

l?umūr hādi the following items/matters

labbayka here I am! at your service!

laga/yilāgi *v.tr.* to find

laḥas/yilḥas *v.tr.* to lick

laḥālhum by themselves

laǰnat alʿafw addōliyya Amnesty International

lammaʿ/yilammiʿ *v.tr.* to shine, polish

laʿlaʿ/yilaʿliʿ *v.intr.* to roar, resound, clang, reverberate

lā samaḥ allāh God does not permit, God forbid

lā waffagu llāh may God not grant him success

lā yigil ʿan no less than

lā ʿād tʿīdaha Don't you ever do it again.

lāḥga *adj.* following

lēlat azzafāf wedding night

lḥāf *n.pl.* luḥuf comforter; cover

li gh̲āyat until

li ṣāliḥ for the well-being (of), for the benefit (of)

li ttasǰīl for registration, for recording

li/a ḥālu by itself, alone

lilḥīn until now

liwā? *n.* major general

lubān *n.coll.* frankincense, gum resin

lugh̲m *n.pl.* algh̲ām mine, explosive device

lugma *n.pl.* -āt, lugam mouthful, morsel

luṭf *n.* kindness, goodness

m

ma?sāt *n.pl.* ma?āsi tragedy; misery

ma?zūn *n.* clergyman authorized to perform marriages

mabāḥis *n.* intelligence agency, secret police

mabda? *n.pl.* mabādi? principle, ideology

mablagh̲ *n.pl.* mabāligh̲ amount, sum

mabna *n.pl.* mabāni building

mad/yimi/ud naẓaru *v.tr.* to gaze, look; to glance at

madaḥ/yimdaḥ *v.tr.* to praise s.o.

madfūn *pass.part.* buried, hidden

madkh̲ūl *n.* income

maḍakh̲kh̲a *n.pl.* -āt pump

maḍḍa/yimaḍḍi *v.tr.* to spend (time); to stay

mafhūm *n.pl.* mafāhīm understanding, concept, idea

mafhūmiyya *n.pl.* -āt understanding; mentality

mafrūḍ *pass.part.* supposed; ordered, requested

magāḍi *n.pl.* groceries

magāyīs *n.* measures, standards

magdira *n.pl.* -āt ability

magh̲fira *n.* forgiveness

magh̲sh̲ūsh̲ *adj.* corrupted, debased; adulterated; cheated, fooled

mahma whatever, no matter what

maḥaṭṭat banzīn gas station

maḥram unlawful; unmarriageable, being in a degree of consanguinity precluding marriage; taboo, forbidden

maḥsūd *adj.pl.* -īn envious

maḥw *n.* erasing, wiping out

maǰāl *n.pl.* -āt area, field, subject

maǰāʿa *n.pl.* -āt famine

maǰbūr *pass.part.* obligated

maǰhūd *n.pl.* maǰhūdāt effort

maǰhūl *pass.part. pl.* -īn unknown

maǰlis *n.pl.* maǰālis social gathering; chamber; board; council; conference room

maǰlis attaʿāwun alkh̲alīǰi the Gulf Cooperation Council

maǰnūn *adj.pl.* maǰānīn crazy; fool

makh̲āṭir *n.* risks, danger, hazards

makh̲lūg *n.pl.* -āt creature; created

makkan/yimakkin *v.tr.* to enable s.o.

malak/yimli/uk *v.tr.* to own

malakiyya muṭlaqa absolute monarchy

malakūt *n.* kingdom (of God)

malābis *n.coll.* clothes

malḥūg *pass.part.* in a hurry; followed

manaḥ/yimnaḥ *v.tr.* to grant, give and receive nothing in return

manākh̲ *n.pl.* -āt weather, climate

manākīr *n.coll.* nail polish

manḥ *n.* granting

mankūb *adj.pl.* -īn afflicted with disaster; ill-fated; victim

marāsīm alḥaǰ the hajj rituals, the rites of the pilgrimage

marfag *n.pl.* marāfig facilities

marḥala *n.pl.* marāḥil period, level, stage

marāḥil alḥaḍāra stages of modernization

marḥūma *pass.part.* deceased, the late, May God rest her soul

marǰaɛ *n.pl.* marāǰiɛ reference; resource; origin

martaba *n.pl.* -āt rank

masʔūliyya *n.pl.* -āt responsibility

masalan for example

masāḥa *n.pl.* -āt area

masḥ *n.* wiping, wiping off

masīr *n.* path; journey

masɛa *n.pl.* masāɛi endeavor, effort

mas͟hagga *n.pl.* -āt hardship, toil, trouble

mas͟hāwir *n.* consultation

mas͟hāɛir *n.* senses, feelings

mas͟hhūr *act.part.* famous

mas͟hrūɛ *n.pl.* mas͟harīɛ project

mas͟hrūɛa *adj.* legal, lawful

maṣlaḥa *n.pl.* maṣāliḥ well-being; benefit; business

maṣalḥat azzakā wu ddak͟hl religious income tax office

maṣrūf *n.pl.* maṣārīf expenditure, expenses, costs

maṣɛad *n.pl.* maṣāɛid elevator

matal *n.pl.* amtāl example; proverb; lesson

matāɛib *n.pl.* troubles, pains, discomforts; difficulties, hardships

matīn *adj.* fat

matwāk lʔak͟hīr your last habitation/dwelling/place of rest

maṭrūḥa *pass.part.* presented, broached or raised (of a question/problem)

mawḍūɛ *n.pl.* mawāḍīɛ subject, issue, matter; title

mawhiba *n.pl.* mawāhib talent, gift

mawwal/yimawwil *v.tr.* to supply; to finance

mawɛid *n.pl.* mawāɛīd appointment, date

mawɛiḍa *n.pl.* mawāɛiḍ sermon, religious exhortation, spiritual counsel

maziyya *n.pl.* mazāya *(the pl. form is more common)* merit, virtue; advantage; superiority,

mazɛūr *pass.part.* frightened

maɛ murūr azzaman as time goes by, with the passage of time

maɛaddāt *n.* equipment, machinery

maɛāli his excellency

maɛās͟h *n.pl.* -āt livelihood, living, income

maɛāzīm *adj.* invited guests

maɛdaniyya *adj.* mineral

maɛdūm *pass.part.* executed; beheaded

maɛīs͟ha *n.* way of life/living; livelihood

maɛlūmāt *n.* information

maɛmal *n.pl.* maɛāmil workshop, factory

maɛraka *n.pl.* maɛārik battle

mā ɛada except

mādda *n.pl.* mawād material

māddi *adj.* material; financial, monetary

mālak w māl *+n.* what do you have to do with...?; leave alone

mālḥa *adj.* salty

māniɛ *n.pl.* mawāniɛ objection; obstacle; hindering

mās͟hi *act.part.pl.* mās͟hyīn walking, going; one who walks/goes

mbarmaǰ *pass.part.* programmed

mēl *n.pl.* muyūl desire, inclination

mihani *adj.* vocational

mihr *n.pl.* muhūr dowry

miḥtār *adj.* confused, bewildered

mikyāǰ *n.coll.* cosmetics, make-up

min gibal on behalf of

min k͟hilāl through

min nāḥiyat concerning, with respect to

minǰar *n.pl.* manāǰir apparatus for water distillation

minzaɛiǰ *pass.part.* disturbed, bothered, annoyed

misbil *adj.* unarmed

miṣfaɛ *n.pl.* maṣāfiɛ veil

mitfawwig *act.part.pl.* -īn outstanding, successful; high achiever

mitnaggla *adj.* mobile; portable

mitnarfiz *adj.* nervous, edgy

mitsāwi *pl.* -īn equal

mitɛallig bi attached to; depending on, related to, connected with, linked to

miɛmāri *adj.* architectural

mīlādi *adj.* A.D.

mīna *n.pl.* mawāniʔ harbor, port

mīzāniyya *n.pl.* -āt budget

mīɛād *n.* appointment, date

mōsim *n.pl.* mawāsim season

mṭarraz *adj.* embroidered

muʔahhal *adj.* qualified

muʔakhkharan lately

muʔassasat almusāɛadāt assuɛūdiyya ḥaggat attanmiya the Saudi Fund for Development

muʔlim *adj.* painful

mubālagha *n.* exaggeration; extravagance

mubāshar *adj.* immediate; direct

mubāsharatan *adv.* directly

mudnib *act.part.* offender

muḍḥik *adj.* funny

muḍni *adj.* tiring

mufattish *act.part.pl.* -īn inspector

muftāḥ *n.pl.* mafātīḥ key

mugābala *n.pl.* -āt meeting; gathering; interview

mugāḍāt *n.* punishment; sentence, (judicial, court) ruling

mughallaf *n.pl.* -āt envelope

mughma ɛalē unconscious

mughra *pass.part.* deluded; tempted, attracted, seduced

mugtaniɛ *adj.* convinced

muharrib *act.part.pl.* -īn smuggler

muhādana *n.* truce, suspension of hostilities, armistice

muhāǰir *act.par.pl.* -īn immigrant

muḥaṣṣan *pass.part.* entrenched; fortified

muǰahhaza *adj.* equipped

muǰammaɛ sakani housing complex

muǰarrad nothing more than, mere; bare, naked; abstract

muǰawharāt *n.* jewelry, jewels, gems

mukallaf *pass.part.pl.* -īn authorized; commissioned, delegated

mukayyafa *adj.* cultivated; conditioned; molded

mukāfaḥa *n.* fighting; stopping

mukh *n.* brain

mukhaddirāt *n.* drugs, narcotics; anesthetics, painkillers, tranquilizers

mukhaṣṣaṣ *adj.pl.* -īn specialized

mukhālafa *n.* violation, traffic ticket

mukhālif li violating, against (a law); conflicting, contradictory

mukhāṭaba *n.* conversation, talk

mukhtabar *n.pl.* -āt laboratory

mukhtariɛ *act.part.pl.* -īn inventor

mukhṭi *act.part.* at fault

mulawwana *adj.* colored, colorful

mulzam *pass.part.* obligated

mumayyiza *n.pl.* -āt distinguishing feature, distinctive mark

munawwar *adj.* lighted; shining; radiant; *(with def.art. plus f. ending)* epithet of Medina

munāfasa *n.* competition, rivalry; athletic event, contest, match; bids

murabbaɛ *pass.part.* square

murabbiya *n.pl.* -āt governess, educator; nanny

murakhkhaṣ *pass.part.* licensed, permitted, authorized

murattaba ḥasab alḥurūf lʔabǰadiyya arranged in alphabetical order

murawwiǰ *act.part.pl.* -īn marketer, pusher (of drugs)

murāgaba *n.* observation; supervision; surveillance, inspection; control; censorship (of the press)

murgham *pass.part.* forced, compeled, coerced

murūr *n.* traffic police; passing

musahhir *adj.* stimulant, something that makes one stay up and lose sleep.

musattara *adj.* covered, hidden

mustaḥaggāt *n. in the pl. form* one's rightful due

mustaḥīl *adj.* impossible

mustanad *n.pl.* -āt document; proof; legal evidence

mustawa iǰtimāɛi social class

mustawdaɛ *n.pl.* -āt warehouse, storehouse

mush bi nnisba illi not to the extent that

musharrif *adj.* honorable, noble

mushāraka *n.* cooperation, collaboration; participation

mushtarak *act.part.* common, joint, combined

muṣaddaga *adj.* notarized

muṣaddir *act.part.pl.* -īn exporter

muṣammama *adj.* designed

muṣādara *n.* confiscation, seizure

muṣība *n.pl.* maṣāyib misfortune, calamity, disaster

muṣṭāf *n.pl.* -īn summer vacationer

mutabarriꜥ *act.part.pl.* -īn contributor, donor; volunteer

mutafajjirāt explosives; bombing

mutawaṣṣiṭ *adj.* medium; average

mutābaꜥa *n.* follow up, continuing

mutgaddim *adj.* advanced

muttaham *pass.part* accused, charged; suspect

mutwaffra *adj.* available, provided

mutꜥammid *pass.part.* intentional, deliberate, premeditated

mutꜥāgid *act.part.pl.* -īn contract employee

mutꜥāṭi *act.part.pl.* -īn user

muṭawwiꜥ *act.part.pl.* -īn religious police

muṭrib *n.pl.* -īn (professional) singer

muwajjih *act.part.* guide, leader, instructor

muwallid *n.pl.* -āt generator

muwazziꜥ *act.part.pl.* -īn distributer

muwāfaga *n.pl.* -āt approval; agreement, conformity

muwāṣafāt *n.* detailed description, specification

muwāṭin *n.pl.* -īn native, citizen

muzawwad *adj.* provided, supplied; equipped

muzayyana *adj.* decorated, adorned, ornamented

muzāriꜥ *n.pl.* -īn farmer

muꜥaddal *n.pl.* -āt average; *(as adj.)* amended, modified, adjusted

muꜥaggad *pass.part.* complicated, difficult

muꜥassara *adj.* difficult, hard

muꜥāgaba *n.* punishment, punishing

muꜥḏam most (of)

muꜥīb *adj.* shameful

muꜥīd *n.pl.* -īn intern

muꜥtabara *adj.* considered

mūya ḥulwa fresh water

mwājha *adj.* opposite (direction)

mzaffata *pass.part.* paved

mzargan *adj.* stubborn

n

nabaḍ *n.* pulse

nabaḥ/yinbaḥ *v.intr.* to bark

nabbah/yinabbih *v.tr.* to warn, alert; to awaken; to notify

naddad/yinaddid + bi *v.intr.* to denounce, degrade, expose (someone's faults)

nadīr *n.pl.* warning, alarm; one who warns

nadmān *act.part.* regretful, repentant

naḍḍaf/yinaḍḍif *v.tr.* to clean

nafa/yinfi *v.tr.* to refute, repudiate; to exile; to banish

nafṭ *n.* petroleum

nagaz/yigaz *v.intr.* to be afraid of

nahḍa *n.pl.* -āt boom; growth, rise, awakening; progress

naḥās *n.coll.* brass

nakha/yinkha *v.tr.* to incite; to challenge, urge forcefully

nama/yinma *v.intr.* to grow

nasl *n.* progeny, descendant

nasma *n.* inhabitant; breeze; breath

nashāṭ riyāḍi athletic activity

nashāṭ tagāfi educational activity, cultural activity

nashl *n.* snatching; stealing; extricating (from danger, difficulties, etc.)

nashr *v.n.* spreading; publishing, publication; announcement

naskha *n.pl.* nusakh copy

naṣaḥ/yinṣaḥ *v.tr.* to advise

naṣīb *n.* share; portion; luck, chance; fate

natīja *n.pl.* natāyij result

nazīf *n.* bleeding

naẓar *n.* eyesight

naẓar/yinẓur *v.intr.* to look at

naẓra *n.* glance, look,

naẓẓam/yinaẓẓim *v.tr.* to arrange

nāda/yinādi *v.tr.* to call

nāgid *act.part.pl.* nuggād critic

nāsab/yināsib *v.tr.* to suit, fit, be in agreement/in conformity with

nāṭig *act.part.* speaker

nāzil fi lodging at, staying in

nidāʔ *n.* appeal, proclamation; call

nihāya *n.pl.* -āt end

nisba *n.* percentage, proportion

nisbiyyan *adv.* relatively

niswān *n.* women

niṭāg *n.* confines, boundary; range, extent, scope, domain

niyya *n.pl.* -āt intention

niǰāra *n.* carpentry

niɛma *n.pl.* -āt, niɛam grace, blessing

nōɛ *n.pl.* anwāɛ kind; sort, type

ntagalat/tintagil *v.intr.* to be moved

nuṣḥ *n.* guidance; good advice

q

qarn *n.pl.* qurūn century

qawmiyya *adj.,n.pl.* -āt national; nationalism

qubbaɛa *n.pl.* -āt hat

r

raʔfa + bi being merciful, having pity

raʔiy ɛām public opinion

rabaḥ/yirbaḥ *v.tr.* to profit; to win, earn; to benefit

rabba/yirabbi *v.tr.* to raise (a child, a beard)

rafaɛ/yirfaɛ yaddu *v.tr.* to refrain from s.th.

rafāhiyya *n.* luxury, leisure

rafḍ *n.* rejection, refusal

ragaba *n.pl.* -āt neck

raghba *n.pl.* -āt desire, inclination

raḥamaha llāh May God rest her soul. May God have mercy on her

raḥḥab/yiraḥḥib + bi *v.intr.* to welcome

raḥīl *n.* departure, emigration, exodus; traveling

raḥma *n.* mercy, sympathy

raǰam/yirǰim *v.tr.* to stone

raǰaɛ/yirǰaɛ *v.intr.* to go back, return

raǰīm *adj.* cursed, damned; evil

ramīm *adj.* decayed, rotten (of bones)

rashīda *adj.* rightly guided; enlightened; mature

rashshāsh *n.pl.* -āt machine gun

rasm *n.pl.* rusūm fee, tax; drawing; picture

rasūl, *n.pl.* rusul messenger; prophet; *(with the def.art.)* the Prophet Muhammad

raṣāṣ *n.coll.* lead

raṣīd *n.* fund; capital; balance

raṣīf *n.pl.* arṣifa sidewalk

raɛa/yirɛa lḥafla *v.tr.* to host a party

raɛiyya *n.* citizens; parish; flock

rāghib *act.part.pl.* -īn the person who is interested

rāḥa *n.* rest, comfort

rāsmāl *n.* (financial) capital

rātib *n.pl.* rawātib salary

rāɛi lwalīma the host of the feast

ribḥ alḥarām unlawful profit, illegal profit

riḍa *n.* approval, acceptance; consent, agreement; satisfaction

riǰāl alǰamārik custom officers

riǰǰāl aɛmāl businessman

riwāya *n.pl.* -āt story; drama, play

rizg *n.pl.* arzāg earnings; means of making a living, livelihood

rīfiyya *adj.* rural

rubbama *adv.* maybe, perhaps

rughm *prep.* in spite of, despite

ruǰim/yurǰam *v.pass.* to be stoned

rukn *n.pl.* arkān pillar (of Islam); corner; basis

rukhṣat ɛamal work permit

rutba *n.pl.* rutab (military) rank; grade, level

ruṭūba *n.* humidity

ruɛb *n.* terror, fear

s

sabbab/yisabbib *v.tr.* to cause

sabbat/yisabbit *v.tr.* to verify, prove

safīnat shaḥn cargo ship

sahar/yishar *v.tr.* to stay up late

sahhal/yisahhil *v.tr.* to make s.th. easy, simplify

sahl *n.pl.* suhūl level, soft ground, plain

sahm *n.pl.* ashum, sihām arrow, spear; share (of stock)

sakhi *adj.* generous

salbi *adj.* negative

sallākh *n.pl.* -īn skinner, butcher

sama *n.pl.* samawāt heaven *(when with the definite article)*; sky

samaḥ/yismaḥ *v.intr.* to allow, permit

samm *n.coll.pl.* sumūm poison

samn bagari clarified butter (made of cow's milk)

sarag/yisrig *v.tr.* to steal

sarwa *n.pl.* -āt wealth, treasure

saṭhiyya *adj.* superficial, external, on the surface

sawa together

sayyida *n.pl.* -āt lady, married woman

saɛa/yisɛa + li *v.intr.* to seek, strive, pursue, walk (after); to work (towards)

saɛāda *n.* happiness

saɛādat + (honorific title) your excellency

sāʔil *n.pl.* sawāʔil liquid

sābig *act.part.* previous; former

sāham/yisāhim + fi *v.intr.* to participate in, take part in; to share

sāhya *n.pl.* sawāhi still water; quiet person; absent-minded, distracted

sālfa *n.pl.* sawālif story, past event, fable

sālim aw sālmīn whoever they are, whether this or that

sāwa/yisāwi *v.tr.* to make equal/similar

sāɛat īd wristwatch

sāɛid *n.pl.* sawāɛid wrist, hand, arm

siga *n.* confidence, trust, faith

siǰil tiǰāri commercial register, business credentials

sikir/yiskar *v.intr.* to be drunk

silāḥ alḥudūd border defense forces

silsila *n.pl.* -āt, salāsil episode; chain; range

singhafūra Singapore

sir *n.pl.* asrār secret

sirga *n.pl.* -āt theft

siwa kān...aw regardless; whether ... or

sōlaf/yisōlif *v.tr.* to chat

subḥānahu wa taɛāla (God) to whom be ascribed all perfection and majesty

sufra *n.* dining table

sukhriya *n.* sarcasm

sukkar nabāt rock candy

sukr *n.* drinking, drunkenness

sukūt *n.* silence

sulūk *n.* behavior

sunna *n.* law (of nature), religious law

sunnat allāh God's law

sūʔ *n.* bad, evil

sūg ɛālamiyya international market

swīsra Switzerland

sh

shabaka *n.pl.* -āt net; network

shabakat alkahraba electric power network

shabīha *adj.* similar

shaddad/yishaddid *v.tr.* to emphasize, reinforce, stress

shafag/yishfag + ɛala *v.intr.* to feel pity, sympathize, have compassion, commiserate, have a tender heart

shag aṭṭurg opening up roads

shaḥma *n.pl.* -āt, shaḥm piece of fat; pulp(of fruit)

shaǰar nakhl palm trees

shakhṣiyya *n.* personality

shal/yishil *v.tr.* to paralyze

shanīɛa *adj.* horrible, brutal; ugly, disgusting, disgraceful

sharaf *n.* honor

sharika musāhima joint-stock company, corporation

sharīk *n.pl.* shuraka companion; partner

sharṭ *n.pl.* shurūṭ condition, stipulation

shatam/yishtim *v.tr.* to curse; to vilify; to insult

shaṭāra *n.* skill, cleverness

shawīr *n.* counselor

shaɛar/yishɛur + bi *v.intr.* to feel

shāḥina *n.pl.* -āt truck

shāmil *adj.* comprehensive, exhaustive, general, overall; complete shāsha *n.pl.* -āt screen (of a television, a computer, a watch)

shāyif ḥālu conceited

shēk siyāḥi traveler's check

shēṭān *n.pl.* shayāṭīn devil, Satan

shibh alǰazzīra lʕarabiyya the Arabian Peninsula

shihāda *n.* declaration; certificate; witness

shiʕār *n.pl.* -āt credo; emblem; slogan; motto

shōṭ *n.pl.* ashwāṭ round

shugga *n.pl.* -āt, shugag apartment

ṣ

ṣabr *n.* patience

ṣadaga *n.pl.* -āt alms, giving for charity (normally in memory of the deceased)

ṣaddigni *v.imp.* believe me

ṣadma *n.pl.* -āt shock, jolt, blow; difficulty

ṣaḥa/yiṣḥa *v.imp.* iṣḥa to wake up; to be alert

ṣaḥāfa *n.* journalism

ṣaḥḥa/yiṣaḥḥi *v.tr.* to wake s.o. up

ṣaḥīfa *n.pl.* ṣuḥuf newspaper

ṣalla llāh ʕalē wu sallam God bless him and grant him salvation

ṣandūg amānāt safety deposit box; baggage checkroom

ṣarakh/yiṣrukh *v.intr.* to scream, cry with a loud voice

ṣarāḥa *n.* frankness, frankly

ṣarrakh/yiṣarrikh *v.intr.* to scream

ṣawwar/yiṣawwir *v.tr.* to make copies of; to draw; to take a picture of

ṣayyaf/yiṣayyif *v.intr.* to spend the summer vacation

ṣāḥib alʕilāga the person concerned, the person involved

ṣārma *adj.* severe, harsh, stern; fierce; strict

ṣiyāna *n.* maintenance (of a machine, a car), upkeep; protection

ṣōm *n.* fasting

ṣudfa *n.pl.* ṣudaf coincidence

ṣudg *n.* truth

t

taʔammul *n.pl.* -āt devotion, hope; inspiration

taʔassasat/titʔassas *v.intr.* to be established, founded

tabarruʕ *n.pl.* -āt contribution, donation

tadbīr *n.* planning; management

tadgīg *n.* doing with precision/exactness/accuracy

tadmīr *n.* subversion; destruction

tadrīb *n.* training

tafashsha/yitfashsha *v.intr.* to spread (often of an epidemic)

tafashshi *n.* spreading, outbreak

tafāha *n.* silliness, stupidity, insignificance, paltriness, tastelessness

tafāṣīl *n.pl.* details

tafkīr *n.* thinking; comtemplation; thought

tagaddum *v.n.* advancing, improvement

tagdīrāt *n.* evaluation

tagharrab/yitgharrab *v.intr.* to go west, to go abroad; to immigrate; to emigrate

taghṭiya *n.* covering

taglīd copying

taglīd *n.pl.* -āt, tagālīd traditions, rituals

taglīʕa *n.pl.* -āt fad, trend

tagwīm hiǰri the Islamic calendar

tagyīm shāmil comprehensive evaluation

tahashsham/yithashsham *v.pass.* to be broken, destroyed, wrecked

tahawwur *n.* hastiness, recklessness

taḥaddi *n.* challenge

taḥarrash/yitḥarrash + bi *v.intr.* to meddle with, interfere with, provoke

taḥḍīri *adj.* preparatory

taḥliya *n.* desalination; sweetening

taḥlīli *adj.* analytic

taḥt taṣarrufhum at their disposal

taǰannub *n.* avoiding

taǰāwub *n.* response, reaction; cooperation

taǰriba *n.pl.* taǰārib experiment; experience; temptation

takhalluf *n.* backwardness, underdevelopment

takharruǰ *n.* graduation

takhaṣṣaṣ/yitkhaṣṣaṣ *v.intr.* to specialize

takhrīj n. graduating, graduation
takyīf markazi central air-conditioning
talāsha/yitlāsha v.intr. to vanish, disappear; to be ruined; to fade
talj n.coll.pl. tulūj snow
tamar n.coll.pl. atmār fruits; results
tamdīdāt ṣiḥḥiyya plumbing, installing pipes for water and sewers
tamīn adj. valuable
tamr n.coll. date
tamwīl v.n. financing
tanmiya n. expansion, advancement; growth
tansīg v.n. arranging, arrangement; preparation
taraddud n. hesitation, hesitance
tarfīhi adj. luxurious, comfortable and pleasant; leisure
tarshīḥ n.pl. -āt nomination
tasdīd almustahiggāt payment of claims
tashīl n.pl. -āt facilitation; facility
tasjīl n. registration; recording, tape recording
taslīm n. handing over; delivery; surrender, submission
tashakkak/yitshakkak + bi v.intr. to doubt, be skeptical
tashāwar/yitshāwar + maɛ v.intr. to consult with, to discuss with
tashghīl amwāl investing money
tashhīr n. exposition, exposé, exposure of something discreditable
tashjīɛiyya adj. encouraging, incentive
taṣmīm n.pl. taṣāmīm design, plan; outline; decision, resolution
taṣnīf n. classification
taṣrīḥ n.pl. -āt, taṣārīḥ permit
taṣwīb n. injury
taṣwīr n. photography, drawing
taṭawwur n. development, progress; evolution
taṭbīgi adj. applied
taṭwīr n. development
tawarraṭ/yitwarraṭ + fi or bi v.intr. to be put in an unpleasant situation, be in a bad fix, be in a dilemma
tawarruṭ n. being in a bad situation/in a bad fix/in a dilemma
tawattur ɛaṣabi nervousness, nervous tension
tawāḍuɛ n. humbleness; modesty
tawgīf n. arrest; stopping
tawjīh n. guidance
tawlīd n. delivering (of babies); generating
tawrīd n. export
tawzīɛ n. distribution; dividing; delivery (of mail, etc.)
tawɛiya n. awareness, awakening, enlightenment
taɛarruḍ n. subjection
taɛāwun n. cooperation
taɛlīm alkubār adult education
taɛlīmāt n. regulations; instructions; information; directions
taɛwīḍ n. compensation, restitution
taɛzīb n. torture
tāb/yitūb v.intr. to repent, turn to God
tānawi adj. secondary
tḍāyag/yitḍāyag + min v.intr. to be bothered by, suffer from
tgaddam/yitgaddam + li v.intr. to ask for a girl's hand, propose marriage
tgaffal alkhaṭ ɛalēna the road was blocked
tḥaggag/yitḥaggag v.pass. to be fulfilled; to be achieved
tḥārab/yitḥārab + maɛ v.intr. to fight with (s.o.)
tijāra n. trade, commerce, business
timshi īd bi īd to go hand in hand
tiɛbāyat n. filling out
tjānas/yitjānas v.intr. to intermarry
tmasak/yitmasak v.pass. to be held, caught, arrested
tōr n.pl. tīrān ox
tuhma n.pl. -āt, tuham accusation
turāb n.coll. dirt, soil; mud
turāθ/t n. culture; heritage; inheritance, traditions
tuɛbān n.pl. taɛābīn snake
tuɛtabar v.pass. to be considered
twaffa/yitwaffa v.intr. to pass away, die
twāna/yitwāna v.intr. to slow down; to neglect
tɛarraḍ/yitɛarraḍ li v.intr. to be exposed, be subjected

ṭ

ṭabaga *n.pl.* -āt layer
ṭabakh/yiṭbikh *v.tr.* to cook
ṭabīb *n.pl.* aṭibba doctor, physician
ṭabīb nisā?i obstetrician, gynecologist
ṭakhkh/yiṭukh *v.tr.* to shoot s.o.
ṭalab *n.pl.* ṭalabāt application; order (for making a purchase); request
ṭalab/yiṭlub *v.tr.* to request, order, ask
ṭamaʿ *n.* greed, avidity, covetousness
ṭammin bālak be calm, relax, let your mind be at ease
ṭarab *n.* music; delight, pleasure
ṭarad/yiṭrud *v.tr.* to expel, drive out, chase away
ṭard *n.* expelling; firing (someone)
ṭarg *n.* knocking
ṭarīg *n.pl.* ṭurgāt road, way
ṭayarān ʿāmūdi helicopter aviation
ṭayarān mugātil combat aviation
ṭayarān nagl commercial aviation, cargo aviation
ṭayyār *n.pl.* -īn pilot
ṭāga intājiyya productive capacity, power of generating
ṭāhra *adj.* pure, clean
ṭāḥ/yiṭīḥ *v.intr.* to fall
ṭāl ʿumrak may God prolong your life
ṭāliʿ mīʿād have an appointment
ṭār/yiṭīr *v.intr.* to fly; fly away
ṭāra *n.pl.* ṭīrān tambourine
ṭēr *n.pl.* ṭuyūr bird; vulture
ṭifl *n.pl.* aṭfāl baby; child
ṭirāz *n.* type, model, sort; fashion, style
ṭīn *n.* mud; clay

u

ukkazyōn *n.pl.* -āt sale
ummiyya *n.* illiteracy
umniya *n.pl.* -āt desire, wish, ambition
uslūb *n.pl.* asālīb method, style, way
usra *n.pl.* usar family
ustāz musāʿid assistant professor
usṭūra *n.pl.* asāṭīr myth; fable, fairy tale
usṭuwāna *n.* (phonograph) record; cylinder (of an engine)
utumātīkiyyan *adv.* automatically

w

waḍ/ẓīfa *n.pl.* waẓāyif job, task
waḍḍaḥ/yiwaḍḍiḥ *v.tr.* to clarify, clear up; to explain; to illustrate
waḍḍaḥ/yiwaḍḍiḥ alkhaṭ to clear the road
waḍʿ māli financial statement
wafa *n.* keeping; fulfillment; faithfulness; loyalty
waffag/yiwaffig *v.tr.* to make successful
wafāt *n.* death
waffar/yiwaffir *v.tr.* to provide, make available; save(money)
wagaʿ fi mushkil get into trouble
waggaʿ/yiwaggiʿ *v.tr.* to sign; to drop; to cause to fall
wahmi *adj.* fictitious; imagined, hypothetical, imaginary
waḥīd *adj.* solitary, the only one
waḥy *n.* revelation; inspiration
wakīl *n.pl.* wukala trustee; guardian; agent
waraga *n.pl.* awrāg māliyya bank note, paper money
warsha *n.pl.* wurash workshop
wasīga *n.pl.* wasāyig document
waṣaf/yūṣif *v.tr.* to describe
waṣīṭ *n.pl.* wuṣaṭa mediator, middleman
waṣl *n.pl.* wuṣūlāt receipt, voucher
wazn *n.pl.* awzān weight
waʿd *n.pl.* wuʿūd promise
wādi *n.pl.* wudyān valley
wāfag/yiwāfig + ʿala *v.intr.* to agree, approve
wāḥa *n.pl.* -āt oasis
wārda *adj.* mentioned; found
wāsig min nafsu confident of oneself
wāʿi *adj.* alert, aware, vigilant
wigāya *n.* protection; prevention
wikāla *n.pl.* -āt agency

wild *n.pl.* awlād son
winsh *n.* tow truck; winch
wisikh *adj.* dirty
wudd *n.* friendship, amity
wuḍū? *n.* ablution

y

yad ɛāmla labor, labor force
yamāni *adj.* Yemeni
yamīn right side; right hand
yanbūɛ *n.pl.* yanābīɛ spring, well, source
yasār left side, left hand
yatīm *n.pl.* aytām orphan
yā dūb barely, hardly
yā imma either
yā ǰamāɛa people! (vocative)
yā sātir one who covers man's shortcomings (an attribute of God)
yā tura I wonder if...
yākhud bi yad to stand by s.o.
yi?is/yiy?as *v.intr.* to give up hope, despair
yōm alfaraḥ wedding day
yōm annaḥr the Day of Immolation (on the 10th of zu lḥiǰǰa)
yuɛtabar *v.pass.* to be considered, be regarded; to be respected

z

zabūn *n.pl.* zabāyin customer, client
zaka *n.* intelligence, cleverness
zall/yizill *v.intr.* to slip; to slide off; to make a mistake
zamm/yizimm *v.tr.* to purse (the lips); to tie up, fasten, tighten
zanb *n.pl.* zunūb offense; sin
zay ma ngūl as we might say
zād/yizīd *v.tr.* to increase
zāgh/yizūgh + ɛan *v.intr.* to depart from, leave; to deviate from
zākar/yizākir *v.tr.* to study
zākira *n.* memory
zāni *act.part.pl.* zunāt adulterer
zēt khām crude oil
zir *n.pl.* zrār button, push button; bud (of plant)
ziyāda *n.* increase
zōg *n.* taste, inclination, liking
zuḥlēga *n.* slippery slope
zuka *n.* almsgiving

ẓ

ẓahar/yiẓhar annu it seemed/seems that
ẓāhira *n.* phenomenon

ع

ɛaba *n.pl.* ɛuby cloak, aba
ɛabāl ma + *v.* until, while
ɛabbar/yiɛabbir + ɛan *v.intr.* to express
ɛadal/yiɛdil + ɛan *v.intr.* to give up, abandon, relinquish; to leave off; to drop
ɛadam *n.* nonexistence; nothingness; lack, absence
ɛadam khibra lack of experience
ɛadāwa *n.pl.* -āt enmity, hostility, animosity
ɛaddal/yiɛaddil *v.tr.* to revise; to adjust; to amend, modify
ɛadl *n.* justice
ɛaduw *n.pl.* aɛdā? enemy
ɛaḍ/yiɛuḍ *v.tr.* to bite
ɛaḍḍam/yiɛaḍḍim *v.tr.* to make great, make big; to exaggerate
ɛaḍma *n.pl.* ɛiḍām bones
ɛafu *n.* pardon
ɛagl *n.pl.* ɛugūl mind, intellect; brain
ɛaǰab *n.* wonder, astonishment
ɛaǰala *n.* haste
ɛaǰǰal/yiɛaǰǰil *v.intr.* to hurry, speed, hasten, expedite
ɛala asās based on, on the basis of, according to

ɛala ākhir ramag at the point of death, on one's last legs; on the verge of exhaustion

ɛala lgalīla at least

ɛalam *n.pl.* aɛlām flag

ɛalanan *adv.* publicly, openly

ɛalāma *n.pl.* -āt grade, mark, sign

ɛamīd *n.* brigadier; dean (of a college)

ɛamīl *n.pl.* ɛumala agent

ɛanza *n.pl.* -āt, ɛanz goat

ɛarabiyya *n.pl.* -āt carriage, cart

ɛaraḍ/yiɛriḍ + ɛala *v.intr.* to bring up; to suggest; to offer, propose

ɛaraḍ/yiɛruḍ *v.tr.* to present, exhibit

ɛarḍ *n.pl.* ɛurūḍ offer, proposal; honor; width; exhibit

ɛashīra *n.pl.* ɛashāyir clan, tribe, family

ɛaṣa *n.pl.* ɛuṣy rod, staff; stick

ɛaṣa/yiɛṣa *v.tr.* to disobey; to resist, to oppose; to defy; to rebel

ɛaṣāya *n.pl.* -āt, ɛuṣiy stick; staff; cane; baton

ɛatm *n.* dark, darkness; night

ɛaṭash *n.* thirst

ɛaṭf *n.* sympathy

ɛawwaḍ/yiɛawwiḍ *v.tr.* to make up to s.o. for a loss; replace

ɛayyan/yiɛayyin *v.tr.* to appoint; to specify

ɛazam/yiɛzim *v.tr.* to invite

ɛazāb *n.* suffering, pain, torment, agony, torture; punishment, chastisement

ɛāda *n.pl.* -āt habit, customs, traditions

ɛādatan *adv.* usually

ɛād/yiɛīd *v.tr.* to repeat an action

ɛāgil *adj.* wise

ɛāli *adj.* high

ɛālim *n.pl.* ɛulama scientist, scholar, learned person

ɛām *n.* *(with def.art.)* last year

ɛāmil ḥālu fahmān acting clever, pretending to be intelligent

ɛār/yīɛir *v.tr.* to lend

ɛibād allāh God's servants, human beings, mankind

ɛibāda *n.* worship

ɛibāra *n.pl.* -āt expression

ɛilāj *n.pl.* -āt treatment

ɛimāra *n.pl.* -āt, ɛamāyir building

ɛiṣāba *n.pl.* -āt gang

ɛiṣyān *n.* revolt, rebellion

ɛīdiyya *n.* a present given on the occasion of a feast

ɛugda nafsiyya mental/psychological complex

ɛugūba *n.pl.* -āt punishment

ɛulba *n.pl.* ɛulab box

ɛulūm insāniyya the humanities

ɛumrāniyya *adj.* constructional, construction

ɛunṣur *n.pl.* ɛanāṣir element

ɛanāṣir mutnāzɛa hostile factions

ɛurbūn *n.* token, symbol, pledge

ɛuzr *n.pl.* aɛzār excuse

ɛūd *n.* wood; branch, twig

Bibliography

Bakalla, Mohammed Hasan. *The Morphological and Phonological Components of the Arabic Verb (Meccan Arabic)*, Longman and Librairie du Liban, 1979.

Cantarino, Vicente. *Modern Arabic Prose*, Indiana University Press, 1974.

Holes, Clive. *Colloquial Arabic of the Gulf and Saudi Arabia*, Routledge and Kegan Paul, London, 1984.

Ingraham, Bruce. *North East Arabian Dialects*, Kegan Paul International, London, 1982.

Johnstone, T.M. *Eastern Arabian Dialect Studies*, Oxford University Press, London, 1967.

Omar, Margaret K. *Saudi Arabic Urban Hijazi Dialect*, Foreigh Service Institute, Washington, D.C., 1975.

Prochazka, Theodore Jr. *Saudi Arabian Dialects*, Kegan Paul International, London, 1988.

Qafisheh, Hamdi A. *A Short Reference Grammar of Gulf Arabic*, The University of Arizona Press, 1977.

Sieny, Mahmoud Esma'il. *The Syntax of Urban Hijazi Arabic*, Longman Group Limited and Librairie du Liban, 1978.

Van Wagoner, Merril Y., Arnold Satterthwait and Frank Rice, *Spoken Arabic (Saudi)*, Spoken Language Services, Inc., 1977.